D1450906

# DENMARK VESEY'S REVOLT

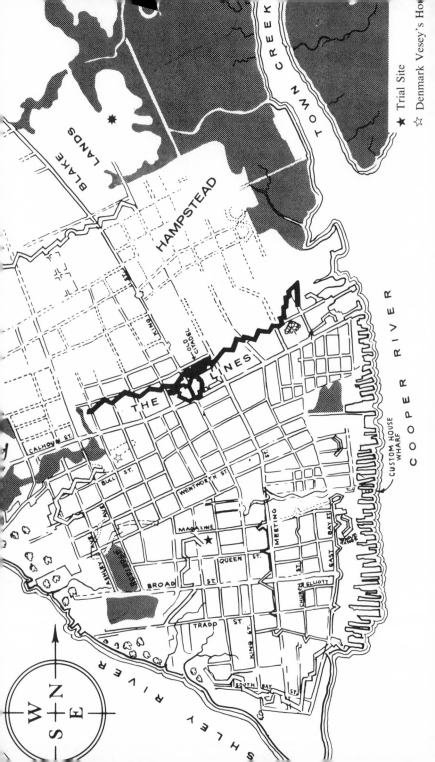

★ Trial Site

☆ Denmark Vesey's Hou[se]

# Denmark Vesey's Revolt

## The Slave Plot
## That Lit a Fuse to Fort Sumter

*by*

## JOHN LOFTON

681883

## THE KENT STATE UNIVERSITY PRESS

**Library of Congress Cataloging in Publication Data**

Lofton, John.
    Denmark Vesey's revolt.

    Updated ed. of: Insurrection in South Carolina. 1964.
    Bibliography: p.
    Includes index.
    1. Charleston (S.C.)—Slave insurrection, 1822.
2. Vesey, Denmark, 1776 (ca.)–1822. 3. Slavery—South Carolina. I. Title.
F279.C49N44    1982              973.5'4'0924              83-11267
ISBN 0-87338-296-X (pbk.)

# PREFACE TO THE PAPERBACK EDITION

● Had Denmark Vesey succeeded in carrying out in full his plan for a black slave insurrection in Charleston, S. C., in 1822, he would have wreaked terrible carnage on the community. Hence, it is not surprising that Vesey aroused strong emotions in his own time. His white judges found him guilty of "treason" and other "crimes of the blackest hue." What is perhaps a little more surprising is that similar emotions are still evident in modern times. When this book was first published in 1964 (under the title of *Insurrection in South Carolina*), a reviewer for the *Charleston News and Courier* took the occasion to retroactively denounce abolitionists, whom he accused of fomenting "just such cruel and destructive schemes" as Vesey's; he also excoriated abolitionists for applauding Vesey "as a martyr."

Another commentator on the book in the same newspaper referred to "Vesey and his voo-dooed band of brigands" and chided this author for his portrayal of the circumstances that led eventually to what the reviewer called "the War of Northern Aggression (1861–65)." He also castigated the author for holding that Southerners are (in the reviewer's words) "always the villains and Negroes the heroes."

Taking a sharply different view, a top official of the National Association for the Advancement of Colored People, after reading advance proofs, wrote to the publisher that he could not commend the book. "I have always thought of Denmark Vesey," he said, "as a Negro hero and martyr; Mr. Lofton pictures him as one who unheroically disavows his principles and who was a most reluctant and unwilling martyr." What I tried to do, of course, was to portray Vesey as neither god nor devil but as a man with those human strengths and weaknesses that were attributed to him by contemporary observers. Although it seems to me that he emerges as a man with strong leadership qualities and a fierce determination to free his people, I leave to the reader the judgment of his character.

Was Vesey a traitor or a martyr? The answer depends on one's perspective. In 1822 many blacks visualized Vesey's cause as being supported by God, which meant they hardly saw their leader as a traitor. A pamphlet written by a black and published in 1850 dubbed Vesey and his followers as patriots. In a pamphlet published in 1901 by the American Negro Academy under the title, "Right on the Scaffold, or the Martyrs of 1822," Archibald H. Grimke lauded the Vesey conspirators as heroes.

Each side in a revolutionary confrontation extols its own virtues, accepts the necessity for violence in defense of its own rights, and denounces violence on the other side. Thus, while Charleston authorities condemned Vesey for planning "to riot in blood, outrage, rapine . . . and conflagration," they proclaimed God to be on the side of the slaveholders and consigned Vesey and thirty-four of his followers to the gallows for trampling "on all laws, human and divine."

Although South Carolina officials in 1822 charged Vesey with being "totally insensible of the divine influence of that Gospel, 'all whose paths are peace,' " they themselves eschewed the gospel of peace when they condoned an 1823 vigilante attack on runaway slaves in which a woman and child were killed and one of the runaways was decapitated and his head stuck on a pole and publicly exposed as a "warning to vicious slaves."

Like the leaders of other unsuccessful revolutionary efforts, Vesey suffered the obloquies of those who suppressed his movement. On the other hand, when revolutionists win and write the history of their country, their leaders are celebrated as patriots and heroes. Thus, when slaves of St. Domingue revolted in 1791 and triumphed over their French masters, Toussaint L'Ouverture and other leaders became patriots of the new country of Haiti. In South Carolina during the Revolutionary War, rebel guerrillas, on the one hand, and supporters of the king, on the other, engaged in ferocious and indiscriminate acts of pillage, burning, and killing against each other. After the war, the guerrillas were honored as patriots; the loyalists were ostracized as Tories. Ironically, South Carolina slaveholders, like the earlier rebels against the king, were to adopt their own modes of insurrectionary activity—in their case, against the federal government. And after their unsuccessful counterrevolution of 1861–1865, they were themselves the targets of the historical obloquies of the victors.

For obvious reasons, then, Denmark Vesey has not achieved a generally recognized status as patriot or hero. But since this book was first published in 1964, his importance has been far more generally recognized both in the historical literature (which will be dealt with further on in this comment) and in the popular media. In 1982 the Public Broadcasting Service aired nationally a ninety-minute television drama entitled "Denmark Vesey's Rebellion." Produced by Yanna Kroyt Brandt and directed by Stan Lathan, it attracted much favorable comment by press reviewers. An oratorio, "Denmark Vesey," written by Waldemar Hille and Aaron Kramer, has been widely performed. At the W. E. B. Dubois Institute of Harvard University, as this was written, composer Walter Robinson was at work on a folk opera, to be entitled "Look What a Wonder Jesus Has Done" (after an old slave hymn), based on the Vesey affair.

Even in Charleston, where the historical attitudes of victor over vanquished still flourish, Vesey has now won a significant measure of recognition. In the 1970s the city of Charleston commissioned a portrait of him. Since no likeness of Vesey survives, the picture shows him addressing a black audience, with his face featureless and seen from an oblique angle. The portrait was hung in 1976 at the Gaillard Municipal Auditorium. At the ceremony at which it was put on display, Mayor Joseph P. Riley, a white, made a speech that would have been remarkable in 1964, when the new civil rights movement was just gaining momentum and was still encountering strong resistance in white Charleston and elsewhere in the South.

Mayor Riley said: "[T]his is . . . part of the effort . . . of the administration to see that parts of history heretofore forgotten are remembered—because it is important that all of us have the opportunity to consider our heritage and those who came before us. And that has not been the case in these United States for a great part of our history, our black history." The mayor added, perhaps with political wistfulness: "There have been writings of history that would attribute to Mr. Vesey actions and attempts that were not his. We should not see him as a man, as reported by some, who sought to kill, because I do not believe that was the case. . . . I find it difficult to believe his plan was to annihilate his city." The mayor observed that Vesey should be considered in present day history "not as a person of hatred, but as a man of love, as a man of compassion, a man who was interested in righting the wrongs, a man who was free and a man who was ahead of his time." He called upon his listeners to make the ceremony one "of white and black Charlestonians because it's a victory when we can come together so soon after a time of such great difficulty and look back to a very dark past and see someone as a hero, who gave his life so that man may be free."

Bishop Frank M. Reid, Jr. of the Seventh District of the AME Church responded in the same spirit as he addressed 250 black citizens and City of Charleston officials attending the unveiling. "We know who Denmark Vesey was," he said, "and we know who we are. We know what he intended to do to them and we know what they did to him. . . . I say this is a creative moment for it recognizes that Vesey was no wild-eyed monsterminded racist. . . . He was not a black against white people. He was a liberator who God had sent to set the people free from oppression."

Mayor Riley's conciliatory words may have been prompted more by a desire to bring the black and white communities together—a not unlaudable objective—than by a true reading of history. Bishop Reid subtly affirmed Vesey's harsh revolutionary purpose without departing from the conciliatory spirit of the occasion. But many white Charleston commentators were not placative. Ashley Cooper, a *News and Courier* columnist, wrote: "If black leaders in Charleston had searched for a thousand years, they could not have found a local black whose portrait would have been more offensive to many white people." Several writers of letters to the paper attacked the mayor—one of them (presumably white) declaring: "If Vesey qualifies for such an honor, we should also hang the portraits of Hitler, Attila the Hun, Herod the murderer of babies. . . . " Black letter writers—including black City Councilman Robert Ford, the legislative sponsor of the portrait—defended the project and the mayor.

But the person who perhaps put the occasion in the most understandable perspective was Bobby Isaac, a black reporter for the *News and Courier*. He wrote: "Blacks—and understanding whites—are not honoring Vesey to upset their white neighbors. Most of us are interested in giving long overdue recognition to a man who is a true black hero. Many whites cannot appreciate black sentiments in this regard because of their tunneled vision of history, which to them has only white heroes. . . . [R]espect for other people's history, language, religion and customs is critical."

The unveiling of the portrait in Charleston was followed soon afterward by the designation of a house, believed to have been Denmark Vesey's, as a National Historic Landmark. The comparatively small house, located at what is now 56 Bull Street, was number 20 in Vesey's time. Its landmark status was achieved through the application of the Afro-American Bicentennial Corporation of Washington, D.C. But a proposal to name a public school after Denmark Vesey was never acted on.

On the national scene, a flurry of attention was focused on Vesey by historians and publishers after the initial publication of this book. The historian who perhaps aroused the most discussion was Richard Wade, whose book (*Slavery in the Cities—The South 1820–1860*. New York: Oxford University Press, 1964) was published a few months after this book. Wade's book devotes some fourteen pages to the Vesey affair. Wade had addressed the same subject a little earlier in a journal article (Wade, "The Vesey Plot: A Reconsideration," *Journal of Southern History*, May 1964). Wade's main conclusion in both publications was that no conspiracy existed or that at most it was never more than loose talk by aggrieved and embittered men on both sides (*Cities*, pp. 237, 241), with whites needing an insurrectionary plot to justify their suppression of blacks, and blacks needing one to prove their urge to freedom. To buttress this thesis, Wade cited: the skepticism of some top officials; the failure to discover conspirators' records and slave caches of weapons; discrepancies in the trial record; the comparative freedom from discontent of urban slaves, which would have given them less incentive to revolt; and, finally, better policing in the city than in the country and the more nearly equal numbers of urban whites and blacks, which would have made revolt in Charleston more difficult.

Several authors have challenged Wade's interpretation. William W. Freehling (*Prelude to the Civil War—The Nullification Controversy in South Carolina, 1816–1836*. New York: Harper & Row, 1965) observed that, while Governor Thomas Bennett, one of the skeptical officials, questioned the breadth of the conspiracy, he believed that a serious plot *was* afoot. Freehling concluded (p. 54) that "Bennett's position, but not Wade's, is consistent with all the evidence." Sterling Stuckey ("Remembering Denmark Vesey—Agitator or Insurrectionist?" *Negro Digest*, XV, February 1966, 28–41) and Robert S. Starobin (*Denmark Vesey—The Slave Conspiracy of 1822*. Englewood Cliffs, N.J.: Prentice-Hall, Inc., 1970) also disagreed with Wade. Their major points were: that the top leaders died without disclosing any information; hence the shortage of confirming testimony was explainable; that the failure to find records and arms was not significant, since leading conspirators, including Vesey, were free after the investigation began and had time to dispose of arms and other evidence, and that, in any event, the insurrectionary plan envisaged the capture of arms; and, finally, that discrepancies between the published testimony and the manuscript testimony were irrelevant to the existence of a believable conspiracy (Starobin, pp. 178–80).

I agree with the interpretations of Freehling, Stuckey, and Starobin rather than Wade's. But with regard to Wade's suggestion that urban slaves would have had less incentive to revolt because of their better condition, I would make two points that Wade's other critics did not—first, that policing of slaves in Charleston often became lax (*Insurrection*, pp. 187–88) and, second, that revolutionary movements have usually been led and widely supported, not by the most deprived class but by those who were better off, those who already enjoyed certain privileges and who wanted to remove remaining vestiges of tyranny precisely because they could visualize and appreciate the advantages of freedom. This phenomenon was repeatedly evident in revolutionary movements in Europe and America.

Ultimately the dispute over whether Vesey had an extensive plan for insurrection comes down to an intellectual exercise based largely on conjecture. Although I believe such a plan existed, the important point—which I made in a comment on the evidence (Chapter 10, note 18, p. 259), and still would emphasize—is that contemporary white leaders believed that insurrectionary activity was in progress and acted on this belief in a way that helped to shift the course of American history.

That shift in course, for which Denmark Vesey was the chief impetus, is one of the main themes of this book (one, incidentally, that few reviewers at the time noted). The point is made in Chapter 14, where I observe that South Carolina, frightened and provoked by the Vesey incident, adopted the Negro Seamen Act, enforced it in defiance of the federal government—in effect, nullifying a United States treaty—and then moved inexorably by stages to nullification of a federal tariff, secession, and civil war—all in defense of slavery. "Nullification, however camouflaged at first," I noted, "was devised as a political defense of slavery, as was the whole arsenal of so-called state rights" (p. 228; see also pp. 222, 229, 233–36).

Other authors were to advance this thesis later. Freehling, in his book, published in 1965, devotes considerable attention to the Vesey conspiracy and to the effect that slavery and the fear of servile insurrections had on South Carolina's shift to defiance of the federal government and eventual withdrawal from the union. (See especially pp. 64, 86, 109–15, 348.) Stephen A. Channing (*Crisis of Fear—Secession in South Carolina*. New York: Simon and Schuster, 1970) refers to Vesey and adopts the same thesis. (See especially pp. 21, 45, 50, 293.)

Of the material on Denmark Vesey that has been published since this book appeared, two books are particularly noteworthy—Robert Starobin's, already mentioned, and *The Trial Record of Denmark Vesey* (Boston: Beacon Press, 1970), which has an introduction by John Oliver Killens, a black novelist. These books are valuable not so much because they provide new material on Vesey but because they make more widely available to researchers and to the general reader material that was previously available only in archives or scholarly journals. Starobin's book, which he edited and for which he wrote an introduction and an afterword, contains, in part one, important excerpts from the Vesey trial record; in part two, reactions from contemporary observers to the 1822 plot; and, in part three, the analyses of later commentators, including Wade, on the Vesey conspiracy. The Beacon Press edition of *The Trial Record* represents the first complete republication of the record. Killens, author of the introduction, published a fictionalized account of the Vesey affair (*Great Gittin' up Morning*. New York: Doubleday, 1972) that dramatizes Vesey as larger than life but provides a lively text for those who like a simplified approach to history.

Since 1964 other publications pertaining to slave insurrections in general and including segments on Vesey have also been reprinted and thus made more widely available. One such volume is Thomas Wentworth Higginson, *Black Rebellion* (New York: Arno Press and The New York Times, 1969). Along with other material written by Higginson, this book contains Higginson's 1861 *Atlantic Monthly* article on Vesey. There is a new preface by James M. McPherson of Princeton. In 1968 Negro Universities Press, a division of Greenwood Publishing Corp., New York, reprinted Joseph Cephas Carroll's pioneering study, *Slave Insurrections in the United States, 1800-1865*, originally published in 1938 by Chapman and Grimes, Inc. of Boston. And in 1969 International Publishers of New York reprinted with a new preface Herbert Aptheker's *American Negro Slave Revolts*, originally published in 1943 by Columbia University Press. All of these works were consulted in their original editions by this author, although Carroll's was inadvertently omitted from the bibliography.

Besides the literature already mentioned, there have been since 1964 one book and several articles that dealt in part with Denmark Vesey. Among them are Nicholas Halasz' book, *The Rattling Chains—Slave Unrest and Revolt in the Antebellum South* (New York: David McKay Company, Inc., 1966) and Max L. Kleinman's article, "The Denmark Vesey Conspiracy: An Historiographical Study" (*Negro History Bulletin*, XVII, Feb./Mar. 1974, 225–28). But none of the studies that I know of has revealed significant new information or offered new insights on the Vesey plot.

The most unusual information touching on Denmark Vesey that has come to my attention since the 1964 publication of this book was communicated by Stephen C. Crane, a Dallas lawyer who is a descendant of Captain Joseph Vesey, the master of the ship that brought Denmark Vesey to Charleston after the Revolutionary War. In naval records, most of which were published after 1964, Mr. Crane discovered information about the captain's activities during the Revolutionary War that was not available to me.

As related in a note in *The Trial Record*, I wrote in Chapter 1 that Captain Vesey was engaged during the war in supplying the French of St. Domingue with slaves. But the records called to my attention by Mr. Crane show that Joseph Vesey, although he may have made some voyages to St. Domingue to haul slaves, was also an active participant on the American side during much of the war. In the latter part of 1775 and early in 1776, he served in the South Carolina navy, commanding a pilot boat that cruised the east coast, warning American vessels of the presence of British warships, attacking British merchant vessels, and transporting emissaries to northern ports in search of recruits for the South Carolina navy (William Bell Clark, ed., *Naval Documents of the American Revolution*, 8 vols., Wash-

ington: U. S. Navy, 1964–, vol. 2, pp. 889, 890, 1275, 1313; vol.
3, pp. 211, 596, 647; vol. 4, p. 16, note 2). In 1776 and 1777,
Vesey served in the Continental Navy under John Paul Jones,
in the positions of first lieutenant on the sloop *Providence* and
master of the brig *Cabot*. He was assigned as acting master of
several vessels taken as prizes and shared in prize money (*Naval
Documents*, vol. 6, pp. 745, 1374–75; vol. 7, pp. 991, 993; vol. 8,
pp. 46, 65–66, note 2; 98–99, 301, 372; Charles R. Smith, *Marines in the Revolution—A History of the Continental Marines
in the American Revolution, 1775-1783*, Washington: U.S.
Marine Corps, 1975, pp. 412, 413 [Vesey's name misspelled in
*Marines*] ).

Between 1778 and 1781, Captain Vesey was issued various
letters of marque to become a privateersman on the American
side. In 1778 Vesey was master and part owner, along with
North and Trescot of Charleston, of the privateer *Adriana*, a
sloop of fifteen guns with a crew of forty-seven. In 1781 he
commanded the privateer *Prospect*, a brigantine of twelve guns
with a crew of sixty (*Naval Records of the American Revolution, 1775-1788*, Washington: Government Printing Office,
1906, pp. 220, 421). The *Prospect* may well have been the vessel
that Vesey was sailing when he picked up Denmark Vesey at St.
Thomas. Records of a 1781 voyage describe the captain as then
a man of thirty-four years of age, 5 feet, 10 inches in height and
having a light complexion. Mr. Crane says that Vesey family
records indicate that Captain Vesey was versed in a number of
languages, which would further explain Denmark Vesey's facility in languages.

Besides the new material relating to Denmark Vesey and
slave revolts that has appeared since the initial publication of
this book, another development merits noting. Literature on
black history and culture has assumed a new status since the
mid-1960s, coinciding with the growing civil rights movement.
Not only were there new studies, but, as a result of demands for
fairer and fuller treatment of black contributions to history and
culture, there were revisions and additions as new editions of

old textbooks appeared. Meanwhile, courses in black history and culture were introduced at a rapid pace in American colleges and universities. After the initial burst of activity, such courses and programs went through a settling down period in which greater discipline and sophistication were demanded by faculties and students alike. But black studies on campuses seem here to stay. Joseph J. Russell, the dean of Afro-American Studies at Indiana University and executive director of the National Council of Black Studies, said early in 1983 that his organization recognized 525 black studies programs, of which 150 were full-scale departments (*New York Times*, Jan. 13, 1983, p. 8).

At this point a word should be said about the present almost universal use of the term "black" instead of "Negro," which formerly was in general use and which is used throughout this book. The change in usage came about in the 1960s through the influence of black leaders. But it should be noted that the term "Negro" had no invidious connotation. Most black scholars used it themselves, as is indicated by its inclusion in the name of well-known black publications like *The Journal of Negro History*. The new usage is merely one of preference.

When this book was first published, a *New York Times* reviewer called it "an exciting account of an almost forgotten chapter in American history." But the chapter was apparently soon forgotten again. When Killens' fictionalized treatment of Vesey appeared in 1972, a reviewer in the *New York Times Book Review* said Killens had "rescued Vesey from obscurity." After the television drama, "Denmark Vesey's Rebellion," went on the air in 1982, a reviewer for the *New York Times* said the show had done "a remarkably good job of taking this little known revolt of black slaves in Charleston, S. C., in 1822 and elevating it from footnote to an important part of American history." Perhaps the republication of this book—still probably the most comprehensive treatment of the Vesey affair, the Charleston social milieu of the time, and the plot's impact on history—will revive again the forgotten chapter, rescue Vesey again from obscurity, and elevate the Vesey conspiracy permanently from a footnote to an important place in American history.

In closing, I must acknowledge my indebtedness to Stephen C. Crane for the valuable new information he supplied on Captain Joseph Vesey. For their help in confirming certain facts connected with recent efforts in Charleston to commemorate Denmark Vesey, I wish to thank Thelma R. Woods and Delbert L. Woods, officers of the Charleston branch of the National Association for the Advancement of Colored People. I also wish to acknowledge the help of my wife, Joanne B. Lyon, who rounded up recently published historical literature dealing with Vesey and made useful editing suggestions.

John Lofton
January 30, 1983

# PREFACE

● The abolitionist Thomas Wentworth Higginson assessed the plan of ex-slave Denmark Vesey for a revolt of Negroes in and around Charleston, South Carolina, in 1822 and called it "the most elaborate insurrectionary project ever formed by American slaves." In "boldness of conception and thoroughness of organization," he asserted, "there has been nothing to compare with it." He concluded that it "came the nearest to a terrible success."[1] The men at Charleston who sat in judgment over Vesey and his followers declared that "Carolina has been rescued from the most horrible catastrophe with which it has been threatened, since it has been an independent state."[2]

Thus it is evident that the significance of the Vesey undertaking was conceded both by those who might have been expected to be sympathetic with its promoters and by those who were the targets of the design. Despite this concurrence of opinion on the part of those who lived with slavery, there has since been no definitive attempt to assess the significance of the Vesey project in the perspective of history.

Perhaps, as Charles Johnson has suggested, "Denmark Vesey is a symbol of a spirit too violent to be acceptable to the white community." There are no Negro schools named for him, and for Negroes to take any pride in his philosophy and courage might be considered "poor taste."[3] And Gunnar Myrdal has observed: "American Negroes, in attempting to integrate themselves into American Society, have had to pay the price of forgetting their historical heroes and martyrs."[4]

Though Denmark Vesey has not been given a recognizable role in history, his plan for insurrection has been accorded considerable repetitious attention in various narratives of American slavery. Such treatment has been facilitated by records of the evidence collected and the trial procedures employed against Vesey and his fellow insurgents. Though the authorities at Charleston were among the intended victims, they saw a need to justify to society the means they used to thwart the revolt.

The official story of the abortive uprising of 1822 has been preserved in three contemporary accounts: (1) a 48-page report written by Charleston Intendant James Hamilton, Jr., at the request of the city council, and first published in the summer of 1822 while the trials of the insurrectionists were still in progress; (2) a 202-page volume, published in October of the same year under the authorship of Lionel H. Kennedy and Thomas Parker, presiding magistrates of the court which tried the first "conspirators" to be discovered;[5] (3) a letter by Governor Thomas Bennett of South Carolina, dated August 10, 1822, and published in Washington on August 24 in the *National Intelligencer* and in Baltimore on September 7 in *Niles' Weekly Register*.

But while the contemporary accounts give fairly exhaustive treatment to the plan itself and to the trials of the accused slaves, none of them reveals very much on Denmark Vesey's background. Nor have later researchers disclosed much additional information, since they have apparently not looked far beyond the three major primary sources.

In an attempt to shed light on those aspects of Denmark Vesey's story not heretofore touched, this writer has examined the Charleston newspapers and public records of the period and has studied the historical literature of South Carolina and the West Indian Islands where Denmark Vesey and his owner, Captain Joseph Vesey, once lived or visited. This search has produced a substantial cache of specific new information bearing directly on the lives of Denmark Vesey and his owner and much general data that helps to put Vesey's activity within the context of a chronicle of his times.

The objectives of this volume are: (1) to portray the thread of the captain's life from the time it was first interwoven with that of the young slave, (2) to examine what effect

this inter-weaving may have had on the fabric of Denmark's*
character and what effect the social milieu of man and slave
may have had in producing a man of revolution, (3) to tell
the story of the insurrection and its aftermath, (4) to suggest
how all these events influenced the Negro's advance toward
freedom, and (5) to indicate how South Carolina politicians
were led to extremes of reaction by their commitment to
slavery and their effort to police it.

For their helpful co-operation in putting research materials at my disposal and for making available the base maps
used for the end papers of this book, I wish to acknowledge
my indebtedness to Miss Virginia Rugheimer, librarian, and
Mrs. Beulah T. Sheetz, assistant librarian, of the Charleston
Library Society. Research courtesies were also extended by
the late Dr. J. Harold Easterby, director of the South Carolina
Archives Department and the late Dr. Robert L. Meriwether,
director of the South Caroliniana Library at the University of
South Carolina. Samuel Gaillard Stoney of Charleston was
good humoredly obliging in suggesting sources of obscure
information.

For reading and criticizing portions of the manuscript, I
want to express thanks to Dr. J. Cutler Andrews, chairman of
the History Department at Chatham College, Dr. Don E.
Fehrenbacher, associate professor of history at Stanford
University, Dr. Fletcher M. Green, professor of history at
the University of North Carolina, and Professors Alfred P.
James and James A. Kehl of the University of Pittsburgh—
though none of them is responsible for any errors that may
have crept into the final product.

J.L.

---

*On occasion in this work Denmark Vesey is referred to by his
first name alone. This usage is followed to avoid confusing Denmark with his owner, Joseph, and to avoid the alternative stilted
usage of the whole name, Denmark Vesey, whenever the man is
mentioned.

# CONTENTS

*They never fail who die*
*In a great cause; the block may soak their gore;*
*Their heads may sodden in the sun; their limbs*
*Be strung to city gates and castle walls—*
*But still their spirit walks abroad. Though years*
*Elapse, and others share as dark a doom,*
*They but augment the deep and sweeping thoughts*
*Which overpower all others, and conduct*
*The world at last to freedom.*

From Lord Byron's *Marino Faliero*, II, ii.

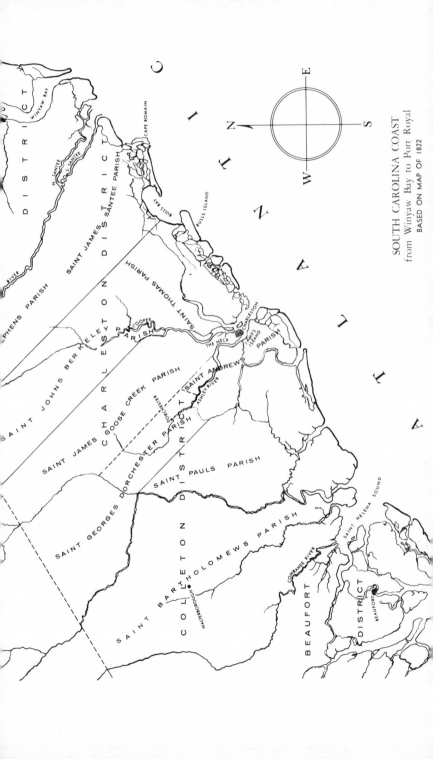

SOUTH CAROLINA COAST
from Winyaw Bay to Port Royal
BASED ON MAP OF 1822

# INTRODUCTION

● Down through the centuries of man's recorded history the acceptance of slavery has been more common in various societies than revulsion against it. Slavery was an acknowledged facet of life in ancient Israel, in Greece, in Rome, in Europe, and in antebellum America. The individual who was trapped in that condition was unfortunate, but his was not a unique status. He was a member of a recognized caste. And since his caste was the lowest in the community, the members of it, however brilliant they might be, were not accorded any significant place in the recitation of their society's story. The written record has more often depicted slaves as objects than as subjects.

Not until relatively recent times did societies become generally conscious of the inappropriateness of slavery in a civilized community and of the moral obligation of the community to terminate the institution. As this consciousness became more widespread and steps were taken to dissolve the slave caste, liberation efforts became a part of the history of states and their political and intellectual leaders. The ending of slavery in the British and French empires constitutes a relevant portion of the chronicle of these peoples. In France merited recognition has gone to J. P. Brissot de Warville and the Society of Friends of the Blacks, and in Britain Thomas Clarkson and William Wilberforce have fittingly been credited with important roles in bringing about slavery's demise. In America the influence of John Woolman, William Lloyd Garrison, Wendell Phillips, and many others has been appropriately noted. The effects of the cataclysm of civil war have been weighed and analyzed.

All of this is as it should be. These interpretations are essential to an understanding of the decline and fall of slavery. And yet they do not tell the whole story. The common attribute of such historical treatises is that they assess the way in which external activities and persons shaped the course of slavery, largely overlooking the disquieting turmoil within the institution itself and the influence that individual slaves had on the system and on the societies in which it existed. Written from the viewpoint of the free citizen, they represent the dominant group's account of its own contribution to freedom rather than a fully-rounded chronicle of the passing of slavery.

In recent years such scholars as Melville J. Herskovitz (*The Myth of the Negro Past*, Harper, 1941) and Herbert Aptheker (*American Negro Slave Revolts*, Columbia University Press, 1943) have emphasized the bearing of internal forces on the history of slavery. But these studies and a few others of their kind have, because of their nature, dealt with the broad sweep of events rather than with details of how the lives and activities of single servitors may have swayed the destinies of themselves and their fellow bondmen.

Yet it should be obvious that individuals within the slave system had at least some effect on its evolution, even as individual participants have molded other human institutions. They were thinking, free-willed human beings with power to communicate their thoughts and aspirations to others. The technique of this work is to examine how the life and example of one slave impinged on the events of his time and to show, by concentrating on the story of an individual, that slaves were not merely pawns in the hands of their rulers but were themselves actors on the stage of history.

Had Denmark Vesey never lived, the twists and turns of American history would not have been quite the same. Though he himself was not a recognized mover and shaker, his actions were demonstrably significant enough to stimulate the thinking and the public acts of those who were. Therefore a portrayal of his life and the world that produced him should constitute a pertinent item in any study of man's emancipation from involuntary servitude.

## A KEY PORT

● The sloop *Warwick* was an insignificant vessel even by eighteenth century maritime standards. And her commander was hardly a man who in that day would have attracted much attention. But when the *Warwick* sailed into the harbor of Charleston, South Carolina, on a mid-summer day in 1770, the little ship was helping to link that city to a fortuitous destiny. She was taking her master, Captain Joseph Vesey, on the first leg of a trading route which, through his instrumentality, would have a portentous bearing on the history of the South Carolina port and indirectly on the history of the nation.

In the early days of the American nation port cities located at points where rivers met the sea were naturally key centers of cultural and mercantile commerce. Linked to the interior by the most convenient mode of transportation and to the transoceanic world by the only means of contact, ports were much more vital conduits in the exchange of commodities and ideas than are trading centers in an age of multiple methods of movement and communication. There were only a few such cities in eighteenth century America. Charleston was one of them. As late as 1774 an English visitor said, after a tour of the United States, that in all the southern states Charleston was the only town worthy of notice.[1]

Captain Vesey was not then a Carolinian. He was a Bermuda islander. But in the period 1770-1775 his real home was the sea, as he commanded a series of no less than five vessels and conducted a lively shipping business between trading points ranging from Carolina to Barbados, a distance of some 1,900 miles. Charleston during these years was one of his regular ports of call.[2]

As a Bermuda islander, Captain Vesey had chosen the

calling which attracted most of the inhabitants of that British colony during his day. The Bermudians in this period built sloops and brigs—as many as sixty in one year—and sold them in the West Indies or North America. Along with the occupation of ship-building went that of navigation. From eighty to a hundred Bermuda vessels were constantly at sea, each manned by a skeleton crew of two whites and four Negroes. In this way fully half of the able-bodied men of the islands became expert mariners. Though some of the ships were owned by their captains, a good many were the property of the better-off Bermudians, who employed the crews. In the case of the Vesey family, several members were masters of vessels which had been acquired as prizes.[3]

During the early months of the year Bermuda's maritime traders often repaired to the Tortugas and to Turks Island. (The latter especially was one of Joseph Vesey's rendezvous.) Here the Bermudians raked salt for sale to passing American vessels or for use as cargo. And from these points they would proceed to South Carolina or Virginia in search of corn, or to Philadelphia or New York in order to exchange their salt or money for such necessities as salt pork, beef, flour, peas, lumber, and candles. Some of the islanders sailed directly home from the continent, while others proceeded to the sugar islands and disposed of their American merchandise there for cash. They reserved part of their receipts for new cargoes to the mainland and put the rest into bills of exchange to be used for purchases in England. By these means Bermudian mariners made a living, and some of them became wealthy.

It may have been on one of his early visits to Charleston that Captain Vesey first considered how he would settle down from the rigorous life of a mariner. A month's visit in port in 1770 gave him ample time in which to view the town as a place to secure permanent moorings.[4]

Charleston in 1770 was the fourth largest city of British America, being exceeded in size only by New York, Boston, and Philadelphia. Shipping, of course, was a major business activity in colonial Charleston, since the city was the commercial capital of the South and the port for a vast territory with few other trading outlets. The volume of trade in 1770 was below average, however, because of the colonists' non-importation policy instituted as a protest against the various tax laws imposed on them by Parliament.

While an embargo on slaves from both Africa and the West Indies was complete during much of the non-importation period, intercolonial commerce between Charleston and the West Indies (except in slaves) continued. Imports from the West Indies included rum, sugar, and molasses. Exports from Charleston to the islands consisted of pine and cypress lumber, cattle, slave provisions, salt meat, and rice. Slave muscles supplied the energy to move these commodities between wharf and ship's hold.

Lumber or slave provisions probably made up the *Warwick's* cargo as she weighed anchor for Turks Island and the Barbados on August 25, 1770. During those intervals before the Revolution when the non-importation policy against slaves was not in effect, Captain Vesey's cargoes may well have consisted partially or wholly of African slaves picked up at relay points in the West Indies. It is not likely that he hauled West Indian slaves, since the Carolinians were prejudiced against Negroes from places other than the coast of Africa. They believed that slaves from the Spanish colonies incited others to escape, and that slaves from the English colonies were of questionable value because they might have been sent away by the courts for crimes or by their owners for their bad qualities.[5]

When the slave trade was resumed in full force in 1772, the figures indicate that the number imported from the West Indies was small in comparison to the number coming from Africa. Whatever the source of Captain Vesey's "merchandise" was, the market in the pre-war years was bringing inflated prices. In May and June of 1773 Captain Vesey could have gotten 350 pounds each for "prime men" in the South Carolina market, and 290 pounds each for "prime women."[6]

As the showdown between the American colonies and Great Britain approached, times became more troublous for maritime traders like the Bermuda captain. In the latter part of 1773 and during 1774 protests against Parliament's tax on tea took the form of dumping tea in the harbor or storing it unused in warehouses. In September 1774 the Continental Congress in Philadelphia adopted an "Association" pledging the colonies to commercial non-intercourse with Great Britain, Ireland, and the West Indies. By this agreement, non-importation was to take effect after December 1, 1774, and unless grievances were redressed, non-exportation on September 10, 1775. Such strictures would obviously threaten the livelihood of the trading Bermudians.

Captain Vesey could perceive during a visit to Charleston in January, 1775, that serious trouble with Britain was brewing. On January 11 South Carolina's First Provincial Congress met to hear a report from the colony's delegates to the Continental Congress at which the non-importation policy had been formulated. After much debate, members of the South Carolina body approved without a dissenting vote the proceedings of the Continental Congress, which included a call for another ban against the slave trade.

When the captain arrived in Charleston in June, 1775, news of the battle of Lexington had reached the city. On August 24, 1775, as Captain Vesey brought the brigantine *Rebecca* into the South Carolina port, the revolutionary storm was too plain to ignore.[7]

By early 1775 South Carolina's accession to the Non-Importation Association had cut off practically all slave imports. The same agreement reduced the value of the total volume of imports from 378,116 pounds sterling in 1774 to a mere 6,246 pounds in 1775. Thus the prospect for West Indies trade could hardly have been encouraging to the Bermuda captain when he sailed into Charleston in the late summer of 1775. In fact, the sickly character of this commerce was attested to by a petition to the House of Commons by the sugar planters of the West Indies, who complained about the American Association and begged for relief because their prosperity depended on free and reciprocal intercourse with the North American provinces.

On September 15, 1775, while the *Rebecca* was reported windbound in Charleston Harbor, the situation in the colony reached such an explosive point that the royal governor, Lord William Campbell, fled to H.M.S. *Tamar* lying in Rebellion Road. Though no newspaper took note of her departure,[8] the *Rebecca* presumably sailed when the weather permitted. That was the last sign Charleston had of Captain Vesey until the Revolutionary War was over. He was occupied during the war in supplying the French of St. Domingue with slaves.[9]

While the uncertain conditions of Carolina trade on the eve of the Revolution led Captain Vesey to transfer his operations farther south, the Bermuda mariner as early as April 15, 1774, had incurred business obligations which called upon him to maintain contact with Charleston. On that date he had signed a bond in which he acknowledged his indebtedness in the sum of 2,400 pounds to Joseph Darell, a Charleston merchant.[10] In addition to being the captain's creditor, Joseph Darell was the owner of his vessel, the *Rebecca*, a square-sterned, fifteen-ton craft that had been built in Bermuda in 1767. Before what seems to have been a remodeling operation in Charleston during the summer of 1773, the *Rebecca* had been the sloop *Robert*.[11]

The captain's signature on the bond, whether he intended it or not, symbolized the tying of his destiny to that of the Carolina port. He would be absent for several years of maritime activity before settling in Charleston. But the signature was a public act, presaging other public acts that he would take as a more solid citizen in the years to come. As a man who assumed responsibility, Captain Vesey would become known in the community, and his influence would be exerted in several fields. Through a former slave, his influence was later to be given expression in a way he could hardly have anticipated.

# SLAVERY
# IN THE ISLANDS

● The spotlight of history, in playing back over the personal world of a child slave, cannot focus on details of character and event. By design of its rulers, the captive society in which the child lived offered no outlets for personal expression, no medium for a personal record to be inscribed on. Though the slave might be kindly treated, he was expected to display more of the responsive nature of a draft animal than the individuality of a human being. If the slave was capable of mental creativity, he had less opportunity to register it than even the most lowly members of non-slave society.

Yet in the almost animal environment of slavery, there were cultural forces and accidents of timing that shaped individual characters. Despite the difficulties of narrowing retrospective vision to a well deliniated scene at St. Thomas (Virgin Islands) in 1781, the historian can note that that place and that time were influential in producing a significant individual career. On this West Indian island in this year lived an unknown slave boy whose personality, while it was being ignored by his masters, was inevitably being molded by an impersonal and uncaring world. For want of any record of an earlier name, call the boy "Denmark," the name he later acquired.

That part of the slave boy's life story which preceded 1781 remains curtained in mystery. He may have been born of slave parents on the West Indian island of St. Thomas, or he may have been born in Africa and have been brought to St. Thomas as a child.[1]

In the years immediately preceding 1781 the Danes were bringing about 1,200 Negroes annually to their island colony of St. Thomas.[2] Since most of the slave cargoes came from Guinea, it is likely that if the character of Denmark himself was not shaped by the culture of Guinea, his antecedents were a product of this society. The Guinea coast at this time had highly organized kingdoms with well recognized social strata signified by forms of deference and prestige differentials. These were all part of the African native's experience before he reached the New World. Most of the slaves in the Danish colony in 1767 (the year of Denmark's birth, according to a later estimate) had been captured in inter-tribal warfare or through some form of treachery. A few had been sold by relatives to satisfy debts. A very few had been sold as punishment for some crime. They came from all levels of the highly stratified African society.[3]

Upon their arrival in St. Thomas, the Africans were received by the island slaves with an initiation ceremony in which the neophytes were baptized and prayed over in the Congo tongue. They were given several lashes across the back to atone for their sins in Guinea. This ceremony had no relation to religion but was a part of the introduction of the new arrival to a pair of foster-parents or god-parents who would take some responsibility for his adjustment to his new life.

Conditions of life among the slaves of St. Thomas varied according to the nature of their work. Laborers on the plantations lived in crude slave houses which were lined up in rows, with as many as fifty or sixty to the row. These dwellings were primitive huts, their roofs thatched with cane stalks and their walls plastered with mud and cow manure. Each family was allotted a house and a piece of land, which it was expected to till and from which it was supposed to obtain most of its food.

Slaves who were skilled craftsmen—masons, carpenters, coopers, tailors, barbers—and the warehouse workers lived for the most part in the town of Charlotte Amalia. Their quarters gradually grew in the savannahs between the hills on which the town was built. The skilled craftsmen, warehouse workers, and house servants enjoyed much more comfortable circumstances and worked shorter hours than did the field laborers, who were at the bottom of the social ladder in slave society.

In addition to the stratification according to occupation, another division which emerged as the colony grew older was that between slaves born in the West Indies and those newly arrived from Africa. A contemporary St. Thomas observer reported that the West Indian Negro looked with scorn on the African-born, referring to the African by the insulting name of "salt head" and classing him with oxen so far as intelligence went. Because the West Indian Negro was born in the land of the whites, he considered himself, according to the white observer, not only much higher socially than the other but also much cleverer.

There was also a social distinction between the slaves and the free Negroes in the colony. In 1773 "336 free negroes and colored persons"[4] were counted in the island's census. They in all likelihood provided for Denmark's first contact with free persons of his own race.

To learn the cost of a fight for freedom, young Denmark had only to observe the Danes' methods of discouraging slave rebels. Their laws for those who aspired to freedom were designed to supply a memorable lesson. One of these laws provided that leaders of runaways should be "pinched thrice" with red hot irons and then hanged. A Negro found guilty of conspiracy was to lose a leg, unless the owner requested a lightening of the sentence to 150 lashes and the loss of the culprit's ears. Slaves failing to report a plot of which they had knowledge were to be branded on the forehead and to receive 150 lashes.

If the Danes' administration of the institution of slavery "educated" Denmark by the harsh precept of the lash and the branding iron, another institution on the island offered education by the gentler method of an appeal to the spirit. In 1732 the Moravians had organized a mission to minister to the slaves on St. Thomas. Between 1732 and 1782 the missionaries to the Danish West Indies baptized 8,833 adults and 2,974 children. Although the Moravians at first took the institution of slavery as they found it and made no protest against it as such, they sought to mitigate its evils by securing their converts as laborers on the mission estates. In the end this militated against the success of their effort because of a not unnatural suspicion among the intended proselytes that those who were at the same time taskmasters and religious teachers could not be wholly devoted to their pupils' spiritual welfare. Eventually the mission came to be intimately connected with the movement for the abolition of slavery. Late in the eighteenth century J. P. Brissot de Warville, founder of the Society of the Friends of the Blacks, reported that the Moravians had "a pretty little settlement near the town" in St. Thomas and that "they have never received a Negro whom they have not liberated."[5]

In the years just prior to 1780 the missionaries were using native assistants, especially for the instruction of potential church members and for the administration of discipline. Among these was Cornelius, a gifted and devout freed-man who served the mission for forty-seven years before he died at eighty-four. Speaking Danish, Dutch, English, and German, he enjoyed universal respect among all classes. His visits to slaves on scattered plantations day and night won him their devotion, and his preaching attracted men of rank and education. While Denmark in later years may not have exhibited the same compassionate nature as Cornelius, the mental accomplishments which were attributed to Denmark were not unlike those of the Moravians' native assistant. Denmark's acquaintances later credited him with great lingual ability and with familiarity with the scriptures. Cornelius demonstrated that Denmark had available on St. Thomas the font for such learning.[6]

At the time of Denmark's boyhood stay there, St. Thomas was used as a slave trading center as well as an area for producing sugar and cotton. Except on the occasion of hurricanes which sometimes ravaged the island, it was not a climatically uncomfortable place to live. In 1773—with Denmark remaining neutral during the course of a European war—prosperity blossomed on St. Thomas and the population greatly increased. The island's harbor was crowded with

vessels of all nations. The town limits of Charlotte Amalia
were extended. Business establishments multiplied. Thousands of refugees, adventurers, and capitalists visited the
island's shores.[7]

In 1775 the total population of St. Thomas was 4,684.
Out of this total, only 336 persons were white. The 4,348
Negro residents of the island included 1,457 living in Charlotte Amalia and 2,891 living in the country. This heavy
proportion of Negroes, many of them townspeople rather
than rural residents, was indicative of the small island's importance as a slave trading center.[8] Many of the residents
were destined to be on the island only temporarily. It was
with the object of removing some of the Negro residents that
Joseph Vesey, the slaver captain, put in at St. Thomas in
1781. At this time he took on board his vessel a fateful cargo
of 390 slaves. Among them was the boy, Denmark.

When a slave trader during the latter part of the
eighteenth century first saw one of the hapless human chattels
in which he dealt, there was ordinarily nothing significant
about the meeting. Slaves were simply a form of merchandise,
and slave trading at this time bulked large in the world's
commerce. In Britain, Wilberforce and Clarkson were yet to
begin their campaign against the traffic in humanity. During
the year 1771 British ports alone sent 195 ships, with a combined capacity of 47,146 slaves, to participate in the trade.
Slave cargoes had been moving toward British America since
1619, with few strong voices being raised in protest until the
late 1700's. Forty-two slave ships bearing cargoes totaling
8,050 black bondmen arrived at the single port of Charleston,
South Carolina, during 1773.

Since the West Indies was one of the principal importing
areas, the voyage of a slave ship between two of the islands
would hardly have been a noteworthy occurrence under ordinary circumstances. More than the usual stake was involved,
however, in the meeting in 1781 of Captain Vesey and the
young slave whom he took on board his vessel at St. Thomas.
The voyage from St. Thomas to St. Domingue which the four-

teen-year-old St. Thomas boy experienced on Captain Vesey's ship was not the kind of passage to which slaves were accustomed. The captain and his officers were struck with the appearance and intelligence of the youngster from the Danish slave market. They made a pet of him by taking him into the cabin and giving him presentable clothes. His name became Denmark Vesey.[9]

Denmark, as a result of this most unusual treatment aboard ship, would naturally remember the Caribbean voyage with longing after being put ashore at Cape Francais to be the slave of one of the French planters of St. Domingue.

In comparison with tiny St. Thomas, Denmark's next home represented a community of metropolitan proportions. French St. Domingue in 1781 was widely regarded as the richest colonial possession in the New World. Its population was estimated at 536,000, including 32,000 whites, 24,000 freedmen, and 480,000 slaves. It supplied not only France but half of Europe with sugar and cocoa. Its 10,695 square miles dotted with numerous great plantations represented vastness beside the thirty-two-square-mile area of St. Thomas.

When Denmark arrived at St. Domingue in 1781 the French were already sowing the seeds of revolution by their severe treatment of their slaves. Their rigorous discipline provided ample fuel for slave talk of violence. And young minds such as Denmark's were waiting receptacles for explosive ideas.

Denmark reached Cape Francais not long after another young Negro emigrant who was destined to lead a violent slave reaction against oppression. It was in 1779 that a twelve-year-old Negro boy ran away from his home, reported to have been either on the West Indian island of Grenada or St. Kitts. The boy was given refuge by a French sailing master who took him to Cape Francais. In a little more than ten years his new island home of St. Domingue would be torn by a revolt of black men against white. And Henry, the runaway, would be starting his climb toward imperial heights as Henry Christophe, King of Haiti.

Though the period which Denmark spent in the French colony as the property of a planter was relatively short, it was long enough for him to experience something of the life of a West Indian plantation. The shell was blown at daylight to call the field slaves to their work, and if they were not there on time they were flogged. Assigned to gangs, they labored in rows under drivers who used whips to force the weak to keep up with the strong. And if death was hastened by this treatment, it was the price of being physically inferior. Work continued until sunset with two intermissions, one for a half hour in the morning and the other for two hours at noon.

The daylight-to-sunset schedule, however, was followed only during what was called the "out of crop" season of the year—or the time when the slaves were preparing the lands for the crop. In the crop season their labor was of longer duration. On estates where manpower was limited (the most numerous kind) the slaves were formed into two shifts which changed at noon and midnight. The "boilers" and others about the sugar cane works were relieved at noon. They then had a rest period which was terminated by "shell blow" at 1:30 p.m. From this time till dark they carried cane tops or grass to the cattle pens. They were then allowed to rest till midnight, at which time they in turn were required to relieve the shift in the boiling house. Estates with larger work forces divided them into three shifts.

On the typical West Indian plantation slave laborers were considered more as work units than as men, women, and children. Births and deaths were counted in terms of profit and loss, and the cost of rearing black children was balanced against the cost of bringing in new Africans. Cruelty and kindliness were given balance sheet value.

Though the exact length of Denmark Vesey's stay on St. Domingue has not been recorded, it was probably for a period of three months or less. Upon Captain Vesey's return to the French colony on his next voyage, he was again confronted by Denmark.[10] The planter who had purchased him maintained that he was "unsound and subject to epileptic fits." In accordance with the custom of the slave trade on the island, the boy was examined by the king's physician who agreed that he was unsound, whereupon Captain Vesey was required to take him back. Denmark thereupon became Vesey's personal servant.[11] From that time, on ocean voyages and ashore, he shared the observations of the seasoned Bermuda voyager.

Denmark Vesey, upon visiting his master's one-time island home of Bermuda, would have found little reason to prefer it to the society to which he was accustomed. Slavery had existed in Bermuda from 1616 or earlier, and during most of this time the slaves had outnumbered their masters. In 1774, however, the population of the Bermudas numbered 5,632 white persons and 5,023 blacks. In 1622 an act to "restrayne the insolencies of Negroes" was passed. Under its terms, Negroes were forbidden to carry weapons or to be out at night except by order of their masters, who were to be held responsible for thefts committed by their slaves. With regard to a Negro found straggling later than a half an hour after the setting of the sun, "any English man" was authorized "to kill him then & thiere without mercye." Moreover, if in such a situation the Negro resisted apprehension and the Englishman failed to give speedy pursuit and then give information on the episode to the nearest magistrate, he would be liable for 100 pounds of tobacco.

Slaves in Bermuda were allowed very few religious privileges and very little education for the most part, but the severity of the restrictions on learning and religious expression varied with the times.

Insurrections by the free colored people and slaves against the whites were found in the making on several occasions. As a result of conspiracies or fear of insurrections, many free Negroes were banished after 1650. In 1673 a plot was discovered among the Negroes of the island, and several confessed their guilt. Six were condemned to be branded or "stigmatized in ye face [forehead] with an hott iron, and their noses slitt, and whipped; and ye rest of ye negroes stigmatized and whipt." The hot iron bore the letter "R."

After a slave plan to rise and massacre the whites was

discovered in 1761, there was great alarm, and the governor declared martial law. One Negro slave who was thought to be the leader was convicted, then burned and hanged in Warwick Parish. The evidence against him, however, was later described as "not very positive." At the time several persons were believed to have been poisoned by the slaves.[12]

As the servant of a sea captain, Denmark would have had only a transient's opportunity to see slave discipline on Bermuda. Yet even a limited observation was enough to reveal something about the universality of the stern measures needed to keep men in bondage. From St. Thomas to St. Domingue to Bermuda the harsh hand of the owners was ever raised in readiness. And in his experience at sea Denmark had a chance to note the taut rein of the traders—the men who exercised temporary authority in the interval between the strict regimens of different masters.

# SLAVE LIFE
# AT SEA

● In 1781, the year in which Captain Joseph Vesey acquired his undisposable chattel, Denmark, the captain was in the business of supplying slaves to the French on the island colony of St. Domingue where premium prices were paid.[1] Since the French in the 1780's were importing about 20,000 slaves a year to St. Domingue, this trade alone was enough to keep Captain Vesey and others busy on the sea lanes between the slave marts and the West Indian island.

During this maritime interval of his life, Denmark had an opportunity to increase his facility with languages[2] by hearing French and Spanish in addition to the English he heard spoken on shipboard. (He had already been introduced to Danish.)

The extent of Denmark's travels by sea, while something less than worldwide (as suggested by one writer[3]), were sufficient to give any bright youth an instructive cosmopolitan experience. Captain Vesey's voyages, as early as the 1770's, had linked such divergent points as St. Eustatius, St. Vincent, St. Kitts, Dominica, Hispaniola, New Providence, Jamaica, St. Croix, Tobago, and Martinique. While most of these ports of call were British, several other cultures were represented among them. St. Eustatius was Dutch; St. Croix, Danish; and Hispaniola (west part) and Martinique, French.[4]

By the time Denmark Vesey joined him, Captain Vesey had probably begun transatlantic crossings to Africa. With mainland North America and many Caribbean ports cut off by war, a busy slaver was not likely to find in the West Indies all the human cargo he needed. Moreover, it was in 1781 that a monopoly of the Danish West Indian slave trade was granted to a single company.[5]

For Denmark, the broad Atlantic and the coast of Africa offered far more challenging horizons than the cane fields which hemmed in most West Indian slaves. The three to ten months required for a trading foray to the slave coast[6] provided time for contemplation and for kaleidoscopic observations.

Africa at this time had already been exploited and degraded for several centuries by European slave traders. While domestic slavery had long existed in Africa, the overseas slave trade induced wholesale horror and debasement that changed the relatively peaceful, generous, and even gentle character of the African society of an earlier time. Africans themselves participated in and were corrupted by the transoceanic trade, but Europeans and Americans were prime movers in the activity which by Denmark Vesey's time exhibited brutality and contempt for human life on a continental scale.

A typical American slave ship of Vesey's time was a sloop, schooner, or barkentine of about fifty tons burden. Captain Vesey commanded vessels of all three types while sailing between Charleston and the West Indies. Such a ship, when engaged in ordinary freighting, had but a single deck. For a slaving voyage, however, a temporary second deck was constructed some three feet below the regular main deck. Barrels of water and food were first stowed in the hold so as to occupy as little space as possible, then a row of staunchions rising just above the barrels was erected fore and aft along the keelson. These were connected by a ridge pole from which rafters were extended to the sides of the ship. Common unplaned boards were laid on the rafters to form the temporary deck which served as slave quarters. A captain, two mates, and from three to six men and boys usually handled a craft of this kind. The ship captains (if they were not owners) generally received, in addition to their salaries, commissions of 4 slaves in 104 on gross sales; and they also were permitted to buy, transport, and sell specified numbers of slaves on their private accounts.

Though Captain Vesey had sailed ships similar to the

American slavers, by 1781 he evidently was master of a ship that was comparable with the English slave vessels of the day. These were generally twice as large as the typical 50-ton American slaver. Judging by the report that Captain Vesey in 1781 took on 390 slaves at St. Thomas, we may infer from the practice of the transatlantic trade that his ship was a vessel of about 255 tons.[7]

On a voyage to Africa, Vesey in all likelihood employed methods similar to those of the English slavers. They arranged their ships so as to make maximum use of the available space. They built platforms six to eight feet wide in the 'tween decks area of their vessels, thus nearly doubling the floor space on which slaves could be stowed.

During the time that a ship was loading its human cargo and water and provisions on the slave coast, the Negroes were ordinarily kept in a temporary stockade on deck for the sake of fresh air. While the ship was at sea, however, the slaves were kept below in their cramped quarters at night and whenever the weather was bad. They were allowed on deck for food, air, and exercise only during daylight hours. It was at this time that the crew cleaned the quarters. To compel prompt compliance with orders, some masters did not hesitate in using the whip.[8]

On the first part of the voyage, men slaves were usually kept shackled to reduce the risk of mutiny. When insurrections did occur, severe repressive measures were taken. It was customary for captains to flog the slaves after an uprising was put down. Some captains used tongs to burn the flesh of offenders, and some employed thumb screws to torture them. On some occasions insurrectionists were put to death by torture. The whole crude drama of a slaving voyage was for young Denmark a visible re-enactment of a tragic chapter in his family history.

It was not uncommon for slave ships to lose from a quarter to a third of their slaves to disease or suffocation on the "middle passage"—the designation given to the trip to the West Indies because it was the second leg of the vessels' triangular voyage: from America to Africa, from Africa to the Caribbean, and from the Caribbean back to America. Slaves with ailments incurred in the passage frequently died shortly after delivery to their purchasers. The crews of the African slavers also suffered from the effects of the middle passage. Captains often reported that seamen of slave ships arrived in the West Indies in a sickly, debilitated state. One captain related that he had frequently seen them with their toes rotted off, their lower legs swelled to the size of their thighs, and in an ulcerated state all over. He observed them lying under the balconies of the houses near the waterside in Barbados and Jamaica.

The life that Denmark Vesey experienced as the servant of a slaver captain can perhaps best be pictured by referring to descriptions of the trade in which his master was engaged during the early period of the young Negro's service with him. Denmark may actually have seen service on more than one kind of ship. A small vessel like most of those which Captain Vesey commanded carried, besides her master, perhaps ten men: two mates, a cooper, a cook, a boy, and five sailors. Her equipment consisted of a pair of swivel guns and 100 grape shot, padlocks, a dozen pair of handcuffs and shackles, a twenty-one-foot boat, some twenty-five gallons of vinegar to wash down the slave quarters between decks, and a medicine chest well stocked with Peruvian bark containing quinine. Her cargo consisted largely of rum made in Newport.[9] The larger ship which Captain Vesey commanded in 1781 carried, of course, a comparably larger company. Her complement of men would have approached sixty, with three mates and two surgeons.[10]

Acquisition of a full cargo of slaves took, in a typical case, some four months of cruising and trading on the African coast.[11] The slaver, in visiting the kingdoms of Ashantee and Dahomey in West Africa in the sections popularly known to the English as the Gold Coast and the Slave Coast, would commonly have to stop at a dozen towns and settlements in order to fill her hold with human freight. Among the trading points along this section of the coast were Agah or Agga,

Anamboe, Calabar, Cormantine, Dix's Cove, Gaboon, Ningo, Popo, Pram Pram, Quashie's Town, Salt Pond, Whydah, and Williams Fort. Traders did not travel inland themselves, depending rather on factors or natives to bring the slaves to the coast.

Goods bartered for slaves included tobacco, rum, gin, guns, powder, knives, cutlasses, kettles, pots, pans, needles, fish hooks, iron and lead bars, beads, shells (much used by African tribes for currency), linens, and cotton material.[12]

The Africans who were rounded up and thus traded for material wealth were in the process subjected to innumerable cruelties and indignities both by their original captors and by their purchasers. Though the treatment accorded the shipbound captives undoubtedly varied with different captains, the literature of the time suggests that brutality was common. Whatever Captain Vesey's tendencies might have been, Denmark in the course of his travels undoubtedly witnessed enough inhumanity in the trader and slave relationship to intensify the dislike for slavery which his personal status had already induced. Denmark's familiarity with the trade, however, went beyond his personal experiences. One of his associates later told of a pamphlet on the slave trade which Denmark possessed.[13]

A factual account of the life slaves experienced on shipboard should be a relevant part of a report on Denmark's career, since he did extensive voyaging on a slave ship. One of the most dispassionate and yet vivid descriptions of a slaver in the literature on the subject is contained in a letter written from Barbados in the West Indies sometime in 1795-96 by Dr. George Pinckard of London.

The doctor and a companion visited an American slave ship not unlike one of Vesey's vessels. She had just arrived from the Guinea coast and was bound for Savannah, Georgia. The ship's master and mate greeted them courteously and readily answered their questions. Of the cargo of 130 slaves, two-thirds were males and one-third females, with a majority of the whole group being between the ages ten and eighteen.

The sexes were kept separate below decks by a bulkhead across the ship, with the waist allocated to the men and the quarterdeck to the women.

Bare planks served as their common bed, each individual having to use his arm as a pillow if he wanted one. When they were lying down they were so close together that it was scarcely possible to set foot between their naked bodies. And the men could not stand between decks without stooping. Even though the slaves were always taken on deck early in the morning and their berths thoroughly washed, the sleeping quarters were still highly offensive to European noses, the doctor reported. No measures could subdue the stench created by the slaves sleeping in such crowded fashion and depositing their excrement where they slept.

The Negroes' food was chiefly rice, which they prepared by simple boiling. To eat it, they sat on their heels around bowls, each putting his hand in the container to claw out what he wanted. Some of the time when they were on deck was occupied in beating the red husks off the rice. The doctor observed several of them pounding the grain, standing upright and indolently raising a pestle and then letting it fall of its own weight into a mortar containing unhusked rice. This was done to the accompaniment of a song and seemed to be a labor of cheerfulness.

Some members of the human cargo were used in working the ship, several of them becoming expert sailors and making themselves highly useful during the passage. All of the involuntary passengers seemed to regard the master of the vessel more in affection than in fear, said the doctor. And though they were strictly obedient, they did not seem to be at all under the influence of terror.

During the day the slaves were dispersed about the ship and roused to bodily exercise to divert their minds "from dwelling upon their change of state and loss of home." As Dr. Pinckard and his friend walked through different groups of them, they observed an air of general cheerfulness and contentment, noting signs of despondency and dejection in only a few. Both sexes were without clothes except for a narrow band of blue cloth tied about the waist and running through the crotch from front to back. Boys were inclined to be playful and to exhibit youthful tricks. In the girls, whose reserve was unchecked by education, the doctor detected an occasional "expressive look" or "significant gesture." Many individuals had marks on the skin which appeared to have been made by a cutting instrument. The visitors learned later that these were distinctive of the nation to which the Negroes belonged. Some of the company had their teeth cut or filed to sharp points, which gave them "a hideous and canine appearance." Although some of the slaves had an eruption on the skin called "Cra-Cra," the group for the most part looked healthy and well fed.

Encouraged by the music of the banjo, the captives sometimes danced and sang while on deck during the day. The doctor reported that they scarcely moved their feet but waved their arms about, writhed and twisted their bodies "into a multitude of disgusting and indecent attitudes." Their song was "a wild and savage yell," chanted "loudly and in harsh monotony," and "devoid of all softness and harmony."

Having finished his tour, the doctor said he had seen no marks of the cruelties said to be practiced on board the ships engaged in the traffic in human flesh. Chains and severities did not seem to be among the devices used in conveying this cargo of Negroes to their American masters. Care evidently was taken to promote their health and comfort. But the doctor nevertheless felt compelled to record that his mind and that of his companion necessarily "suffered in contemplating the degrading practices of civilized beings toward the less cultivated heathen of their species."[14]

Dr. Pinckard's observations on the Guinea man were recorded in the mid-1790's. The scene was one that would have been familiar to Joseph Vesey. Only a few years before, his ship had ridden at anchor in the same harbor.

# SLAVE CITY
# IN A FREE REPUBLIC

● Although South Carolina's capital city had a spacious harbor, it was not an easy one for an eighteenth-century master to enter. A sand bank, with only a few breaks in it, extended almost from shore to shore across the mouth of the bay. Ships could enter by one or the other of the openings where the water even at low tide was about twelve feet deep. But the channels were not easily distinguished, and the passage at night was especially difficult. Moreover, the anchorage ground outside the bank was only usable when the sea was calm.[1]

The sand barrier and the twelve-foot low water depth at the Charleston bar did not, however, prevent big ships of the time from entering the port. Vessels sailing between Charleston and Europe in colonial times ranged up to 500 tons burden. The great majority of vessels engaged in the Charleston trade carried from 1,000 to 1,200 barrels of rice, which meant that their capacity was from 250 to 300 tons. Ships drawing about eleven feet and of less than 200 tons burden could easily pass the Charleston bar even at low water.[2] While the sloops, schooners, and brigantines which Captain Vesey commanded during the colonial period were in the fifty-ton class, the vessel which he commanded at the close of the war was in a class with the big ships in the Charleston trade.

When he headed for Charleston again after the war, the Bermuda captain was an experienced veteran in maritime commerce, both in terms of the variety of craft he had commanded and the number of voyages he had made. As he sailed by Sullivan's Island into the harbor mouth and caught sight of the oaks and lofty pines along the shore, the scene was one that had become familiar to him in visits of the previous decade. This same view had greeted Captain Vesey many times during the 1770's as he sailed into the bay from St. Kitts, Dominica, or some other Caribbean port. But in 1783 the captain's perspective changed from that of a visitor to that of a settler. He would no longer have to worry about negotiating the bar or be prepared for such things as the disciplinary roar of a cannon shot aimed at an absent-minded or disobedient captain. "Vessels," warned a Charleston newspaper of 1783, "which shall attempt to pass the battery, without paying regard to the instructions, will pay Two Dollars for the first charge and Four Dollars for every other charge which should be fired at them."[3]

As the voyager sailed inward, the outline of the town rose out of the fertile fields and wooded country on either side of the Ashley and Cooper rivers. The Carolina coast was one more different landfall for the young Negro aboard, now, at sixteen, a veteran sailor. Charleston's skyline was flat except for a few protuberances such as St. Michael's whose 192-foot steeple was often visible from vessels before they made any land.

Located at the confluence of the Ashley and Cooper Rivers about five miles above the point at which they flow into the Atlantic, the city was well placed as a center of inland plantation and transoceanic trade. Canoes, small boats, and pettygues plied the rivers, bringing down plantation produce and returning with necessities for the planters. Pettygues were the work boats of the river and coastal trade. They were decked vessels forty or more feet long, ordinarily propelled by oars but sometimes having sails mounted on two removable masts. These and other boats were likely to be competing with ships for space along the crowded waterfront. Most of the wharves were located along the Cooper River, which was the busiest of the two streams. The Cooper on the north side of the city could accommodate ships for twenty miles of its course and smaller vessels for forty miles. The Ashley River on the other side was navigable for only a short distance.[4]

During the summer of 1783 Captain Vesey signified his intention to establish himself in Charleston. On July 16 of that year he leased from John Christian Smith, shopkeeper of Charleston, two lots of land, one on King Street and the other in the village of Dorchester, paying five shillings for a one-year agreement. The public record of the lease gave the city as Vesey's place of residence but identified him as a "mariner." Two months later, however, the former master of the *Rebecca* had become a land-based slave merchant. In late September of 1783 the schooner *Dove*, a fast, Bermuda-built vessel of some fifty-seven tons,[5] put into Charleston from St. Thomas. The issue of the *South Carolina Gazette and General Advertiser* which noted her arrival also contained an advertisement directing anyone interested in buying the *Dove* to apply at the place of "JOE VESEY" at 27-1/4 Bay. In addition to the *Dove*, J. Vesey & Co." was advertising the forty-five-ton schooner *Polly*, and her cargo of slaves, which had arrived from Tortola a few days before the *Dove*. A second batch of slaves, said to have been brought in by the schooner *Eagle*, was offered for sale by Vesey's company at the same place as the *Polly's* cargo.[6]

Customers were solicited by the following words:

Negroes,
On Wednesday the first of October, at Mrs. Dewees, No. 43,[7] Queen-street,
Will be exposed for sale, 104 Prime Slaves, just imported in the schooner *Eagle*, Captain David Miller. The Sale will continue every fair day (Sundays excepted) until all be Sold.
The conditions will be made as convenient as possible to the purchasers.

J. Vesey & Co.[8]
No. 27-1/4 Bay.

The nature of this appeal to the buyer suggests that at this time the slave market was not too promising. The advertiser evidently did not expect the cargo to be disposed of in a single day's sale, as it might have been in other times. Moreover, the human merchandise was offered on conditions "as convenient as possible to the purchasers." And to make sure that knowledge of the sale was as widely disseminated as possible, Captain Vesey advertised in no less than three newspapers.[9]

Vesey and Company's auction, assuming that it followed Charleston slave-selling procedure of that day, was one more event guaranteed to impress on a sensitive Negro youth the indignities to which his race was subject.

> . . . The negroes [said a contemporary observer] are sold in the market of Charleston like bullocks and horses; the day of the intended auction being previously advertised in the newspapers. They are exposed to sale on a sort of stage, turned about and exhibited from all sides, by the common cryer, put up and adjudged to the highest bidder. This spectacle, which is offered four or five times a week, renders the spectators callous . . .[10]

It is not known how successful the captain was in selling the two lots of slaves. But the fact that the schooner *Polly* departed for Savannah on October 18, after being twice advertised, indicates that he may have found a buyer in that city for the Virginia-built vessel.[11]

Captain Vesey's efforts at this time to dispose of the ships as well as their cargoes indicated that he was ready to get out of the slave-carrying business and into a different occupation. Certainly this particular time was not auspicious for setting up shop as a slave merchant. Henry Laurens, one of the greatest of the South Carolina slave factors, regarded the season for selling Negroes as practically over by September because of the greater danger of losses from sickness in cold weather. The immediate postwar period was also one of declining demand for slaves.

Within eleven years after the Declaration of Independence every state except Georgia had by law prohibited or severely restricted the traffic in human chattels. South Carolina in 1784 placed a duty of three pounds sterling on Negroes imported from Africa and Asia, and a duty of five pounds sterling on those from any other part of the world. Although slaves from any part of the United States were still allowed to come in duty free after a residence of six months, the state for economic reasons in 1787 prohibited the foreign slave trade altogether[12]—a restriction that was to be renewed from time to time until 1803 when an expansion of rice and cotton cultivation was to make a re-opening of the traffic profitable. From 1792 to 1802 the importation of slaves from other states was also forbidden.[13]

Even before the trade was cut off by statute, the flow of Negroes had shrunk below what it had been in some prewar years. A visitor to Charleston in January 1784 reported that a company had been formed there for carrying on the slave trade to the coast of Africa and, "in the space of two years since the peace proposals," had brought in some 3,000 blacks to the Charleston market and sold them. In September 1785 John Rutledge told a committee of the legislature that in the period since the peace not more than 7,000 slaves had been imported. This two-year figure compared with a total of 8,050 in the single year of 1773. Moreover, the legislators were even then debating the advisability of prohibiting slave importations for three years because of the strain on credit caused by the trade. So if Captain Vesey had chosen to remain in the business, he faced a declining patronage unless he later participated in the illicit trade that was conducted by land and sea during the prohibition period.[14]

Another factor militating against Captain Vesey's remaining in business as a slave broker was that he could hardly have been well known to Charleston area planters. A successful slave merchant had to have trusting acquaintances throughout a wide territory, since the planters were cautions about bonding themselves to a little-known dealer. Slaves represented a heavy investment, with "prime" men in a good year (1773, for example) selling for 350 pounds currency (about 50 pounds sterling) on the Carolina market, and "prime" women bringing 290 pounds currency (41 pounds sterling).[15] Boys and girls sold for proportionately less. In a less favorable year a merchant received from 25 to 35 pounds sterling a "head" for his slave merchandise.

If Captain Vesey did not in 1783 yield to the difficulties of continuing large-scale slave marketing in Charleston, he

did within a few years. A shift in the captain's business interests from slave-selling to merchandising ships' supplies began
as early as 1784 when he was listed in ship manifests for the
port as the consignee for various shipments of hardware,
anchors, grapnels, salt, rum, and sugar. During this same
year, however, he was also the importer of three Negro wom-
en, one child, and a slave simply listed as a "new negro."[16]

The captain's Bay Street neighbors in 1783 were obviously shipping agents who could be helpful to one going into
the business of marine merchandising. In November John
William Nusum of 27-1/2 Bay (Vesey's slave-marketing
address had been 27-1/4 Bay) sought to charter a vessel of
200 or 300 tons for a voyage to the West Indies with a stop
for loading at Savannah. A week later James Blair of 29 Bay
advised those desiring to send freight or book passage to
London to apply to Captain Benjamin Sproule of the ship
*Flora* moored at Prioleau's wharf. (Twenty years later Captain Vesey was to marry a Mrs. Blair.) Enterprises such as
these would be quite likely to disclose a need for outfitting
supplies.[17] By 1790 the Charleston Directory identified Joseph
Vesey of 281 King Street simply as a "ship chandler," an
occupation for which the former captain was undoubtedly
suited by both experience and acquaintanceship.[18]

While the ex-Bermuda mariner, Captain Joseph Vesey,
was settling himself in Charleston, the city itself was settling
into life under the new American republic. The Revolution
had left its scars as well as the necessity for readjustment to
an economy independent of a mother country. Slavery was
one aspect of the economy which the war had affected in a
noticeable way. The British fleet in 1782 carried away from
South Carolina 5,333 Negroes, and, according to the contemporary David Ramsay, the total number of slaves taken
off during the war was 25,000—a figure that may, however,
have been exaggerated.

The French nobleman, the Duke de la Rochefoucauld-
Liancourt, reported in 1796 that the number of Negroes
(whether in Charleston or all of South Carolina was not

specified) who were slain or escaped from their masters during the war was not less than 30,000, including between 600 and 700 whom the English carried away when they evacuated.[19]

Although the formal evacuation by the British had occurred in December, 1782, a Charleston business man on March 18, 1783, was warning slave owners to guard against the seizure of their slaves by the British. In a letter to a newspaper "an old suffering Merchant" noted that he had seen a British "picaroon" in the harbor and observed that it would be embarrassing to have a cargo consigned to him captured after it reached port. "Inhabitants of Charleston," he urged, "keep a strict eye over your black walking property."[20]

Negroes themselves, however, were not necessarily unwilling passengers of the British. During the war Negroes had sometimes fled from the plantations to the British camp. And they had been known to inform British troops of American movements.[21] South Carolina Negroes naturally had no particular stake in the American cause. In fact, a committee of the Continental Congress in 1779 reported, on the basis of information supplied by South Carolina officials, that the state could not effectively employ its militia against the British because much of that force was needed as a home guard to prevent rebellion and flight on the part of the slaves. Subsequently South Carolina rejected a suggestion from Congress that it free and arm some 3,000 slaves and employ them against the English.[22]

As a result of the departure of some of the slaves, Charleston was faced with the task of repairing its war damage with a smaller work force than it might otherwise have counted on. The great plantations, on which the life of the city largely depended, had been put out of commission. Most of the houses in the city had suffered from enemy fire, with those south of Broad Street having been hit by ships' guns and those in the northern part having been bombarded by the land batteries of the invaders. Pillaging and burning had reduced stocks of goods. The paper money in circulation had become valueless.

Despite these difficulties, Charleston began quickly to revive. In 1783 the city was incorporated by act of the legislature under the name of Charleston.[23] With its corporate area divided into thirteen wards and including all of the peninsula south of Boundary Street (now Calhoun Street), it was to be governed by thirteen wardens (one from each ward), from among whom an intendant was to be chosen by the people. On September 11, 1783, Richard Hutson was elected to the post. Several weeks later Captain Robert Cochran was appointed harbor master for the port.[24]

Among the signs of the city's recovery were the brigs, scows, and schooners in the harbor. A German physician, Dr. Johann David Schoepf, who stayed in Charleston from January 14 to March 9, 1784, reported that trade had again reached pre-Revolutionary levels. In 1786 the Reverend Francis Asbury commented on the city's "flourishing condition." And in February, 1793, he mentioned that the list of vessels in the harbor included fifty-three ships, fifty-five brigs, twenty-five sloops, twenty-five schooners, seven snows, and two barques, besides pilot boats and coasters. Obviously such a volume of shipping created opportunities for dealers in marine supplies. But these signs of business activity did not tell a story of uniform prosperity. There was a postwar economic lull. The shipping figures were most impressive when viewed against the dormant commercial period of the Revolution. Josiah Quincy, on visiting Charleston as early as 1773, had noted that "350 sail lay off the town."[25]

From a pre-war population of between 10,000 and 12,000, as reported by Dr. Schoepf, Charleston grew very rapidly until 1790, when the first federal census gave a total population of 16,920, of whom 8,089 were white people and 8,831 were Negroes.

Another indication of Charleston's postwar rejuvenation was the number of new houses of brick and stone replacing the wooden ones burned during the war. Schoepf gave the total number of houses in the city in 1784 as 1,500.

As they rebuilt, Charlestonians managed to give their community some degree of architectural individuality by covering brick with stucco in delicate shades of blue, green, pink, and yellow, and by using colored instead of drab slate shingles. Although most of the dwellings followed the Georgian style, with its balanced facade and ornate classical doorway, owners often departed from the strict integrity of the design by hiding three-tiered piazzas behind false walls with doorways on the street side.

Charleston houses were described by Dr. Schoepf as having "airy and cool rooms . . . spacious yards and gardens, and the kitchen . . . always placed in a separate building . . . to avoid the heat and the danger of fire."

The Duke de la Rochefoucauld-Liancourt, who landed in March, 1796, reported that, despite the large number of slaves in Charleston, the houses were not kept as clean as in the northern states. He observed:

> . . . Every thing peculiar to the buildings of this place is formed to moderate the excessive heats; the windows are open, the doors pass through both sides of the houses. Every endeavour is used to refresh the apartments within with fresh air. Large galleries are formed to shelter the upper part of the house, from the force of the sun's rays; and only the cooling north-east wind is admitted to blow through the rooms. In Charleston persons vie with one another, not who shall have the finest, but who the coolest house. . . .
>
> Houses, otherwise commodious and well furnished, make often but a poor appearance outwardly. They are indifferently painted, or perhaps not at all. The doors and railings are in very bad state. The air being so thick and so saline, soon destroys the colouring.

At the time of Captain Vesey's early residence in Charleston the chief public buildings were St. Michael's and St. Philip's churches, the State House, the Guard House, and the New Exchange (all on Broad Street) and Vaux Hall and the St. Cecilia Society building (on Tradd Street). The county jail was built between 1783 and 1800 on property bounded by Queen, Magazine, Back (now Logan) and Masyck streets. Like the city's private residences and most of its structural work, these buildings stood as solid testimony to the contribution of slave labor to the community.

Charleston's streets were almost all narrow and unpaved.

Because of the scarcity of stones, paving was expensive. A little paving was done with stones brought as ballast in ships; but the streets were mostly of sand which blew about when the wind rose and drifted into the houses. When heavy rains came, the sand held the water in puddles, adding to the discomfort of pedestrians who had to use the streets. Some of the streets had foot paths at the side, but these were narrow and broken by doors of cellars, and therefore of limited value.

Yet Charleston, despite its defects, was a comparatively comfortable place in which to live—at least for the well-to-do. Its manner of life, dress, equipages, furniture, according to a contemporary foreign visitor, denoted a "higher degree of taste and love of show, and less frugality than in the northern provinces." Charlestonians, he reported, "live rapidly, not willingly letting go untasted any of the pleasures of this life." At the same time, he observed, "there is courtesy here, without punctiliousness, stiffness or formality."

George Washington was prompted to praise the city's hospitality and gaiety after a visit in 1791,[26] while the Duke de la Rochefoucauld-Liancourt was so captivated that he said he knew of no town in the United States where the visitor would enjoy himself more or which he would leave with greater regret.

From John Bernard, the English comedian who visited the city at the turn of the century, came an appreciative assessment of Charleston's preoccupation with life's pleasures. The "citizens" he said, "seemed a world in themselves, very leisurely and happily taking things as they went, and twining the locks of old Time as though their hue were not gray but golden."[27]

The social season in Charleston, from January to March, was filled with concerts and balls of the St. Cecilia Society, as well as with private dinner parties at which the raconteur was accorded more honor than the epicure. The climax came with race week in February, followed by the Jockey Club ball. Numerous coaches, richly ornamented and bearing family crests, transported hundreds of spectators to the track grandstands.

The dinner parties, the concerts, the dances, the races, and other gay events—usually attended by slaves in a menial capacity—all presented glittering scenes for the servitors, including Denmark Vesey, to contrast with their own drab life.

Yet Charleston, with all its social glitter, was still not far removed from the frontier. In December, 1783, a large wolf was killed in Broad Street by a member of the city guard. He had been alerted by a man at the beef market whose meat the wolf was eating. The night before he was dispatched the animal had bitten two men and killed several dogs.[28]

Nor was the city cosmopolitan enough to escape the criticism of a young immigrant from the North who set his observations of 1785-1786 down in his diary. Timothy Ford found the productiveness of the soil sufficient to provide opportunities for planters and commercial interests and to invite further immigration. But he thought the ease with which money might be made conducive to pleasure-seeking and unlikely to encourage work and efforts at self-improvement. He noted little activity in science and a tendency on the part of the inhabitants to regard such pursuits as "tasteless" and a preoccupation of the needy. With science "in a state of degradation," he didn't see how art could flourish. He observed a disinterest in manufactures and a readiness to rely on the goods of foreign markets. Military art in South Carolina, according to Ford, had become "empty pajeantry and artless parade." The residents, in his view, seemed willing to forget the dangers and hardships of war amidst the "alluring baits of pleasure." Despite the obvious spending of money, Ford found the sought-after luxuries unworthy of the name. Food in particular he thought was poor.[29]

But Ford, for whom opportunity was hedged in by no restrictions of caste, was soon to be defending the culture into which he had moved against other attackers.

# BURDEN BEARERS
# IN SOUTH CAROLINA

● By the final decade of the eighteenth century, slavery had been allowed to take an almost unshakeable grip on the destiny of South Carolina. Yet the imprint of the system on the state is not fully apparent in a glance at the figures from the first federal census in 1790. The census showed that the white population that year constituted 56.3 per cent of the total, one of the highest white ratios in the history of the state. In colonial times and in the nineteenth century, Negroes held a big lead. The overall 1790 figures, signifying the temporary numerical ascendancy of the non-slaveholding farmers of the upcountry, did not, however, portray the realities of Carolina society.

To appreciate the real impact of slavery, one must look not to the total state population of 249,000 in which whites held a 31,000 lead but to the figures for the lowcountry which shaped South Carolina's true political and economic character. In the Charleston district—composed roughly of the present counties of Charleston, Berkeley, Dorchester, and Colleton—there were in 1790 only 15,402 whites as against 51,846 Negroes (775 of them free). Yet the lowcountry— made up of the Charleston district and two other big slave-owning areas—ran the state government (as will be seen in the next chapter) and spoke for South Carolina in national councils.

In the lower part of the state the heavy concentration of slaves bespoke wealth, a considerably more direct lever for political power in 1790 than it is today. It also provided a commentary on the nature of the economy and on the division of labor. The plantation character of the Charleston district was suggested by a density of 13.4 Negroes per square mile, greater than in any other area in the state. In the city of Charleston itself, where employment considered more compatible with free white status was available, the population ratio was nearly even. This population equilibrium of urban society was in sharp contrast to the extreme disparity between black and white on some of the nearby plantations. One traveler of the period reported that M. Bligh, who lived in England but had several plantations in South Carolina, owned between 1,200 and 1,500 Negroes. Ralph Izard, whom the census of 1790 reported to be the next to the largest planter in the state, owned 594 slaves distributed on eight plantations in three parishes, and had besides ten other slaves in Charleston. The number of slaves employed on the average plantation, however, seems to have been between twenty-five and thirty.[1]

By 1800 the state ratio of whites to Negroes was roughly 9 to 7 (196,255 to 149,336), the widest margin the slave-holding race was to hold until the mid-twentieth century when the proportion of Negroes began to decline sharply. But in the Charleston district in 1800 the ratio was more than three to one in favor of Negroes (63,615 to 18,768). In that same year the average price of "prime field hands" in the Charleston district was $500. The dollar figure gives a clue to the wealth of the slave-holders of the area, while the population totals suggest the relative strength of arbitrarily harnessed manpower and hence the potential for Negro revolt. The potential was sometimes recognized by the dominant group but at other times was discounted because owners preferred to believe that no slave leader would emerge who would see the significance of the numbers.

The Negroes who formed such a substantial part of the population of South Carolina performed a great many of the essential tasks which kept both the rural and urban economy of the state going. Without knowing it, they held the power to paralyze the economy of the lowcountry. A visitor reported in 1784 that there was hardly any trade or craft which had not been learned and was not being carried on by Negroes.

"The gentlemen in the country," he observed, "have among their negroes, as the Russian nobility among their serfs, the most necessary handicraftsmen, cobblers, tailors, carpenters, smiths, and the like, whose work they command at the smallest possible price, or for nothing almost."

Field slaves, though they were the key workers in an agricultural economy, did not always constitute a majority of the plantation Negro population. La Rochefoucauld-Liancourt noted that, in a plantation with seventy slaves, no more than forty worked—the rest being the old, the sick, or children. Moreau de St. Mery remarked that field slaves made up only a third of the total number of Negroes on the plantations. Estimates of a single slave's productive capacity ranged upward from five barrels of rice a year, and his value to his master was placed at anywhere from eight to nineteen times the cost of his maintenance.[2] These figures, while suggestive of exploitation, do not, of course, depict the actual profit picture, since they do not reflect the cost of maintaining economically non-productive slaves.

In Charleston the market was perhaps the greatest single field of employment for Negroes. There were three markets in the city—two for vegetables, meat, and other provisions, and one for fish. They opened each morning at sunrise with the ringing of the market bells. Any persons who offered anything for sale before the signal by the bells was subject to a penalty. If the offender was free, the penalty was a fine: if a slave, it was thirty-nine lashes and confinement to the stocks for not more than six hours.

Conditions in and near the market were indicated by the frequent references in contemporary writing to the vultures in the city. The German visitor, Dr. Schoepf, wrote: "They eat up what sloth has not removed out of the way, and so have a great part in maintaining cleanliness and keeping off unwholesome vapors from dead beasts and filth."

Much of the merchandising activity in the markets was conducted by slaves who sold provisions, fruit, and garden stuff for their planter masters. Owners were required only to furnish their slaves with tickets specifying the quantity and quality of the produce offered for sale. Although Negroes were strictly forbidden to sell in the public markets anything not produced at or received from their masters' plantations or to buy anything in order to sell it again, these regulations were obviously extremely hard to enforce.

Slaves employed by the big planters eventually monopolized the market business. The man with small capital and a few acres of land could not hope to supply the market as cheaply as the big plantation owner. Moreover, the white property owner who tilled his land himself felt (according to the social code of the day) humiliated when he attempted to sell his produce in the market and was jostled by competing slaves. There were a few white farmers in this class near Charleston who owned the necessary fifty-acre freehold of an elector. But the more energetic among them began to emigrate to the West.

Fishing was another occupation which was carried on principally by Negroes. Licensed fishermen were required to register with the city clerk the dimensions of their boats, the tackle, and the number of hands employed on board, along with their names and to whom they belonged. Punishment for failure to make such an entry within a specified time might be thirty-nine lashes and the withdrawal of the fisherman's license. Fishermen were the only class of slaves who could lawfully own vessels, but this law was frequently violated.

It was because fishing was largely given over to Negroes that they were active in the fish market. Sometime after the passage of the authorizing law in 1770, this market was located on a "low water lot" opposite the bay end of Queen Street.

In addition to marketing and fishing, Negroes in Charleston were also employed as butchers, carpenters, bricklayers, blacksmiths, wheelwrights, pump or blockmakers, cabinet makers, painters, glaziers, gold and silversmiths, tailors, tinmen, tanners, curriers, coopers, shoemakers, barbers, hatters, ropemakers, turners, handicraftsmen, and mariners. A few of these craftsmen were free Negroes, but most of them were slaves working for their masters or hired out to other employers at a profit.

Denmark Vesey as a free man in later life was to earn his living at carpentry, a trade in which he presumably had some experience as a slave.

The business of hiring out Negroes was widespread, and its practitioners ranged from the indolent owners of a few slaves who "farmed" them out and lived on their wages, to the big slave-owners who looked to their hiring arrangements to add to their other financial dividends. Regarded as capital, the slave let out on hire was expected to earn his food and clothes and bring in annually to his master from 15 to 20 per cent interest. Masters, however, viewed hired-out slaves as an unstable investment because they might run away, become incapacitated through sickness, or be lost through death. The hirer was therefore required to give bond immediately for the payment of stipulated sums at stipulated dates. Wages were payable monthly, yearly, or otherwise, depending on the individual agreement. Sometimes a slave, instead of finding employment for himself or having his master find it for him at a specified price, had his services put up at auction to the highest bidder.

A substantial portion of Charleston city revenue came from masters who let out slaves for hire and who were required to purchase licenses or badges for these workers. Badges or tickets good for a year sold in 1783 for the following sums: for a butcher, forty shillings; carpenter, bricklayer, fisherman, blacksmith, wheelwright, pump or blockmaker, cabinet maker, painter, glazier, and gold or silversmith, twenty shillings; for a tinman, tanner, or currier, fifteen shillings; for a mariner, cooper, shoemaker, barber, hatter, ropemaker, turner, or any other handicraft tradesman, ten shillings; and for all others the sum was five shillings. The same prices were charged free Negroes who let out their own services.[3]

While wages, of course, varied, one cabinet maker who owned slaves for hire was getting as much as twenty pounds per month for skilled handicraftsmen as early as 1776. In 1795 La Rochefoucauld-Liancourt reported that carpenters' wages at Charleston were $2.50 per day for white workmen and $1.50 per day for Negroes. Because of the social stigma attached to manual labor, mechanics in Charleston, according to one observer, came to bear nothing more of their trade than the name. Slaves did their work for them. Meanwhile many of them emigrated northward as a result of the competition of Negroes in their crafts.[4]

An indication of how arrangements were made for the hiring of slaves is provided by some of the advertisements of the period. In an advertisement in the *Gazette of the State of South Carolina* for April 21, 1789, Anne Hawes advised that she carried on a painting, glazing, and paper hanging business "on reasonable terms for cash or short credit," and hired out Negro painters by the day.[5]

In October of 1793 the following notice appeared in a Charleston newspaper:

> Wanted to Hire,
> Five or Six
> Negro Carpenters,
> To work about 30 miles from town.
> Enquire at No. 264 Meeting-street.[6]

An advertiser a few years later was more specific:

> Twenty Negro Carpenters,
>      And Thirty Women,
> Are immediately wanted to cut Live Oak Timber upon Bull's Island; the former will be engaged for six months, and the latter for one year certain. Their owners may depend upon their being well taken care of, and their wages punctually paid every month by
>                    Thomas Shulbrick:
>      Who will contract for the Cutting and Delivery of the Frames of Two or Three Brigs or Schooners, in June next.[7]

The measure of such workmen's efficiency can be gauged by a contemporary estimate that two slaves could saw 600 feet of pine or 780 feet of cypress, cedar, red bay or poplar per week, "provided the trees are cut, squared and pitted to their hands."[8]

Such out-of-town projects as these may well have given

Denmark Vesey his first view of the rural area around Charleston and an acquaintance with country slaves, an acquaintance he was to find useful later.

Owners of hired-out slaves were not always happy about the hiring situation, as the following advertisement suggests:

> All persons are forbid employing my ship Carpenters, Frank and Charles, without their being engaged of me; and are also forbid paying any money to either of them; the first of who has, in direct contradiction of my orders, employed himself to work in the country. The person now employing him will therefore be sued for the money.[9]
>
> John Chamneys

While slaves were assuming an increasing share of the physical burdens of South Carolina, their role was having an effect on white residents. "The number of slaves," wrote Timothy Ford in 1784, "supply the almost total want of instruments of husbandry; & the dint of muscular force the want of invention and improvement." The Duke de la Rochefoucauld-Liancourt put it thus: "A child has a number of Negro children to attend him, and comply with all his humours; so that the little white man learns even before he can walk, to tyrannize over the blacks."[10]

In drawing up legislation to control slaves, South Carolina took its cue from Barbados, with which the Carolina colony had had a connection from the time of its founding. The West Indian island, where the English had early developed the plantation system with Negro labor, had slave enactments dating from 1644. These were broadened and incorporated into a general statute in 1688, the preamble of which declared that the "barbarous, wild and savage nature" of Negro slaves made them "unqualified to be governed by the laws, customs and practices of our nation. . . ." In 1712 the Carolina Assembly copied virtually verbatim the preamble and some of the clauses of the Barbadian law of 1688. This statute served as the colony's basic slave law until the Stono insurrection of 1739 roused the legislature into passing the more complete law of 1740.

Aimed mainly at preventing revolt, the act of 1740 provided, among other things, that no slaves were to be taught to write, no more than seven men were to travel in a group on the high roads unless accompanied by white persons, no slaves were to be kept on any plantation where no white person lived. In addition to these clearly counter-revolutionary clauses, the statute also forbade the sale of liquor to slaves without their masters' approval, forbade servants to wear anything but coarse clothing unless they were in livery, and limited the slave's work day to fourteen hours in winter and fifteen hours in summer. In later years this basic act was supplemented by curfew and patrol provisions, amended to increase penalties against Negroes for striking white persons, and to require masters to provide adequate food as well as clothing. But it was never repealed while slavery existed in South Carolina.

The first patrol law of 1702 was intended to protect the home front against possible rebellion by the "worst class of negroes," who were left there in time of invasion, while nearly all of the whites and "the better class of negroes" were called into military service. After the Stono uprising of 1739 the Assembly divided the province into patrol districts and increased the powers of patrol riders. Under this law, militia captains were required to keep lists of all persons liable for patrol duty in their areas. Those not owning or interested in slaves sixteen years old or older were excepted. Female slave-owners were required to furnish substitutes. And any regular patrolman could send a substitute between the ages of sixteen and sixty. If any responsible person failed to do his duty, the captain was authorized to employ a substitute at thirty shillings per night and to collect the cost from the defaulter by action for debt.

Every male inhabitant, upon reaching the age of eighteen, was notified that he was a member of the militia. Companies assembled on one day each month, and regiments or battalions on two days a year for exercises. At each muster the captain was required to pick a certain number of men (not more than seven) living near each other to do patrol duty until the next muster. Their rides were not to include any circuit of more than fifteen miles. In case of an insurrection, the militia officers had discretionary power to make the best use of arms, ammunition, and vessels wherever they found them. But despite the elaborate provisions for patrolling, there were frequent complaints about the failure to put the patrol act into force. A Charleston grand jury listed this failure as a general grievance in 1766.[11]

The apprehension and punishment of Negroes for violating the rules was facilitated by a law empowering ad hoc courts to handle their cases. Any justice of the peace, on being informed of the commission of a crime by a slave or free Negro, was authorized to send a constable to arrest the alleged criminal. Within three days he was to summon another justice from nearby and from three to five freeholders and proceed to try the accused. Conviction was permitted on the vote of one justice and two freeholders or one freeholder and two justices. Broad discretion was allowed in the assessment of penalties. And there was no appeal from these courts during much of their history.

The shortcomings of this system of justice were obvious even to critics within the state. There was no trial by jury and no assurance of the impartiality of the judges. The verdict did not have to be unanimous. There was no requirement that counsel be provided, or that the master or guardian be present.

In commenting on the slave law, the Duke de la Rochefoucauld-Liancourt questioned South Carolina justice. He declared:

. . . No defender is allowed to the poor wretched accused; and his judges have the power to condemn him to whatever mode of death they shall think proper. Simple theft by a negro is punished with death. When the crime is not such as to deserve capital punishment, a justice of the peace, with a single freeman, may, in this case, condemn to whatever lighter punishment they shall please to inflict. For the murder of a negro with malicious intent, a white man pays a fine of three thousand six hundred and eighty dollars. If he had only beaten the negro, without intention of murder, till his death ensued, the fine is but one thousand five hundred dollars. He who maims a negro, puts out his eyes, cuts off his tongue, or castrates him, pays only a fine of four hundred and twenty-eight dollars. In all these cases, the white man is imprisoned till the fine be paid. It is easy to see, that a white man can, in such case, seldom be convicted; as negroes are incapable by law of giving evidence; and no white man will readily offer his testimony in favour of a black, against a person of his own colour. A negro slaying a white man, in defense of his master, is pardoned. But, if he do the same thing, or even but wound a white man, in defense of his own life, he will eventually be put to death.[12]

In contrast to the duke's report, another French visitor of the period noted that a white man who killed a Negro was fined only $200. Still another writer refers to a newspaper account of 1809 telling of a fine of fifty pounds assessed against a white man for slaying a Negro.[13]

Slaves in South Carolina condemned for crimes considered particularly heinous were sometimes burned alive. Several such sentences were carried out after the Revolutionary era. Thomas Wentworth Higginson reported that two Negroes were burned at Charleston in 1808. And a contemporary newspaper story tells of the flogging and cropping of the ears of two Negroes convicted in 1802 of stealing merchandise. Two cases of the hanging of Negroes for witchcraft in South Carolina (one in Charleston) were reported in 1793.[14]

Evidently slaves sometimes escaped punishment for capital offenses because their owners did not want to lose them. La Rochefoucauld-Liancourt observed that they were on occasion shielded by their masters because the latter would receive only $128 for an executed slave. In some instances masters were squeamish about administering punishment. They preferred to send their slaves to the jail to receive a specified number of lashes.[15]

Floggings might also be administered by the patrol to slaves who absented themselves from their homes without a pass. A switch or cowhide was the specified instrument. The regulation was that no slave should be found away from his master's place, without a written pass from his master, unless he were accompanied by a white person (even a child of ten) who could vouch for the reason for his absence. In substance the pass was an order to any person or patrolman to allow the slave to "pass and repass" from a given hour on a certain day to a given hour on a later day. In practice, however, the pass usually gave the bearer permission to be absent from the plantation for a given length of time. The law of 1734 required that the document show the destination of the slave and state that he rode a horse, if he happened to be mounted.

Special regulations were adopted for slaves in the city of Charleston. With a view to limiting the number of Negroes, the law in force in 1786 provided that no master or mistress should keep for daily attendance to wants more than four slaves for the head of the house and one for each white person in the family (exclusive of children). The penalty for violation of the provision was double taxation on the slaves.

To help keep order in the city, any two commissioners of the fish market were authorized to confine riotous, disorderly, or drunken Negroes in the stocks for not more than two hours. Repeating offenders might be publicly whipped on the order of a majority of the commissioners or two justices of the peace. (The public stocks were located at the fish market.)

Under a city ordinance of 1784, a white person who broke a lamp was subject upon conviction to forfeit twenty pounds currency. A slave, however, was to be whipped through the streets to the tune of not more than thirty-nine lashes, unless the owner paid his forfeit. For wearing a free Negro's badge, a slave might be whipped up to a maximum of thirty-nine lashes and put in the stocks for at least one hour.

Masters of vessels who brought any persons of color, whether bond or free, into port were required to notify a city official as soon as they arrived.[16] The existence of this regulation suggests that Charleston officialdom would have known about Denmark Vesey some forty years before he was to give them any cause for concern.

Living conditions for slaves in postwar South Carolina did not add up to the comfortable picture painted by apologists for the system. The lot of slaves in the state was described in 1784 by Dr. Schoepf as in general harder and more troublous than that of their northern brethren. On the rice plantations, said Schoepf, they were "allotted more work and more tedious work." The treatment which they experienced at the hands of their overseers was capricious and often tyrannical, he reported. As evidence of the "bad situation" in which the slaves lived, the doctor cited the fact that they did not multiply in the same proportion as the white inhabitants. He noted also that "their severe handling" had already caused several uprisings among them.[17]

La Rochefoucauld-Liancourt observed that South Carolina's ban on slave imports in 1788 induced a softening of the cruel treatment to which Negroes had formerly been subjected.[18]

Another French visitor to the state during the next decade reported, however, that the treatment of slaves was made extremely bad as a result of fires which unexpectedly broke out. Arson by Negroes, particularly those recently brought from St. Domingue, was suspected. On June 14, 1795, Charleston was struck by a conflagration which lasted twelve hours. Before it was subdued it had destroyed all the houses on Queen Street from the bay to the corner of Church Street, all but two houses on Church Street between Broad Street and St. Philip's Church, on the north side of Broad Street from the State House to four doors below Church, and five houses of the Bay at the corner of Queen Street. There were recurrent fires in the spring of 1796. Some Negroes were arrested and reportedly confessed. In November, 1797, three slaves were executed and two banished for conspiracy to burn the city. Early in 1798 a plan among "French Negroes" to burn Charleston, repeating the technique used at St. Domingue, was believed to have been thwarted by timely discovery. In March of 1800 there were suspicious fires. Charleston newspapers offered a $500 reward for the identification of a band of incendiaries who had recently made several attempts to destroy the city.[19]

When fears of fiery destruction were aroused, the citizenry could forget that a few years before a slave had been rewarded for his heroism during a fire. In 1796, when the steeple of St. Philip's caught fire as the French Protestant Church nearby was burning, a Negro man climbed up to the burning shingles and tore them off.[20] For this service he was given his freedom.[21]

In general the life of the slave was hardly comfortable even when he was kindly treated. Schoepf remarked that plantation hands received "wretched food." In the coast region north of Charleston, he reported, rice was "almost" their only food. Other items mentioned by various observers as making up the slaves' monotonous diet were corn, potatoes, salt meat, and fish, with corn most often reported as the staple. In addition to the staples such as rice and corn issued to them from the plantation supply, the slaves' fare included such items as they might have time to raise for themselves on plots of ground allocated for the cultivation of "provisions."[22]

Slave quarters in the city consisted of small houses in the rear of owners' residences, and on the plantations a row or cluster of cabins somewhere on the grounds. These dwellings were hardly more than huts.[23] And even those that might be sturdily constructed contained only crude furnishings.

Well disposed planters in Carolina gave each slave once a year a suit of coarse woolen cloth, two rough shirts, and a pair of hose. Cotton summer clothing was distributed by some. The kind of clothing which might be worn by ordinary slaves, however, was prescribed by law. Specified fabrics in the late colonial era included "Negro Cloth, Duffils, Kersies, Osnabrugs, blue linen, chest linen, coarse garlix, check cottons or Scotch plaids." Livery men and waiting boys were allowed more latitude in their dress. But the law on Negro clothing was often as laxly enforced as was the law prohibiting dram shops from selling or delivering strong drinks to slaves without the consent of their owners or the persons having charge of them. These regulations, like any regulations, required an expenditure of effort to compel obedience. Hence—even though they were adopted for the protection of the ruling group—they were sometimes ignored out of sheer apathy. Fear or provocation periodically evoked crackdowns.

During times of depression, the economic distress of owners was likely to be visited upon slaves in the form of greater privation. In one such period a Charleston citizen wrote that the "wretched situation of a large proportion of our slaves is sufficient to harrow up the feelings of the most flinty heart."

Contemporary observers in South Carolina frequently inveighed against the illegal practice of teaching slaves their letters. South Carolina's slave code of 1740 imposed a fine of 100 pounds on anyone teaching a slave to write. The reason for the restriction is obvious. The ability to write could give the slave a tool with which to gain anything from a minimum of extra freedom to the ultimate reward itself. He might write himself permission to buy whiskey or engage in a trade. He might write a pass which would get him by the patrol and to a life of liberty in which he might come to be accepted as a free man. Or he might communicate with his fellows for the purpose of plotting insurrection. As has been noted, the occasion which gave rise to the passage of the revised act of 1740 was an insurrection near Charleston in 1739. At the time of the Camden, S.C., slave conspiracy of 1816 it was noted that two of the participants could read and write.[24]

Yet despite fears of what education might bring, hundreds—perhaps thousands—of slaves were taught to read and write. Some, like Denmark Vesey, came to the state's shores having already acquired some education. Besides the personal instruction given by some owners to young slaves, there were schools for the education and Christian conversion of Negroes. One was opened in Charleston in 1743 by Dr. Alexander Garden, rector of St. Philip's Church. Though this school ended in 1764 or a little later, its teaching may well have been passed on privately to a later generation. It had upward of sixty pupils at one time.[25]

While education may have contributed to the danger of

revolt, it undoubtedly also increased the slave's usefulness to the master. Thus arose the tendency to ignore the law, except in periods of apprehension, whereupon it would be pointed out that literate Negroes had access to incendiary writings. Such teaching as there was, however, reached only a relatively small percentage of the Negro population. One iconoclastic Southerner viewed slavery as the inevitable parent of ignorance, not only among Negroes but among whites as well.[26]

For many years all but a few masters opposed religious instruction for their slaves on the ground that to make the slave a Christian brother might start a trend toward manumission. There were also the objections that religion injured the slave as a laborer or involved a danger of insurrection by facilitating assemblies of slaves. (This objection was to be proved well founded in Denmark Vesey's case.) But eventually the zealous evangelists won out.

Religious instruction of the Negro in South Carolina during the late eighteenth century and the early part of the nineteenth was carried on principally by four denominations: The Baptists, the Methodists, the Presbyterians, and the Episcopalians. Well before the Revolutionary War, the Anglican Church's Society for the Propagation of the Gospel in Foreign Parts had established a school for Negroes in Charleston. This activity was, until the close of the war, the most effective effort to reach the colored population. After the war the Episcopal Church began to lose its dominant position, and the Baptists, Methodists, and Presbyterians gained in strength as a result of the revision of the laws (beginning with the drafting of the constitution of 1776) which had given the Episcopal Church (formerly the Church of England) a favored status.[27]

Unlike the Methodists, the Baptists maintained no societies expressly for evangelizing Negro slaves. The Baptist church operated primarily through its local associations. In the long run the Baptists and Methodists were more successful than the Episcopalians and Presbyterians in evangelizing South Carolina Negroes, because the former two denominations were more universally distributed throughout the state and because the simple and emotional character of their rituals appealed more to the uneducated slaves.[28]

Among the circuit and station preachers who served Negroes, Methodist Bishop Francis Asbury, in his journal, left one of the most demonstrative records of the relationship. The tireless bishop, who covered the eastern United States in almost ceaseless riding for thirty years, often paid tribute to the superior receptiveness of "the Africans." ". . . My heart sinketh," he wrote on January 21, 1797, "and I am ready to conclude we are not sent to the whites in this place [Charleston], except a very few; but to the poor Africans."[29]

During his visits to Charleston between 1785 and 1799 Bishop Asbury had some meetings attended exclusively by Negroes and others by blacks and whites together. "I had about a hundred blacks, and nearly fifty whites to hear me," he noted on Sunday, March 22, 1789. Four years later he was telling about presiding at "the women's class, white and black," and having "a powerful meeting." Other assemblies, large and small, were held for Negroes alone, with the bishop on one occasion holding a "love-feast" for nearly 250 members of the African society, and on another spending a "happy . . . evening" with the "poor slaves in brother Wells's kitchen." In their conference on February 17, 1790, the Methodists resolved to establish "Sunday-schools for poor children, white and black."[30]

In his journal entry for Sunday, January 22, 1797, Bishop Asbury offered one of his few descriptions of how he actually appealed to the slaves in Charleston. "I have met the African people every morning between five and six o'clock, at my lodging, with singing, reading, exhortation, and prayer," he reported. Evidently the bishop's efforts were at least rewarded by warm personal response from the slaves, for they frequently came to see him when he was in the city. At the end of a visit in 1795 he was touched when a group of "poor Africans brought their blessings, and wishes, and prayers" on the eve of his departure. On another such occasion two years later a Negro woman, sixty years of age, who supported herself by picking oakum and by the charity of her friends, brought him a French crown because she said she was distressed on his account. But, though he had only three dollars for a trip of 1,000 miles, he would not take it.[31]

If the Negroes were responsive to his ministrations, the city as a whole apparently was not. "I lament the wickedness of this city, and their great hatred against us," Asbury wrote in January 1797.[32]

Bishop Asbury's apparently warm personal relationship with slaves and his differentiation between the responsiveness of whites and blacks was probably not a typical clerical reaction. The more common attitude of white pastors toward Negroes was likely to be a paternalistic one directed toward instilling certain Christian virtues that were compatible with the master-slave relationship. Moreover, it is well to remember that in the eighteenth and early nineteenth centuries religious ministrations to Negroes, whatever they were, were largely confined to those who were near at hand. Plantation house servants and Negroes living in the cities and towns were the ones to receive religious instruction because they happened to come within the scope of the already existing ecclesiastical machinery. The plantation mission, reaching into remote areas, was instituted largely after 1830.[33]

# SEEDS
# OF INSURRECTION

● In South Carolina the liberalizing repercussions of the American Revolution met stronger resistance perhaps than in any other state. The firmly entrenched slave system of the Palmetto State had something to do with it. In this connection, the attitudes of the South Carolina delegates to the federal constitutional convention were significant. The slave trade might have been prohibited by the federal Constitution, one observer asserted, but for the delegates from Georgia and South Carolina. Spokesmen for Delaware, Maryland, and Virginia all denounced the traffic, even though all of them were slave-holders. As a result of the insistence of other Southern delegates, however, the Constitution permitted the slave trade to continue until 1808. Presumably Charles Cotesworth Pinckney of South Carolina spoke for a major portion of the region's electorate when he reminded the convention that, if the drafting committee failed to provide some security to the Southern states against an "emancipation" of slaves, he would be bound by duty to his state to vote against the report.[1] John Rutledge said he did not believe the South would encourage the slave trade, nor was he afraid that slave insurrections would occur as a result of more importation. He was willing to exempt the northern states from the obligation to protect the South from rebellion.[2] (He was not around to be reminded of this sentiment when South Carolina, fearful of servile revolt, requested a reinforcement of its federal garrison in 1822.)

When the national Constitution was debated in the South Carolina legislature in 1788, Rawlins Lowndes, who opposed ratification, wanted to know, among other things, why the northern delegates opposed the importation of slaves, why the slave trade should be limited to twenty years and why a tax should be placed on it even before the time limit expired. In the first Congress of 1789 Representatives William Smith and Thomas Tucker of South Carolina both vigorously objected to a ten-dollar tax on slaves imported into the country.

The drafting of the state's first postwar constitution was also affected by a constant concern for property, especially slaves. Even though South Carolina had participated in the war to shake off the monarchial rule of George III, one of the rewards of the Revolution in the state was not government by the people. The state constitution of 1790 provided for the most strongly centralized and aristocratic government that could have been set up under the limitations imposed by the Constitution of the United States.[3] The state was controlled by an elite class of coastal merchants and slave-holding planters. Its political institutions were designed to protect them against the alien notions that might be entertained by non-slave-owning back country immigrants. Coast country immigrants such as Joseph Vesey, since they helped to maintain the slave system, were not considered a cause for concern.

What trend there was toward democratic institutions in South Carolina can only be appreciated by viewing it from the perspective of the period prior to the drafting of the 1778 state constitution. That document disestablished the Episcopal Church and provided that it was no longer to be supported by taxation. But while that particular church was "disestablished," there was not complete disestablishment. "The Christian Protestant religion" was constituted and declared to be "the established religion of this State." The governor, lieutenant governor, members of the privy council and the legislature all had to be of the Protestant faith. Dissatisfaction with this charter among the people of the state brought proposals for reform. Even so, Ralph Izard, the second largest planter in the state, was complaining to Thomas Jefferson in a letter in 1785 that: "Our governments tend too much to Democracy. A handicraftsman thinks apprenticeship necessary to make himself acquainted with his business. But our back countrymen are of the opinion that a politician may be born such as well as a poet."[4]

It was the democratic element, made up of the "back countrymen," which worked for a constitutional convention to draw up another charter to replace that of 1778. Meeting in May of 1790, the convention, although dominated by delegates from the lowcountry, drafted a document which nevertheless made some concessions to the small farmers of the upcountry. Primogeniture was ordered abolished. Civil officers were to replace church wardens as supervisors of elections, and there was to be no religious qualification for voting. The payment of a three-shilling tax might be substituted for possession of a fifty-acre freehold in order to meet the requirements for suffrage. Property qualifications for office were reduced in the case of the governor, from the ownership of a holding of 10,000 pounds value to one of 1,500 pounds; in the case of a resident senator, from 2,000 pounds to 500 pounds; of a non-resident senator, from 7,000 pounds to 3,500; of a non-resident representative, 3,500 to 500. A resident representative had to be in possession of "a settled freehold estate" of 500 acres of land and ten Negroes; or real estate of the value of 150 pounds sterling, "clear of debt." The "clear of debt" provision was appended to each property qualification required for office-holders. While freedom of religion was granted and officials were no longer to be required to be of the Protestant religion, there was a proviso that liberty of conscience "shall not be construed as to excuse acts of licentiousness or justify practices inconsistent with the peace and safety of this state."

Despite this liberalization of the organic law, the lower section of the state remained firmly in power. With more than three-fourths of the wealth of the state under their control, the judicial districts of Georgetown, Charleston, and Beaufort held the upper hand in the legislature, although they contained only one-fifth of the white population of South Carolina. The 28,644 whites of these three districts were to elect seventy members of the House and twenty members of the Senate. On the other hand, the 111,534 whites of the upper judicial districts of Cheraw, Camden, Ninety Six, and Orangeburg were to elect only fifty-four House members and seventeen senators. Slaves, whose influence was exerted as property rather than as humanity, helped swing the balance in favor of the lower part of the state.

The prospective danger to the slave system was used to oppose democratically-inclined South Carolinians who sought more representative government. When the census of 1790 revealed that the upper part of the state contained more than four times the white population of the lower part, residents of the upcountry began to agitate against the injustice of being represented by a minority in both houses of the General Assembly. They organized the Representative Reform Association, and one of its leaders, Robert Goodloe Harper, in 1794 drafted a pamphlet addressed to the people of the state. The reformers declared that it was not democratic for one-fifth of the population to rule the other four-fifths. They contended that representation should be in proportion to population. They rejected the argument that property should be represented, contending that society existed long before private property. As public property was changed to private property, they said, equal political rights were retained. Wealth would always have influence enough without giving it legal weight in apportioning representatives. Instead of having more votes, they asserted, rich men should be given less voting power in order to balance the undue power their wealth gave them.

Henry William DeSaussure, in answering the reformers, denied that equality was the natural condition of man. If such a theory were put into operation, he argued, the white people would be forced to "instantly free the unfortunate slaves," and thus bring ruin to both races. He pointed out that in 1795 no Southern state had adopted the principle of representation in proportion to population and that the federal Constitution, by its three-fifths rule, recognized the justice of concessions to slave-holders. Timothy Ford of Charleston, himself an immigrant, rejected the claims of political rights by the free labor immigrants who had poured into the upcountry, and declared that had they professed half the doctrine of majority rule now publicized by "Appius" (Harper), the lowcountry would have regarded every arrival "as a reinforcement to an internal enemy."[5]

Ford defended slavery as an aid to freedom. The presence of slaves, he wrote, caused free men to strive to preserve their rights and liberties and thus keep above the servant level. Therefore freedom was insured by slavery. Even the spokesmen for the upcountrymen who were seeking greater rights for themselves paid their respects to the institution of slavery. In 1795 a group of senators and representatives, in a message to the people of the lowcountry, denied that their campaign for more equal representation in the legislature threatened slavery. Members from the back country, they said, were already slave-holders, and those who voted against slavery would be in danger of getting a coat of tar and feathers upon their return home.

The lowcountry realized that ultimately it would have to yield on representation. It was determined, however, to hold its legislative power until Carolina education and the spread of slavery into the upcountry transformed that part of the state from a possible enemy to an assimilated friend of the slavery system. The development of cotton culture and the accompanying advance of slavery into the state's middle country and then into the upland hills was to aid the plan. The emancipation sentiment, inspired in some minds by the philosophical liberalism of the Revolutionary era, later all but died out. In 1808 a constitutional amendment was adopted, providing that each election district should have one senator (except that Charleston should have two), and each should elect one representative for each one sixty-second of the white population and one for each one sixty-second of the taxable wealth of the state that it contained.

This new arrangement gave the legal "upper division" control of the House by a majority of sixteen, and of the Senate by a majority of one. But slavery's advance from the coast had already practically assured the lowcountry slave-holders that the upcountry would vote with them in the legislature. With the legislature secured, governmental control in South Carolina was to remain until 1865 in the hands of a propertied, slave-holding aristocracy to a degree unexampled in any other state.

Even in South Carolina, however, the bulwarks erected by the wealthy property owners could not completely stem the equalitarian tide of the Revolution—a tide that would eventually seep through and weaken the foundations of the stratified society they were trying to build. In some ways the conservatives themselves yielded to libertarian sentiments.

Under the influence of the Revolutionary era, a few leaders in South Carolina in the generation before 1800 gave the stamp of social approval to manumission. As early as 1776 Henry Laurens, one of the great Carolina slave factors, was writing to his son: "You know, dear son, I abhor slavery." John Laurens, the son, also expressed disapproval of slavery. Christopher Gadsden, one of South Carolina's Revolutionary stalwarts, pronounced the institution an insufferable crime. Philodemus, in a political pamphlet published in Charleston in 1784, maintained that "such is the fatal influence of slavery on the human mind, that it almost wholly effaces from it even the boasted characteristics of rationality."[6]

In 1792 a South Carolina court, on instructions of Chief Justice John Rutledge, set Sally, a slave, free as a result of a suit brought in the interest of another slave who had saved up her money to purchase Sally's freedom. "Rusticus," of St. Andrews, about 1794 urged that justice, public safety, and better agriculture demanded immediate emancipation, which would be less dangerous then than later. David Ramsay in 1796 condemned slavery. In 1799 Thomas Wadsworth of Charleston liberated his slaves, gave them fifty acres of land each, and put them under the care of the Bush River Meeting, a Quaker group near Newberry, South Carolina.[7]

In the religious forum, as in others in the postwar era, there was discussion which generated a temporary ferment

for freedom. And before it was muffled, it no doubt planted
some seeds of unrest. Because slaves partaking of religious
instruction before 1800 were relatively few and because
most of those who did were in the bosoms of white congregations, their owners presumably did not worry too much
about the anti-slavery pronouncements made by the govern-
ing bodies of some of the churches. Some of the talk, however, was bound sooner or later to reach slave ears.

The Baptists expressed opposition to the buying and
selling of slaves for profit. At first the American Presbyterian
Church was not hostile to emancipation in the abstract, but it
was not inclined to favor wholesale abolition in actual practice. There were, however, some movements within the
Presbyterian Church and some individual ministers aiming
wholeheartedly for manumission. In 1794 the Reverend W. C.
Davis, speaking before the Presbytery of South Carolina,
denounced his fellow Christians who owned slaves. The Reverend James Gilleland accepted the pastorate of the congregation of Bradaway in the Pendleton District with the members' understanding that he favored the emancipation of
slaves but that he would seek their consent before he spoke
on it. In 1804, however, he moved to Ohio rather than live
in a region where slavery prevailed.

In 1799 the Presbyterian Synod of the Carolinas received a resolution calling upon it to appoint a committee to
work with other denominations to use their influence to
secure legislation which would provide for the emancipation
of the children of slaves born after the passage of the proposed act—such children to be free at a specified age. This
proposal was put before the First Presbytery of South Carolina meeting in February 1800. But this body, after "mature
deliberation," advised against acting on it.[8]

In 1780 the Conference of the Methodist Church, North
and South, passed a resolution condemning slavery as "contrary to the laws of God" and "hurtful to society." The
Methodists in 1784 forbade all members to own slaves except in states where manumission was prohibited by law.
This step ignited tempers and stirred much criticism in the

Carolinas and Virginia. Though this rule was indefinitely suspended within six months, concern over slavery was periodically reflected in denominational debates.

Methodists met violent opposition in South Carolina in the postwar era, some of it caused by sectarian differences but some also due no doubt to the attitude of that denomination on slavery. In 1788 Bishop Francis Asbury told in his journal of how, while a colleague was preaching at a church in Charleston, a riot was started at the door, the congregation became alarmed and "ladies leaped out at the windows of the church, and a dreadful confusion ensued." That night, while Asbury himself was speaking, the church was stoned. The next year the bishop was expressing concern because an "unkind attack" had been published against the Methodists because of their "slave rules."[9]

In a 1794 *Journal* entry Asbury noted that some at a conference to provide preachers for Charleston, Georgetown, Edisto, and Santee were afraid that, if the Methodists retained none who traded in slaves, the preachers would not be supported. The indefatigable bishop saw no reason for fear on this point.[10]

A year later he was writing in his journal:

> Here [between Georgetown and Charleston] are the rich, the rice, and the slaves; the last is awful to me. Wealthy people settled on the rice lands of Cooper River hold from fifty to two hundred slaves on a plantation in chains and bondage: yet God is able of these stones, yea, of these slave-holders to raise up children unto Abraham.

That same year Asbury had reported another riot at a Charleston church in which windows were broken and the doors beaten open.[11]

In 1796 the Methodists prohibited the ownership of slaves by church officials and forbade any Methodist to buy or sell slaves "unjustly, inhumanly or covetously." By 1808 they had suffered a relapse and repealed all rules which attempted to regulate a private member's dealings with slavery.

These vicissitudes finally caused Bishop Asbury to come

to the conclusion that it would be better to work for the salvation of the slave's soul and the alleviation of the harshness of his life rather than continue the attempt to have him liberated. As the Methodist Church became strong enough to organize conferences in various sections, the questions of slavery were referred to these bodies and thus localized to an extent.[12]

Eventually the Methodist Church, like all others in the South except the Quaker, began to accommodate itself to the institution of slavery. The resulting decline in fear that their property would be indoctrinated with ideas of freedom led plantation owners to admit the Methodist preachers, just as they had admitted the spokesmen for other faiths earlier. They hoped the spiritual efforts of the preachers would improve and soften the character of their slaves.[13] Ironically, it was a schismatic branch of the Methodist Church to which Denmark Vesey and many of his followers later belonged.

In the period immediately after the Revolution, grassroots political movements began to register popular feeling against aristocratic leanings in South Carolina. The Secret Committee of Correspondence of the Whig Club of Six Hundred and the Marine Anti-Britannic Society sought to stir up sentiment against everything aristocratic and British. An anti-Tory riot occurred in Charleston in 1783, and distinctly class riots in 1784, when, according to the radicals of the day, an armed Tory mob was called out against an unarmed Whig mob.

The Marine Anti-Britannic Society had been formed in Charleston after the evacuation of the British and was especially active in 1783. It was primarily a seamen's aid organization whose purpose was to offer relief to widows and orphans of sailors and to take the leadership in erecting a marine hospital and seminary. But it was also concerned with ferreting out pro-English citizens and counter-revolutionary plots. To counteract what it believed to be misrepresentations of its aims by "the Aristocratic Gentry," the society in 1784 authorized a committee to state its purposes. This group declared that the society's objective was to conserve, "pure and unmutilated, privileges which, being obtained through the dint of a long arduous, and bloody Conflict . . . cannot be viewed with too jealous an Eye." The society's leaders were well-known democrats who later joined the Republican Society of South Carolina and became sympathetic with the spokesmen for the French Revolution in America.[14]

Not long after the slave-holders erected their protective constitutional bulwark of 1790, the equalitarian waves of the French Revolution began to wash against it. In Charleston sometime during 1792 a French Patriotic Society was organized to support the French Revolution. It was soon affiliated with the Friends of Liberty and Equality of Bordeaux. The activity in behalf of the principles of revolutionary France prompted a flood of letters to the newspapers of the state from both critics and defenders. "L" writing in the *City Gazette* of November 17, 1792, claimed to be a Frenchman and denied that Jacobins favored communism. He said the French were liberty-loving people, able to defend their liberties.

At first South Carolina officialdom, not sensing the long-range import of the upheaval in France, responded favorably to the popular expressions of sympathy for French principles. On January 9, 1793, Governor William Moultrie, the president of the Senate, the speaker of the House, and the chief justice of the state appeared at a "feast" to celebrate the adoption of a republican form of government and the recent victories by France.

In August of 1793 the first of what was to become a group of democratic societies in the Carolinas was formed at Charleston. On September 5 it adopted a "Declaration of the Friends of Liberty and National Justice." To these popular societies, which sprang up from one end of the young nation to the other, the basic question was whether the democratic tendency stirred up by the Revolution should be followed or whether the country should turn into more conventional paths of governmental organization. The societies supported the democratic tendency. Many radical and even moderate democrats belonging to them looked with dissatisfaction upon the conservative trends in state and national constitution-making, where direct representation of the people was being compromised.

Most of the activities of the organizations were devoted to promoting public discussions, issuing circulars and memorials expressing their feelings on current political issues. They defended the "Rights of Man" and the French Revolution. They opposed certain acts of the general government and took verbal stands on some local issues. The societies, however, were also involved in direct actions which their opponents considered extra-legal if not illegal. For example, they disarmed British ships, recruited for pro-French projects, and otherwise participated in such activities as insurrectionary plans against the Floridas.

To the democratic societies, the Rights of Man meant the rights of free speech, free press, and freedom of assembly. They insisted upon the right to criticize governmental representatives and to "call them on the carpet" for explanation and questioning concerning their public acts. And they upheld their right to publish their reactions to this accounting.

The attachment the societies felt for France is indicated by a statement of the Republican Society of Charleston:

> If the present eventful European contest should terminate in the dissolution of the French Republic, we have no doubt but that the craving appetite of despotism will be satisfied with nothing less than American vassalage, in some form or other. The interest of absolute power requires that the voice of liberty should be heard no more, and in the event of the overthrow of the French Republic, the United States, then without an ally, may be forced to yield to European confederacy. And in as much as an aristocratic ambition has already manifested itself in the conduct, even of some Americans, and has lately been more strongly marked by its whispers of dissatisfaction to the cause of France, and of mankind, we do therefore intend our signatures to be an

avowal of different political sentiments. And we do hereby declare, pledging ourselves to each other, and to the world, that we and each of us, will contribute to the utmost of our ability towards the support of equal liberty and national justice, as well in respect to the French Republic, as of the United States against tyranny and iniquitous rule, in whatever form they may be presented by any character or body of men, appearing in these United States.[15]

In its war with England and Spain, the new French republic expected the co-operation of the American government. The two nations had signed a treaty of alliance in 1778 under which the United States extended special favors to France, including the right to receive its prizes in American ports and the right to forbid privateers of the enemies of France to fit out in American ports. In February, 1793, France opened all her colonial ports to America, and in May of the same year removed all restrictions on American vessels. But this favorable action toward American shipping, at the same time that Britain was preying on it, did not keep Washington from issuing his famous neutrality proclamation on April 22, 1793. Despite reminders from Edmund Charles Genet, the French republic's minister plenipotentiary who had been greeted by an enthusiastic populace at Charleston as he landed on April 8, the administration remained adamant. It was equally deaf to the importunities of the popular clubs which openly advocated war in behalf of the French ally; the Charleston and Pinckneyville, South Carolina, groups declared that although "war is a calamity," it is better than "dishonourable submission."

Under the circumstances, the Charleston society did what it could to help the French. In August of 1793 the English sloop *Advice* was supposed to be loading rice in Charleston harbor. Suspicions were aroused that the vessel was also arming. So the Republican Society appointed a committee to investigate an evident infraction of the neutrality proclamation. On discovering that the sloop was arming, the society sent a message to its master giving him until eight o'clock the following morning to disarm. When the captain refused, the membership unanimously agreed to board and disarm the ship, with a unit of the militia as a guard. They completed the mission to the accompaniment of cheers from a crowd assembled on the wharf.

A few months later (March, 1794) the Charleston club was attacking the neutrality proclamation, observing that proclamations are for the purpose of informing people of the laws already enacted, whereas this proclamation was a person's own will and was therefore unconstitutional and despotic. (Later the same year, after the Whiskey Rebellion in Western Pennsylvania in which popular club members participated, President Washington in a message to Congress was to denounce the "self-created societies" for "disturbing the operation of the laws."[16])

In any event the neutrality proclamation did not prevent friends of France in Charleston from exhibiting their enthusiasm. On February 13, 1794, the Republican Society of Charleston held a feast which was attended by the French consul and visitors from French ships in the harbor. Members wore hats decorated with "a branch of laurel surmounted with the Cap of Liberty." The flags of France and the United States were displayed over the hotel and in the room. Among the toasts offered were: "May the union of the two Republics be co-existent with time"; "A speedy revolution in Great Britain and Ireland on Sans-Culotte Principles"; and "The guillotine to all tyrants, plunderers and funding speculators."[17]

Nor did the neutrality proclamation prevent officers of the Charleston Republican Society from collaborating with local French officials on plans for the so-called "Genet Project" to attack the Floridas and wrest them from Spain. The bond between the democrats in Charleston and M. A. B. Mangourit, the French consul, was signified by a stone from the Bastille which he gave them and upon which they intended to engrave the cap of liberty. Later in the spring of 1794 they voted to send an address of friendship to the French National Convention.

While all of this pro-French activity was occupying Charleston citizens, Captain Joseph Vesey and his slave, Denmark, were living in the city. The captain's residence had embraced the period of agitation by the Marine Anti-Britannic Society, the leaders of which had later joined the Republican Society of South Carolina and become outspoken in their sympathy for the French Revolution. Although Captain Vesey's membership in the Marine Anti-Britannic Society is not a matter of verifiable record, he was one of the commissioners of the Marine Hospital, an institution in which the society was active.[18] Moreover, he had engaged in anti-British activity as early as the years of the Revolution when he supplied the French of St. Domingue with slaves. Finally, the captain, it must also be recalled, was a former mariner and thus a member of the fraternity in which the society was interested.

Regardless of how obvious the captain's political sympathies were, they did not bar him during the decade after he sailed into Charelston harbor from becoming a man of affairs in the city. He became a citizen of some means whose cosmopolitan associations kept his household in touch with the world. The first federal census recorded him as head of a family, which included a white boy under sixteen, four other members of unspecified relationship, and eight slaves. In 1790 he was living at 281 King Street and operating a business in ships' supplies at 38 East Bay Street, a few blocks away. Ship chandlers Vesey and North were, like other Charleston businessmen of the period, dependent on the skills of slaves. When Jerry, a twenty-five-year-old mulatto rope-maker, ran away during the summer of 1793, their reliance on his services was suggested by their persistent advertisements offering a reward to anyone who would return him.[19]

During the next ten years the captain participated in a number of business ventures and exhibited a willingness to assume public responsibility. He was a party in several property transfers in this period, including the lease of a lot on the west side of Meeting Street in 1793 and the purchase of property on the south side of Queen Street in 1794. He served on occasion as trustee for a debtor and as administrator for a deed.[20]

The city council in November, 1793, elected Vesey to the posts of commissioner of pilotage, of the markets, and of the Marine Hospital, all three positions to be held for the ensuing year. During his first year as a market commissioner, he helped to formulate new rules to curb the crafty practice by slaves of buying articles in their masters' names and returning them the same day, presumably after using them. Four years later the captain was still a market commissioner and, as such, purchased land for a new market on both sides of Queen Street east of East Bay.[21] In 1800 Captain Vesey's interests reached definitely into the political sphere with his appointment as one of the managers for an election of a member of Congress, one state senator and fifteen state representatives.[22] The 1800 campaign was the one in which the Republicans made their successful bid for national power. They put South Carolina in Jefferson's column despite attacks on the Virginian as a man who had favored France and who had on more than one occasion advocated the emancipation of slaves.

In order to subdue the Republican societies and rob them of their leadership, the Federalists repeatedly stressed the threat to existing property relationships in radical democratic activity. Of all the charges leveled against the organizations, the one concerning their threat to the status quo was the most effective in weakening their power. The idea began to spread in the South that it was unsafe for the slaves to gather from ardent Republicans that "equality is the normal condition of man." That slaves might be inadvertently led to adopt such a notion was indicated by the fact that the Republican Society of Charleston had at one time offered a reward to any Negroes who would divulge information concerning undemocratic intrigues of their Federalist masters.

Obviously, if tendencies like those of the French Revolution caught on in the South, the plantation economic system would be undermined. The popularity of the sympathizers with France began to fade because of the risk to which it was believed they were subjecting the whole slave economy.

The drastic change in sentiment was due, however, not to the ideas of the French Revolution alone but to those ideas coupled with an overt demonstration of them within the context of slavery. In the ten years after Denmark first visited St. Domingue, many changes had obviously occurred in the life of the Caribbean isle. In 1791 the whole character of the French island society was turned upside down. It began on the night of August 20, 1791, when a drum sounded a signal that echoed from the Turpin plantation across St. Domingue's Plaine-du-Nord. In the two months which followed, 180 sugar plantations and about 900 coffee, cotton, and indigo settlements were given to the flames as the island's slaves revolted, dragged numerous whites from their homes, and slaughtered them in shocking ways which they had learned only too well from their own experience at the hands of their masters.

As the revolution in St. Domingue progressed, French refugees flocked into the seaboard cities of the United States—as many as 1,500 landing at Baltimore in a single month. Others went to New York and Philadelphia and to Charleston. To cap their harrowing experiences on the island, the Santo Domingan refugees were sometimes searched and relieved of their possessions when the vessels on which they were fleeing were stopped on the high seas by privateers. Discomfiture at sea, ironically, was an experience that many of their slaves had also had, though in more severe form. In one instance citizens of continental France apparently were subjected to harsh treatment by the Negro crew of a Dutch privateer because of the captives' nationality.[23] As the import of the refugee tide began to sink in, the name of the French colony in the Caribbean became more and more one to be mentioned with caution in the South.

Some 500 refugees from St. Domingue arrived in Charleston in 1792. They continued to stream in during the following year, with the newspapers noting their appearance

with such items as, "Upwards of twenty French passengers
have arrived in the brig Harriet, capt. Kennedy; and the sloop
Harriet, capt. Campbell." In October of 1793 a Charleston
newspaper was relaying the information from France that in
July the "calamity at St. Domingue" had been "at its height."[24]

Charlestonians were generous in responding to solicita-
tions for the relief of "the distressed inhabitants of St.
Domingo." A committee, of which Joseph Vesey was treas-
urer, was appointed by the citizens to receive subscriptions
and distribute them to the former French colonists. On September 5, 1793, the "inhabitants of Hispaniola" then in
Charleston held a meeting at the Exchange to return thanks
to the citizens of the South Carolina port for their assistance.
Late in the same month the refugee relief committee urged
Charlestonians to make "further liberal contributions" to help
carry these "unfortunate persons" through the approaching
winter. Although some 1,300 pounds had been paid toward
the relief of 243 persons, there was still a need for money
because many of the French had left the island without clothing or any other necessity. Moreover, there might be more
of the islanders fleeing to Charleston.

During the fall of 1793, sermons were preached in various Charleston churches calling on members to contribute to
the relief of the victims of the upheaval in St. Domingue. The
congregation of St. Philips' donated more than "one hundred
guineas." Methodist, Presbyterian, and Episcopal congregations were notified in advance during October and November
that they would hear pleas in behalf of the distressed refugees.
In December Governor William Moultrie, in a message to
the legislature, pointed out that, despite voluntary donations
to aid the former inhabitants of St. Domingue, many of them
were destitute; therefore he urged the legislators to grant them
further relief.[25]

Meanwhile a controversy had arisen between officials of
the new French republic and spokesmen of the Charleston
benevolent society as to whether the fleeing French citizens
had been aided by their own land. In a letter to the *City
Gazette and Daily Advertiser* of September 5, 1793, a group

of "citizens of Cape Francois," while acknowledging their allegiance to France and her new constitution, declared that they were indebted to Charlestonians for their preservation. Some rancor evidently arose over an alleged failure of France to help her own, for M. A. B. Mangourit, French consul at Charleston, published in the same newspaper a month later a letter in which he purported to answer "political poisoners." To prove that his country had succored its refugees, he made public a correspondence between himself and a French officer who had just arrived in the harbor from Cape Francais and was not permitted to leave his ship. In response to the officer's declaration of loyalty and his appeal for aid, Mangourit said, he sent provisions to the schooner *Maria* with instructions that they were to be distributed not only to the soldiers under the appealing officer's command but to their fellow French passengers as well.

This documentation, even if it offered true testimony in this particular case, did not end the dispute. On November 20 the *City Gazette and Daily Advertiser* published a circular letter from Edmund Genet, in which he advised the various committees of beneficence at Charleston, Baltimore, and Philadelphia that a "considerable quantity of provisions" had been distributed in their localities at the expense of the republic. In the same letter he authorized French officials in these places to organize "patriots of the islands" into corps of "volunteers of France." Genet's statement elicited a prompt rejoinder from the Charleston benevolent society in which the signers, Nathaniel Russel, Joseph Vesey, and Edward Penman, denied any knowledge of largess from the French government and expressed doubt that there had been any. In the face of a reiteration of the claim by Mangourit, a group of former Santo Domingans supported the stand of the benevolent society, asserted their dependence on it, and denied getting any aid from the French consul.[26]

Within a few years the former French colonists were becoming a part of the community. Some of them started a newspaper in Charleston in 1794. By 1795 entire streets in the city—Union Street, for example—were occupied by them.

Some of them earned a livelihood by operating gambling houses. Some hired out slaves whom they had brought with them from the West Indies.[27]

The influx of the refugees inevitably, under the circumstances, created a strain on the social and political structure of the host city. Like St. Domingue, South Carolina—particularly the coastal region—had a society built on a slave base. In Charleston itself the slaves held the edge over the white population, and in the surrounding country they far outnumbered their white masters. Owners were not unaware of the explosive potentiality of their situation if a spark similar to that which detonated the French colony were lighted in South Carolina. Despite precautions, pamphlets telling about the massacres at St. Domingue got into circulation. A Charlestonian, writing to a newspaper in the fall of 1793, expressed the fear that slaves from St. Domingue might relate "what ought to be suppressed." He observed inadequacies in the community's military preparation, called attention to the neglect of patrol duty by the well-to-do and the shifting of that obligation to "overseers and the poor." To counteract the danger, he proposed the formation of a state legion to be made up of artillery, infantry, and cavalry.

An attempted insurrection in Norfolk, Virginia, in 1793 was subsequently attributed to the influence of the uprising at St. Domingue. In a move to eliminate such influences, South Carolina's Governor Moultrie in October of that year ordered all free Negroes and people of color who had arrived in the state from St. Domingue in the previous twelve months to leave within ten days. Those who did not depart were to be confined until removed.[28]

Rumors circulated that agents of the Brissotinic party in France had encouraged the St. Domingue insurrection and were desirous of inciting similar uprisings in the United States. Thomas Jefferson heard of such a rumor and, while he did not believe it, he passed it on to the governor of South Carolina for what it was worth.[29] John Rutledge, who had been a member of the constitutional convention, charged that "too much of the new-fangled French philosophy" had gotten to the Negroes. He asserted that slaves had been "tampered with" by agents of France.

In addition to being perturbed by the possible importation of ideas of rebellion from St. Domingue, the South was alarmed by the decrees of the French National Assembly emancipating slaves in the French colonies. Though Genet himself doubted that there was any danger of revolt in the United States, his reassurances could hardly pacify the South after it was discovered that he was a member of the Society of the Friends of the Blacks. This organization, an outgrowth of the English movement for the abolition of slavery, was formed in Paris and had begun an active campaign to free Negroes from bondage.[30]

An increasing distrust of the French was signalized by a changed attitude among Charlestonians toward the West Indian refugees. By 1799 Robert Goodloe Harper, formerly a Republican and now an active Federalist, was circulating the story that only Toussaint's seizure of authority from Hedouville had prevented an invasion of the Southern states for the purpose of inciting an uprising among the slaves who, he reported, were already being aroused by French secret agents. (This was the same Harper who in 1794 had frightened the slave-holding lowcountry by pleading the non-slave-holding upcountry's case for equal legislative representation.) The Frenchmen in Charleston, for their part, began to murmur against their benefactors. Slaves and slavery were at the root of the discord. The uneasiness of the local slave-holders was not alleviated by the sale of some St. Domingue Negroes to South Carolina citizens and the freeing of others.[31]

As a committee officer who was receiving and handing out contributions to French refugees, Captain Vesey stood at a focal point in the line of tense communications between the visitors and the established community. St. Domingue slaves who accompanied their masters in calling on the captain had a simple opportunity to pass on to Denmark news of what had been happening on the island.

The significance that this episode in Captain Vesey's

life could have on the planner of a future insurrection is obvious. Reports to Denmark of the successful rebellion against the French slave-owners may well have been his first source of inspiration. At any rate there were to be many references by the Vesey insurgents to the hope they gained from the example set by the Negroes of St. Domingue.[32]

In the generation after the Revolution, Southern opinion generally acknowledged slavery to be an evil, but one passively to be endured. There was little conclusive thinking on what the future would be. But later it was to become obvious that if some of the late eighteenth-century tendencies continued, the props might be knocked from under the slavery system, in which the South by then had a greatly increased economic stake. Therefore the ideas spawned by the American and French revolutions, the democratic societies, and the religious emancipationists came to be mistrusted and feared in the South[33]—though by the time their implications came to be fully appreciated, they had already sowed seeds of disquiet.

As plantation owners in South Carolina and elsewhere in the South consolidated their political strength following the patenting of the cotton gin (in 1794) and the resulting greater commercial importance of cotton, they helped to erect an intellectual climate in the region that was to become progressively more antagonistic toward enlightened ideas about slavery and more fearful of real or supposed threats to the system. The comparative tolerance with which attackers of slavery were accepted in the region in the postwar generation was supplanted by an atmosphere thoroughly hostile even to discussion.

While the rest of the nation was beginning to repudiate slavery, the South, led by South Carolina, was becoming rigid in its attachment to the system.[34] If South Carolina's behavior taught anything to would-be emancipators like Denmark Vesey, it was that reliance on white efforts to achieve Negro freedom was likely to be futile.

# THE HALF-FREE
# COMMUNITY

● A few years after Captain Vesey's activity in behalf of the refugees from St. Domingue, Denmark purchased his freedom with $600 of a $1,500 prize he won in the East Bay Street lottery.[1] There is no knowing how long he patronized the lottery, hoping against hope that a lucky number might spell liberation.

With the drawing of the prize money, a new life and a new outlook was to begin for the young "immigrant" from St. Thomas. He had experienced at least twenty years of slavery in many lands and under varying conditions—in St Thomas where probably his master was Danish; in St. Domingue, under the orders of a French plantation owner; on shipboard, under the discipline of a Bermuda sea captain; in South Carolina, under the regimen of an urban society. It was enough to give him a broad education in slavery, and evidently enough to give him a lasting inspiration to work for freedom, whatever the cost.

At least a part of Denmark Vesey's education for freedom may have been given to him, although unwittingly, by organizations that were an outgrowth of South Carolina's own Revolution for freedom. Denmark was living in a city where anti-Britannic and pro-republican partisans were active and where their ideas freely circulated. It was also a city that gave its ear to advocates of the "rights of man" as promoted by the French Revolution. Their talk may not have been meant for slave ears, but words are hard to enslave.

The buffeting the young freedman had undoubtedly taken in the years of servitude—the menial role in which he had been cast, the hauteur toward his race and his status —could hardly have failed to produce a certain acerbity of character and a sourness of outlook toward the society which had imposed such strictures on him.

At the time of his emancipation, Denmark was about thirty-three years old and had been a resident of Charleston for some seventeen years. As he prepared to make his own way in the world, he joined a little community of about 1,000 free Negroes in a district where forty times as many of the members of his own race were slaves. He had to find an occupation in which skill was enough in demand to enable him to compete in the labor market with the compulsory services of bondmen. In this period free Negro artisans in Charleston included carpenters, tailors, seamstresses, and shoemakers. Advertisements in Charleston newspapers during the 1790's had indicated that there were openings in carpentry. Denmark Vesey chose this craft. Negro carpenters in Charleston in 1795 were making $1.50 a day.[2]

Upon leaving the service of Captain Vesey, Denmark was confronted not only with the responsibility of making a living but also with that of finding a place to live. Though he had $900 remaining from his prize money, this did not open for him doors such as would have been opened for a white man. Where should he live? The Charleston Directory indicates that he did not acquire his own address at 20 Bull Street until many years after winning his freedom. Meantime Captain Vesey was himself often on the move during the years after Denmark's liberation, so that any quarters he provided for his ex-slave were changeable.[3]

In any event, the casual conjugal relationships which Denmark maintained precluded the convenience of a residence with any degree of permanence. His wives—taken or dropped as the exigencies of attachment or the Negro regulations dictated—lived in various parts of the city. He was reported to have had seven in the course of his life and at times more than one at the same time. Those who were slaves he could only visit by permission of their owners. Beck, one of his consorts, lived in a house near that of Major James Hamilton at the corner of Coming and Bull Streets. (There was at that time no insistence on segregated housing.)

His relationship to her was such that, even after parting from her, he continued to visit at her house for some time. After he acquired the house at 20 Bull Street, one wife lived with him there.[4]

In addition to wives, Denmark had a family of considerable size. He had one son who was a mulatto and another who was a "black fellow." He had a daughter, a step-daughter, and two or more stepsons. And this list of those who are accounted for by records does not necessarily complete the roster. Despite a multiplicity of wives and relative freedom of movement, Denmark somehow didn't manage to have offspring who were born free of the fetters of slavery. This circumstance and the corollary commitment to slave spouses helped to keep him chained to the ways and rules of the slave community.[5]

To Denmark perhaps the most tolerable link with the white community was Captain Vesey's household. Though the captain was responsible for his long years of bondage and was still a representative of the slave system, the old mariner nevertheless maintained a less rigid relationship with members of other races than did his fellow citizens. In 1790 he had had four free persons of color in his household. One of the captain's circle was a free East Indian woman named Mary Clodner but commonly called "May Vesey." In 1796 she purchased three lots of land near Charleston known as the Grove. When May Vesey died only a few years after making the real estate purchase, Joseph Vesey was named administrator of her estate. The property was duly inventoried and appraised in 1802 and sold in 1804. In subsequent years the name "Vesey" continued to be associated with free persons of color in Charleston. Sarah Vesey kept a store on Market Street. Susan Vesey in 1830 was head of a family of thirteen and lived on the Neck.[6]

If Captain Vesey lent aid and comfort to free persons of color, this did not mean, however, that in the interval of his residence in Charleston he had become ideologically opposed to slavery. He and his wife held an interest in slaves throughout their lives. In 1800 the captain and his business

partner were forced to sell "twenty valuable Negro Fellows"
to satisfy a debt to the United States. But as late as 1824
Mrs. Vesey still held slaves and was conveying to Samuel B.
Henwood in trust for her daughter two female slaves. Among
the items of property which Mrs. Vesey bequeathed to her
husband in 1829 was a "negro wench."[7]

Despite fluctuations in his fortunes, as evidenced by the
proceeding to satisfy a debt, Captain Vesey managed to
retain the esteem of his neighbors. In 1803 his marriage to
"the amiable Mrs. Blair" was duly noted in the Charleston
papers. Several years later the veteran mariner was chosen
president of the newly-formed Marine Society. He served
at least three years in this post, being still president in 1809.
Here the captain was still maintaining his tie with the sea and
presumably with the men who sailed it. The monthly meetings of the society provided an opportunity to keep in touch
with old and new cronies in his former occupation. As in
the days of his service with the relief committee for refugees,
the captain was keeping the channels of communication open.
By exploiting them, Denmark could gain insights into
happenings in the world at large. Whatever their cosmopolitan connections were, however, the Joseph Veseys were not
of Charleston's elite. Mrs Vesey named Robert Stuart, a
carpenter, as executor of her estate. The family sympathies
were undoubtedly more with the city's artisans than with
the planter aristocracy.[8]

Denmark Vesey launched his career as a free man in
an occupation which might as easily have taken him to
Bull's Island, twenty miles away, as to the other end of the
city. The carpenter who hired out his services was naturally
subject to the call of his employer, and carpenters were
sometimes sent away from the city by Charleston business
men on such projects as the preparation of ship timbers. The
workmen labored near the site where the trees were felled.
While away on missions of this kind, Denmark had the
opportunity for making the acquaintance of plantation slaves,
an opportunity that ordinary urban pursuits did not provide.

In later years Denmark was to count on a wide following among Negroes whom he had met in the country around Charleston.

Scarcely had Denmark Vesey won the key to his fetters when the South Carolina legislature decided to restrict the manumission of slaves. Until 1800 the law had placed no curb on a master who wanted to grant freedom to a human chattel. But in that year the General Assembly noted that "many slaves of bad character or indigent or infirm have been set free." It therefore passed an act providing that from that time forward any master desirous of freeing a slave should appear with the slave before a magistrate. The magistrate was to summon five freeholders, and together they would question master and man as to the slave's character and his ability to earn his own living. If magistrates and freeholders approved, they might issue a certificate permitting the emancipation. This certificate and the deed of emancipation were to be recorded by the clerk of court and a copy of the deed was to be made by the clerk and given to the freed Negro. Except for those whose freedom had been bequeathed before the passage of this act, all Negroes set free thereafter without respect for the law's provisions were subject to seizure and enslavement by any citizen. In 1831 the Court of Appeals refused to confirm the freedom of a Negro who had been seized under the terms of this act, although he had been living on a farm as a free man as early as 1800. Had Denmark Vesey been examined by a magistrate and free-holders, according to the requirements of the law of 1800, he might well have been denied eligibility for freedom because of his stay in St. Domingue. Fortunately for him he escaped scrutiny.

Slaves in the South were freed either through the liberality of their masters, unrelated to any special effort on their part, or through extraordinary personal exertion. Among the latter were those like Denmark who acquired enough money to buy themselves and thus demonstrated their financial responsibility. Others earned their freedom by unusual

services such as fighting fires,[9] war duty (as in the case of
John Eady of the South Carolina lowcountry during the
Revolution), or even by revealing insurrectionary plots
among their fellow slaves.

The same influence brought many private manu-
Throughout the North the legal disestablishment of
slavery was prompted largely by the liberal philosophy of
the Revolution which recognized the inconsistency between
maintaining slavery and talking about the unalienable rights
of man. The same influence brought many private manu-
missions in the South. But the majority of Southern free
Negroes acquired their status as a result of the conscience-
prodded liberality of their masters or the desire of masters to
shed an economic burden. Some owners in South Carolina
freed their slaves to atone for cruelty to them. Others sought
to put off old slaves on the public after indigo became
unprofitable and before cotton became a money crop. Many
of those freed could thank their mixed blood and the consequent compulsion on the part of white fathers to cut the
bonds of those they were responsible for bringing into the
world. (While most of these children were not the offspring of formal unions, they were evidence of prevalent
black-white cohabitation; and yet South Carolina did not
outlaw intermarriage between the races until 1865.) The
will was the common legal instrument for effecting manumission, although deeds were also employed.[10]

After 1810 the rate of emancipation in the South was
lowered because slaves were becoming more valuable and
freedmen were increasingly regarded as a source of disturbance of the system.[11] In Charleston County, however, the
free population figures did not reflect the decline until 1830.
The total number of free colored persons there rose from
1,161 in 1800 to 3,615 in 1820. By 1830 it was only 3,632.[12]
Charleston County's almost static free Negro population in
the 1820-1830 decade was offset by a rise in the city. The
Charleston free Negro community numbered 1,024 in 1800,
1,497 in 1820. and 2,129 in 1830.[13] The sharp increase in
the city's free Negroes between 1820 and 1830 suggests

that many had moved in from rural areas where their presence near plantation slaves was discouraged. Denmark Vesey no doubt contributed to this development by his activity among plantation hands.

But antipathy to emancipation began building up before Denmark Vesey aroused any concern. As the number of free Negroes grew, anxiety increased over the possibility of their aid to insurrectionary projects. In 1819 the South Carolina House of Representatives adopted a resolution advising that further introduction of free Negroes into the state be prohibited. In 1820 Governor John Geddes urged strong measures to stop the immigration of such persons in the interest of preserving the state's "domestic tranquility." That same year the General Assembly not only forbade further immigration but also prohibited further emancipation within the state except by its own edict. The man who reported the bill in the legislature was, ironically, John C. Prioleau, a Charlestonian whose slave was later to have a part in Denmark Vesey's undoing.[14]

Free Negro immigration was a recurring problem to slave society. The original ban against it dated from 1794 in South Carolina, when an act was passed forbidding such movement (except from other states) and providing that those who offended should be transported whence they came.[15] This prohibition was renewed in 1800[16] and made perpetual in 1803.[17] But the legislation apparently was not effective enough. And the 1820 ban was accompanied by a proviso that any free Negro entering the state from the outside was to be arrested and hauled before a magistrate who was to order him to leave the state; and in case he failed to do so within fifteen days he was to be fined $20, a procedure that could be repeated indefinitely.[18]

Apart from the curbs on immigration, there were various other restrictions against movement such as license and registration requirements. Masters of vessels were reminded by a notice in the *City Gazette* in 1800 of their obligation under the law to report on "any persons of color, whether bond or free," whom they might bring into the state, and were informed of their duty to assume written responsibility for such persons.[19]

The 1820 act dealing with free Negro immigration contained the first virtually complete barrier to manumission. Although the legislature could approve emancipations, it often ignored requests for such action. The result was that there were some evasions of the law and slaves were allowed to be de facto free. But by and large the people went along with the state's policy of curbing the increase in the number of free Negroes on the grounds that they represented a threat to the peace and safety of the community and that their presence was incompatible with the slave system.

Once they had left slavery behind them, Negroes did not become peers of those who had their citizenship as a birthright. They were assigned to an inferior caste by the dominant white race and expected to derive their main satisfaction from not being slaves. Upper caste whites were inclined to regard black free men indulgently and to welcome their availability in the labor force. White laboring men, on the other hand, were often unfavorably disposed toward free Negroes because they looked upon the ex-slaves as competitors.

Both groups feared the role which free blacks might play in an uprising. R. G. Harper wrote that the free Negro was inferior socially, improvident, lazy, a collaborator in slave theft, a medium for illegal trading, a poisoner of the minds of slaves who envied his condition, a plotter of unlawful meetings and insurrectionary movements. He obviously was trying to summon all the arguments he could to buttress his plea for shipping free Negroes out of the state. But in speaking of the envy which such persons aroused among slaves, he was at the same time refuting the slavery apologists' contention that free Negroes were scorned by slaves. Envy seems to have been a more prevalent emotion than scorn in the light of the frequent efforts by runaways and insurgents to gain the status of free Negroes.

The free Negro community was divided by class lines, with the demarcation sometimes drawn by economics and sometimes by mixed blood. If mulattoes and quadroons occupied a higher status than their black brethren, however, their good fortune did not necessarily arise from any intrinsic value in mixed blood; they might as easily have been the beneficiaries of a more favored treatment because of their kinship with the whites. A Charleston pamphleteer differentiated between mulattoes and blacks, condemning the viciousness and indolence of the latter and lauding the thrift and sobriety of the former, adding that in the event of revolt the mulattoes would be more likely to become allies of the whites. Without specific reference to this theory, Denmark Vesey's contemporaries consistently identified him as a "black man."[20]

Whatever the reason for their prosperity, certain upper caste free Negroes served as custodians of the slave system. They took pride in their free ancestry, their economic position, and their proportion of mixed blood. They married inside a restricted class, dowries apparently being provided for the daughters; they took great care in the protection and transmission of property; they provided for the education of their children. They paid their ransom to slaveholders who let them alone by disclosing plans designed by discontented and underprivileged Negroes for overthrowing the system. Some of these free Negroes actually owned slaves, which they mistreated and exploited even as white masters did.

But it should be noted that some free Negro slaveowners held their fellow human beings in bondage only as a means of sparing them a worse enslavement under other owners. And white owners were known to sell slaves to free Negroes in order to be rid of them. A Charleston citizen sold a man slave to the man's free colored sister for one dollar on condition that the sister take care of him. The slave obviously was physically or mentally defective.

The Duke de la Rochefoucauld-Liancourt told of a free Negro named Pindaim who lived in St. Paul Township and owned a plantation and 200 slaves. He had married a white woman and had given his mulatto daughter in marriage to a white man. Then eighty-five years old, he was exemplary in his conduct except for the severity with which he treated his slaves. Such a plantation master was a phenomenon in Carolina, said the duke. Well-to-do free Negroes were more common in the city. The city offered them more opportunities to use and profit by their intelligence and by their skill in various crafts.[21]

Barred as they were from rising into white society, and anxious to maintain their divorce from slavery, free Negroes formed organizations to help them preserve their status. The Brown Fellowship Society was organized at Charleston in 1790 under rules that admitted to membership bona fide free brown men of good character. The initial fee was $50 and membership was restricted to fifty. Among the society's services were the education of members' children, assistance for orphans and widows, and the provision of burial grounds for their dead. Monthly meetings were held at the society's clubhouse, and special observances were arranged on each anniversary.

Other organizations formed along similar lines were the Humane and Friendly Society in 1802 and the Minors Moralist in 1803. The Friendly Union was organized in 1813, and a little later the Unity and Friendship and the Brotherly societies.

To keep itself ideologically above suspicion, the Brown Fellowship Society had a rule which provided that: "All debates on controverted points of divinity or matters of the nation, governments, states or churches, shall be excluded from the conversation of this society, and whoever shall persist in such shall be fined. . . ." The characteristic of complete docility implied by this proscription was offset, however, by at least one instance in which the society became righteously indignant. In 1817 it expelled George Logan and cancelled rights and benefits for him and his heirs on the ground that he had conspired to cause a free black to be sold as a slave.

By its expulsion action, the society did tacitly register an antipathy to slavery. But its barrier against free black men as members testified to its primary pretension as an exclusive social organization. Because of his color, Denmark Vesey was not eligible for admission.[22] If he had been admitted, the restrictive rules of the Brown Fellowship Society would not have comported with his untamed spirit of protest. The Society of Free Blacks, formed in 1791 as a consequence of the other fellowship's color bar, was more in keeping with Denmark's nature. This was because of its lack of pretense, however—not because it was revolutionary in outlook.

In some of their lodge activities and in a great many of their daily affairs, free colored persons and slaves readily intermingled. Even on the free men's side, the strictures of the society in which they lived often permitted no other course. They worked where they could find employment, whether alongside slaves or not. The number of free persons being limited, they took mates where they could find them among the free and the slave—except for those who sought to maintain their social status by marrying only within the free class. Regardless of the status of free persons of color, white society generally spurned social contact with them.

Prosperity for the free Negro in Charleston was highest in the period from 1790 to 1830, after which the increasingly hostile attitude of the state and of white society in general made his lot more difficult. In 1819 free Negroes in the South Carolina city were listed in thirty branches of work. Among them were twenty-two seamstresses, eleven carpenters (one of whom was Denmark Vesey), ten tailors and six shoemakers. In addition to these artisans, there were at various times also contractors, merchants, and coal and wood dealers. A number of free Negroes reached a financial standing recognized by the banks. Their wealth ranged from $15,000 to $125,000. (Denmark Vesey in 1822 was reported to own property worth about $8,000).[23] Included in Charleston's group of well-to-do free Negroes were Anthony Weston,

William McKinlay, Joseph De Reef, R. E. De Reef, Robert Howard, Charles Holloway, Richard Holloway (who was mulatto, a native of Maryland who had emigrated to Charleston, and who was at one time a seaman), Joshua Wilson, Sr., and Jehu Jones.

Jones in 1815 bought a hotel at public auction for $13,000. Located in the heart of Charleston, this establishment was patronized by the elite of white society, including the governor of the state. Jones lived as comfortably as some of his white patrons, amassed property valued at some $40,000, and enjoyed a reputation for integrity and business talent.

Free Negroes as fortunate as Jones, however, were exceptional. Most of them found a niche in economic society much on a level with slaves. They worked at menial jobs that were available. Along the seaboard they sought out water pursuits such as oystering, fishing, and boating, in which they would not be invading a field generally occupied by white laborers. In earning a living, as in other phases of activity, free Negroes were subjected to restrictions. There were occupational costs such as the $10 tax which Charleston levied on free Negro males from twenty-one to sixty years of age who were "carrying on any trade or art or being a mechanic." Such discriminatory devices were designed to keep free Negroes out of more desirable crafts where they would compete with white artisans.

Free Negroes in South Carolina occupied a sort of limbo between slavery and real freedom. They could hold property, but they could not vote. They were allowed to testify against their own kind but not against white persons. They were excluded from jury boxes. They were excluded from the militia early in the nineteenth century. Free Negro males from eighteen to fifty years of age were subject to a poll tax of two dollars. One who failed to pay the tax might be seized by the sheriff and sold for a period of service (not more than five years) sufficient to pay the costs. A committee of the legislature in 1809 rebuffed a petition by free Negroes and mulattoes of Charleston pleading for repeal of the capitation tax.

Though free Negroes had a measure of liberty, there were no guarantees that they would retain it. They might be seized under fraudulent claims and enslaved despite the law's provisions for freedom.

The Charleston grand jury in 1816 described a ruse by which free Negroes were deprived of their liberty:

> We present as a grievance the show of lawful proceedings, which has been fictitiously given by some persons to the horrible practice of inducing free negroes in jail or in debt to bind themselves for a trifling sum for several years, and by a transfer in the indenture and a chain of inhuman proceedings cause them to be sold into the interior or out of the state, by which means they may be deprived of their freedom.

Sometimes free Negroes, particularly children, were kidnapped without even the pretense of a legal claim. With their color supporting a presumption of slave status and custody indicating ownership, victims of kidnapping were in a difficult position to seek redress. Add to these disadvantages their legal disabilities, their innocent ignorance (if they were children) and the threat of the lash, and the reason why few could reassert their freedom becomes clear. Those who did usually were able to do so only because they were aided by white friends. Apparently the abduction of free Negroes was not forbidden by law in South Carolina until 1837.

When charged with crimes, free Negroes were subject to trial before the same kind of court as was provided for slaves. Two justices of the peace and from three to five freeholders conducted the proceeding and assessed the penalties, which included anything from death to a fine. Convictions were permitted by vote of three members of the court. There was no requirement that counsel be provided, and no appeal. The testimony of a free Negro was not acceptable in court against that of a white person, but a slave was a competent witness against the accused free Negro. (In 1807, however, a South Carolina court ruled that a man

of color, whose mother was a free white woman, could
testify for the prosecution against a white accused.) U. B.
Phillips surmises that many free Negroes were undoubtedly
arrested and convicted in every state under circumstances in
which white men went free. A complete and accurate picture
of criminal prosecutions of Negroes is hard to come by,
however, since the courts which tried them usually kept no
records.

There is evidence showing that free persons of color
in Charleston chafed under the limitations of pseudo-citizen-
ship and sought to improve their status. In 1790 Thomas
Cole, a bricklayer, and P. B. Mathews and Mathew Webb,
butchers, submitted a petition to the state Senate on behalf
of themselves and other free men of color. They noted that,
for the purpose of apportioning South Carolina's representation in Congress, they had been counted among the free
citizens of the state. Yet, said the petitioners, they had been
deprived by the Negro Act of 1740 of the rights and privileges of citizens. The attention of the Senate was directed
to the following grievances:

The petitioners could not give testimony on oath in
prosecutions in behalf of the state.

They could not give testimony in seeking to recover
debts due to them, nor in establishing agreements made by
them within the meaning of the statutes of frauds and per-
juries—except in cases in which persons of color were
concerned. As a result, they were subject to great losses
and repeated injuries without any means of redress.

They were denied the rights of free citizens by being
subject to trial without a jury and subject to prosecution
by the unsworn testimony of slaves.

The signers reminded the senators that, ever since the
independence of the United States had been established, they
had paid their proportionate share of property taxes. They
declared themselves willing to take an oath of allegiance to
the state such as might be prescribed by the law-makers, and
willing to assume the duty of helping to preserve the peace
in Charleston and elsewhere if called upon. In a tactful

conclusion, the memorialists said they did not expect to be put on an equal footing with free white citizens, but they prayed for some relief from their grievances.

But the petition of Thomas Cole, P. B. Mathews, Mathew Webb, and others was rejected.[24] If Denmark Vesey or any other rising leader of the free Negro community was interested in a test of the value of peaceful methods, the legislature in 1791 demonstrated their futility.

Three years later the home of P. B. Mathews, who was evidently under suspicion as a plotter against the state, was searched in his absence. In a letter to the *City Gazette* Mathews complained of the invasion of his home without his knowledge. While he granted that he might have secreted his papers had he been forewarned, he said he was glad the intruders had a chance to examine them, since they demonstrated the lack of incriminating evidence among his effects. He noted that a copy of the fruitless memorial to the legislature had been found and offered to supply the names of its signers if they were wanted. He denied the "report" that a large quantity of arms and ammunition had been found in his possession and called on "the gentlemen" who had searched his house to verify that the only weapons there were an old pistol without a flint, a broken sword, and an old cutlass—all of such little value that they were stuck up in the shingles in an unfinished part of the building.

Mathews declared that it had always been his aim to hold the approbation of the citizens of the state. He recalled that during the British wartime occupation of Charleston he had taken up a collection among the free colored men of the city to be used for the relief of Charleston citizens who were then confined on prison ships. Asserting his readiness then as in the past to defend the country against foreign or domestic enemies, Mathews signed himself "The public's most obedient servant."

In an affidavit printed below the letter, Major John Hamilton testified to Mathew's repeated expressions of willingness to take up arms in the cause of the United States.

And James Bentham, J. P., swore to Mathew's good character.[25]

Despite the ability and the uprightness displayed by Peter B. Mathews and others like him, they did not win any change in South Carolina's basic attitude toward free men of their race. That attitude was exemplified by an 1832 decision of the Court of Appeals in a case challenging the indictment of a white man for an unprovoked assault upon a free Negro. With a great show of benevolence, the court acknowledged that free Negroes had the rights of life, liberty, and property and said these must be protected by the community. Since such persons were capable of committing and receiving injury, they were (said the opinion) liable to punishment for the one and entitled to redress for the other.

But in an obiter dictum that revealed his true feeling, the judge continued:

> . . . Free negroes belong to a degraded caste of society; they are in no respect on an equality with a white man. According to their condition they ought by law to be compelled to demean themselves as inferiors, from whom submission and respect to the whites, in all their intercourse in society, is demanded; I have always thought and while on circuit ruled that words of impertinence and insolence, addressed by a free negro to a white man, would justify an assault and battery.[26]

The lattitude permitted to white men under this opinion illustrates the extent to which control of the Negro population was left to men rather than to laws.[27]

In Charleston one of the purposes of the Brown Fellowship Society was to maintain schools for Negro children. Other societies were organized with a similar objective. Thomas S. Bonneau, the most well known of Charleston's colored teachers, kept a school from 1803 to 1828. Mrs. Stromer, a colored woman, founded a school in 1820, and it ran until the Civil War. Individual upper class free Negroes made special provisions for the schooling of their children. In 1794 George Bedon indicated in his will that he wanted his two sons kept in school until they were fifteen years of age.[28] Taking maximum advantage of these opportunities, some free Negroes of Charleston attained an intellectual (as well as economic) status in which they ranked favorably with their own kind even in the North. Despite these manifestations of progress in education, however, most of the children of free Negroes had little chance for an education. They were, of course, barred from white schools. And their own schools had to be conducted under white surveillance.

Besides the general lack of opportunity for education, there was a statutory discouragement of enlightenment, aimed at free Negroes as well as slaves. In 1800 an act was passed prohibiting all assemblages of slaves and free Negroes for mental instruction (even with whites present) "in a confined or secret place of meeting," behind "barred, bolted or locked doors" which prevented free ingress and egress. This law also forbade all meetings of Negroes for religious or mental instruction between sunset and sunrise. This proviso, of course, effectively curbed many such meetings, since working Negroes had few opportunities to meet during the day. Both civil and military officers of the law were empowered to disperse gatherings held in violation of the act and, if they deemed necessary, to inflict twenty lashes on all free persons of color, or to hand them over to a constable who, at the discretion of a magistrate, might inflict a similar punishment. This statute was aimed at religious meetings, but its terms were broad enough to cover assemblies devoted to any kind of mental activity.[29]

Both the Baptists and Methodists protested that the sunset-to-sunrise restriction interfered with their efforts at religious instruction. In 1801 and again in 1802 the Charleston Baptist Association petitioned the legislature for an amendment to the law in so far as it affected persons of color. Because of the complaints, the law was amended in 1803 to permit their class meetings to continue until 9:00 p.m., provided a majority of those present were white. Such gatherings, however, might still be invaded by objectors with a warrant from a justice of the peace, or without a warrant if no justice of the peace lived within three miles.

Later the Baptists formally thanked General Charles Cotesworth Pinckney, Major Thomas Pinckney, and Henry William DeSaussure for their exertions in behalf of the denomination's appeal. In 1819 the requirement that a "majority of whites" be present was repealed and a meeting of Negroes for religious purposes came to be regarded as lawful if a white man was present to be responsible for their conduct.[30]

Put on the statute books as a result of public apprehension, these restrictions were usually enforced only as long as fears lasted and were revived when some new bid for freedom by Negroes again aroused public anxiety.

During quiet periods when fears of servile explosions were relatively dormant, Negroes were given greater freedom to conduct their own religious affairs. In the Baptist and Methodist denominations particularly, Negroes were sometimes permitted to form separate congregations. White ministers occasionally preached to such groups, and white laymen often sat in them. But pulpits and pews were frequently occupied by Negroes alone. Such activities continued until some white citizens became alarmed and goaded authorities into action.

In 1816 a writer in *The Times* of Charleston complained:

> Almost every night there is a meeting of these noisy, frantic worshippers. . . . Midnight! Is that the season for religious convocation? Even allowing that these meetings were conducted with propriety, is that the accepted time? That the meeting of numerous black people to hear the scripture expounded by an ignorant and (too frequently) vicious person of their own color can be of no benefit either to themselves or the community is certain; that it may be attended with many evils is, I presume, obvious to every reflecting mind.[31]

In the early 1800's several thousand colored Methodists in Charleston had enjoyed a quarterly conference of their own, had custody of their collections and control over church trials of colored members. But in 1815 these privileges were cancelled on the ground that they had been abused. This white action against the Negro quarterly conference prompted a secession movement among Negro Methodists in Charleston. Morris Brown and other leaders of the colored Methodists of Charleston communicated with officials of the African Methodist Episcopal Church which had been launched in the North in 1816 and had congregations in Philadelphia, Baltimore, and other neighboring cities. Two of the Charleston Methodists visited Philadelphia and were ordained for pastorates in the South Carolina city. In 1817 a purportedly independent African Association was organized in Charleston.[32] It was to have several churches: one on Anson Street, one on Cow Alley, and one in Hampstead.[33] Denmark Vesey became a member of the Hampstead church.[34]

It was a dispute over custody of one of the Negro burial grounds that provided the pretext for the secessionist movement in the Methodist Church in Charleston. As a consequence, most of the colored class leaders resigned and more than three-quarters of the 6,000 Negro Methodists withdrew their membership from the white churches. Upon the organization of the schismatic African establishment, one of its members was constituted a bishop.

White officials were quick to register their disapproval of such displays of independence. As a result of complaints that one such separate Negro congregation constituted a nuisance, 469 black worshippers were arrested in 1817 on disorderly conduct charges. Though the arrested group was discharged, they were on notice as to what might happen to them at any time.

The next year city officials moved against the Hampstead church, citing the statute of 1800 prohibiting the assembling of slaves and free Negroes for mental instruction without the presence of white persons. On a June Sunday in 1818 the city guard arrested 140 free Negroes and slaves belonging to this African church and lodged them in the guard-house. The City Council on Monday sentenced five of this group, a bishop and four ministers, to one month's imprisonment or to give security that they would leave the

state. Eight ministers were sentenced to receive ten lashes or
to pay fines of ten dollars each.

This interference with the new African Church aroused
much resentment among members.[35] In 1820 a group of free
Negroes petitioned the legislature to be allowed to conduct
independent worship services at their church in Hampstead,
just outside Charleston. The Charleston delegation to the
General Assembly, to whom the matter was referred,
recommended that the petition be rejected. Despite the re-
pression, the African Church continued somehow to function
until 1822 when its use as a seedbed for revolt brought
a still more severe subjugation.[36]

White authorities were sometimes held back by pangs of
conscience from restraining religious activity, even though
their recurring fears of insurrectionary agitation dictated
such restraint. In 1818 a South Carolina court set aside a
penalty against a Negro class leader who had objected to the
patrol's repeated interruptions of his religious meetings. A
Charleston ordinance of 1789 had excepted funerals from its
general ban against congregations of more than seven slaves
at the house of a free Negro. But in time even funerals came
to be suspected.

Hedged in as they were by restrictions, a few free
Negroes accepted the escape provided by the emigration
program of the American Colonization Society. Organized
at Washington in 1816, the society had impressive sponsor-
ship, including that of Jefferson, Henry Clay, and John
Randolph. Its five branches in 1817 eventually grew to 150
auxiliaries throughout the country. But despite the opportunity for freedom it purported to offer to Negroes, and
the solution it held out for the slave-holders' problems of
excess, the society met a mixed reaction from both groups.
Negroes themselves—a substantial portion of them now
natives of America—didn't relish the idea of being transported to the strange and distant land of Liberia. As
difficult as their situation was, they had put down roots and
had many relatives in their places of residence. In the first

twelve years of the society's operations, only 1,430 Negroes were settled in the colony. Denmark Vesey reportedly said he did not go with Creighton to Africa because he had not the will and moreover he wanted to stay and see what he could do for his fellow creatures.[37]

Supporters of the colonization plan nevertheless worked to gain adherents. Protestant churchmen disciplined Negro ministers under their control for opposing the plan. A relatively small number of Negroes gave willing support to the society. In 1832 a free man of color in Charleston wrote to the *African Repository* saying he favored the idea of African colonization.[38]

Some slave-holders endorsed colonization, a certain number of them with the humane idea that it would serve the welfare of Negroes; but others envisaged it as a way to get rid of both unwanted slaves and freedmen. Robert Goodloe Harper, himself a South Carolinian by adoption, denounced free Negroes as dangerous to slave society and was an early advocate of shipping them away. He originated the name Liberia. John Randolph of Virginia saw the society as a means of ridding slave states of the conspiratorial influence of free Negroes. Robert Mills, a South Carolinian, urged the legislature to ship the Negroes to Africa.[39]

Many abolitionists opposed colonization on the same grounds as Negroes did. John Quincy Adams, partial to this view, observed that the colonists would suffer more than if they remained in the United States.

Much of the opposition to the society stemmed from the great anticipated expense of its project. A South Carolina senator estimated that the minimum cost of transporting one colonist was $500. In 1827 South Carolina's United States senators and representatives were advised by the legislature to take the position that Congress had no power to patronize or make appropriations for the American Colonization Society. Senator Robert Y. Hayne of South Carolina denounced the plan as both unnecessary and too costly.[40]

# MAINSTREAM
# OF REACTION

● Charleston at the turn of the century was still the commercial and social center of South Carolina and of a large part of the South as well. The South Carolina port, now containing 20,473 inhabitants, had dropped from fourth to fifth place among American cities.[1] But the great expansion of cotton cultivation and the resultant export trade promised a growing future. Regular shipping lines with vessels bound for Jamaica, Cuba, France, and England advertised their dates of sailing. On a single day well over a hundred sail, exclusive of coasting vessels, could be counted in the harbor.

Big stores with a variety of merchandise fronted on Broad, Tradd, and Elliott Streets. Items such as men's and women's gold watches, seals and silver knee buckles and wine were ordinary articles of import. Some seventy silversmiths found business in Charleston. Wagons from all over the state and beyond rolled into upper King Street laden with commodities for trade. There were no less than four public markets in the city. The factors who handled business transactions on cotton and rice for the planters had their offices on East Bay. Business dealings were considered by the well-to-do plantation owners to be beneath their dignity.

The Carolina Coffee House at Bedon's Alley and Tradd Street was a popular hotel. Well known public buildings were the state house, the guard house, the armory, the Charleston orphan house, the exchange, and the poor house. Among the places of worship were two Episcopal churches, and one each for the Congregationalists, Baptists, Scotch Presbyterians, German Lutherans, and French Protestants. The Methodists had three churches. Besides these there was a

Roman Catholic chapel, a Quaker meeting house, and a Jewish synagogue.

Homes were frequently built adjacent to the street, leaving room behind for secluded gardens and auxiliary structures. Some of Charleston's most notable houses were built during the first half of the nineteenth century, their erection providing work for artisans such as Denmark Vesey.[2]

The pace of Charleston society was set by the relatively small group of planters who cultivated rice and cotton on the flat low lands of coastal South Carolina and made the city their base of social operations. They lived on their plantations during a part of the year and moved to town houses in Charleston in winter for social events and in summer to escape what they considered to be the unhealthy environment of the fields. Without realizing the true source of the danger, they were in fact following a sensible course in summer and avoiding the low-lying rural areas where disease-carrying mosquitoes were more prevalent. Most slaves were left in the country on the theory that they were immune or expendable. A wealthy plantation family carried with it to the city, however, a retinue of servants which might include a coachman, grooms and a footman, a butler, a housekeeper and assistants, a maid for each woman in the family and for each small child, a cook and an apprentice and a kitchen boy, laundresses, and a man servant for each adult male in the family.

Made comfortable by their attendants, the planters were free to indulge their proclivities for hospitality and European tastes. Like their counterparts in Virginia, they traveled and read. In 1803 Ebenezer S. Thomas, one of four Charleston book dealers, brought from England 50,000 volumes dealing with every phase of literature, art, and science.[3] With the coming of St. Domingue refugees to Charleston, the theater reopened. A number of Charleston teachers were women of French extraction, and they created another tie with the continent.

The February horse races represented the big social

event of the year. Schools were dismissed and judges adjourned courts. Planters matched the blooded horses which they had taken pride in raising. Other social activities were planned to coincide with the period of the races. The St. Cecelia Society, founded to cater to a love for music, gave its attention after 1822 to patronizing annual balls. The Philharmonic Society was chartered in 1810 and was prepared to carry on the city's musical tradition.

In contrast to all the gaiety and sophistication, however, Charleston exhibited another level of activity which was far less sensitive to the finer things of life. On a street off East Bay near the waterfront, slave auctioneers twice a week proclaimed the fine points of their merchandise. Human chattels were placed upon tables and, in various stages of undress, turned around so that prospective buyers could appraise them from different angles. Mouths were opened to show teeth, much in the same manner as an owner might show the teeth of a horse for the inspection of customers. Crowds of bidders and bystanders observed the spectacle.

A Charleston auctioneer of this period gave a typical demonstration of the technique of his calling. He put a sixteen-year-old girl on the table, commented on her qualities, pointed to a protuberance in front in such a way as to suggest that she was pregnant, which would have increased her value. When an eager woman buyer made the highest bid and hastened to examine her purchase more closely, she discovered that the girl was actually in pitiful physical condition and was in fact afflicted with abdominal dropsy (ascites).[4]

So intense was the desire to be waited on by servants that those who could not buy slaves hired them at six to ten dollars a month. Every kind of work was performed by Negroes.[5] Methods for exacting the desired maximum of service were often far from genteel. In 1816 a Charleston Grand Jury said it presented

as a most serious evil the many instances of negro homicide, which have been committed within the city for many years.

> The parties exercising unlimited control, as masters and mistresses, in the indulgence of their malignant and cruel passions, in the barbarous treatment of slaves, using them worse than beasts of burden and thereby bringing on the community, the State and the city the contumely and opprobrium of the civilized world.[6]

Not only was Charleston's gentility offset by such covert severity, but the city's vaunted devotion to culture in the early nineteenth century was soon to be hindered by the planters' overt preoccupation with cotton growing and slave buying. Literature got less attention. Moreover, as intolerance on the slavery question increased, people of intellectual independence, such as the Quakers, were driven out. With the diversion of local talent to more mundane pursuits, South Carolina was forced to import more of such cultural necessities as teachers and books.

South Carolina Federalists played an influential role in national affairs during the early years of the republic, their participation in government indicating the state's important place in the union. President Washington named Federalist John Rutledge an associate justice of the Supreme Court and later nominated him as chief justice. He offered Charles Cotesworth Pinckney the secretaryship of state in 1795 and, though Pinckney declined this honor, he accepted the next year a request to undertake a delicate diplomatic mission to France. Thomas Pinckney, C. C.'s brother, was the Federalist candidate for vice president in 1796. And four years later C. C. Pinckney himself was the Federalist candidate for the same office. In 1804 and 1808 he was the party's presidential candidate.

As residents of Charleston, the Pinckney brothers spoke for the politically potent and strongly Federalist coastal section of the state. But they did not reflect the views of the rest of South Carolina which had been consistently anti-Federalist. Republican Charles Pinckney, a cousin of the Federalist Pinckney brothers, was four times elected governor between 1789 and 1806. South Carolina in 1796 voted for Jefferson and Thomas Pinckney, and in 1800 for Jefferson and Burr. The growing Republican grip on the state extended to the capture of the legislature in 1800. Four years later the Republicans took nearly all of the offices. The state's two United States senators and eight representatives were all of that party. The Federalist congressional candidate was defeated for the first time in the Charleston district in 1804. In contrast to the Republican electors' narrow victory in 1800, this time the electors pledged to Jefferson and Clinton won easily. The legislature chose Republican Paul Hamilton as governor. Among the state legislators only a few Federalists remained in office. In 1808 and again in 1812 the Republicans carried South Carolina. So strong were they in the former year that the Federalists did not even bother to present a slate of presidential electors to the legislature. And in the latter year even Charleston elected a full delegation of Republicans to the General Assembly.

While South Carolina was during the early years of the century anti-Federalist, it was at the same time nationalistic in the Jeffersonian sense. On passage of the administration's Non-Importation Act of 1806, the six South Carolina representatives who were present voted affirmatively, as did one senator. In 1807 all but one of South Carolina's congressmen backed the administration program to strengthen the navy, and all but one absent member supported the embargo. From all over the state came expressions of the general view that the embargo should be enforced until American ships could traverse the ocean like those of a free nation. In December of 1808 the legislature, without a dissenting vote, passed a resolution highly praising Jefferson.

Throughout the Jeffersonian period, the Federalists remained critical. In 1803 they had founded the *Courier* in Charleston to oppose the Republican *City Gazette*. In its issue of December 1, 1808, the *Courier* deplored the "ruinous" effect of the embargo on farmers, mechanics, and merchants, declared that the United States had virtually surrendered its independence, and opined that the expenditure of a little gunpowder fifteen months earlier would have avoided the strangulation of commerce.[7] Yet for all their opposition, the South Carolina Federalists remained loyal to the nation. John Rutledge the younger said that, while he had nothing but severe censure for the administration, he felt that it must be supported in time of attack from another nation. In 1809, with Madison having succeeded Jefferson in the White House, Charleston Federalists and Republicans held a joint meeting at St. Michael's Church and expressed their resolve "to evince confidence in the general government and their determination to support the Union, Constitution and rights of the country."[8]

South Carolina's allegiance to the general government during this period held despite the economically depressing trend. Doleful comments on the effects of the national government's commercial measures were not without foundation. Rice exports dropped in 1807 to what up to that time was close to an all-time low.[9] The next year rice prices skidded in a few weeks from $3.50 to $1.75. Sea island cotton at Charleston slumped from an average of 51.6 cents a pound in 1805 to 24.7 in 1808, the lowest point of the 1800-1810 decade.[10] South Carolina exports totaled $14,807,000 in 1801 and only $5,290,614 in 1810. But no threats of secession came from the Palmetto State. Her leaders at that time viewed the depressed condition of business, not as a punishment imposed on South Carolina by the national government, but as a necessary affliction incurred in the course of the administration's effort to preserve the dignity of the nation.

At the height of its admiration of the Jeffersonian administration, South Carolina in 1808 adopted a fairer basis of representation in the state legislature and in 1810 amended the state constitution to provide that every white man of the age of twenty-one, except paupers, non-commissioned officers and private soldiers of the army of the United States, was to have the right to vote if he was a citizen of the state and had lived in the election district six months. This was

South Carolina's last bow toward democracy until after the Civil War.

The group of rising young leaders whom South Carolina sent to Congress in 1811 were more concerned with nationalism than with philosophical democracy. They looked beyond the borders of their own state to a powerful future for the young republic. Sharing this vision were John C. Calhoun, William Lowndes, and Langdon Cheves. Joining other War Hawks in Congress, they carried the Madison administration along with their view that only by fighting Great Britain could the United States assert its dignity as a nation and stop British interference with its shipping on the high seas. South Carolina's delegation gave strong support to various steps to prepare the nation for the conflict.

Calhoun, in seeking his legislative seat, had campaigned on a war platform. Once in the House and on the Foreign Affairs Committee, of which he was soon chairman, he began backing military preparedness legislation looking toward the fulfillment of his campaign pledge. He had doubted the efficacy of the embargo and supported other measures short of war only as a means to gain time. He introduced the bill formally declaring war with Britain. In his first term in Congress, Calhoun announced that he contended not for his own state alone but "for the interests of the whole people."[11]

South Carolina accepted the War of 1812 as a part of the price of membership in the Union. Republicans welcomed it, and, while it was not popular with the Federalists, most of them dutifully supported it. Even the rabidly anti-Republican Charleston *Courier* declared that the time for argument had passed and now all must carry on the war "with vigor, with unanimity, and we must sincerely pray with glory and success."[12] A large proportion of the officers in the war came from South Carolina. President Madison appointed Federalist Thomas Pinckney commander of the Southeast or Sixth Military district.

Meanwhile, sounds of dissent had been coming from

New Enland, which opposed the war. Congressman David R. Williams of South Carolina chided Joseph Quincy of Massachusetts for predicting that his state would resist the federal government. Williams asserted that successful prosecution of the conflict would benefit the representative from Massachusetts and his friends as much as anyone in the House. Timothy Pickering, one of the leaders of New England states' rights agitation, got summary verbal treatment by the South Carolina Marine Society, an organization which Captain Joseph Vesey had led. The Society drank to the toast: "Timothy Pickering—may the production of a Rope-Walk be the neck-cloth of him who attempts to untwist the political cable of our union."[13]

In 1814 representatives of Massachusetts, Rhode Island, and Connecticut met in the Hartford Convention, talked of secession, and drew up a report condemning the Madison administration and the war and inviting the New England states to nullify the conscription bill before Congress. From Charleston, in the words of the editor of the *Southern Patriot*, a new Republican newspaper, came a biting denunciation of the activities at Hartford:

> . . . we tremble at the influence of State prejudice, wielded by the arm of personal ambition. . . . We abhor all doctrines, that tend to separate those, whose interest, whose glory, whose existence, is union. . . . Increase the powers of the National Congress—amend your constitution where it is too weak for the purpose of *National Defense*; and give your Executive a discretionary power, for which he can always be responsible. This is the key stone that binds the arch.[14]

These rhetorical missiles from South Carolina were well designed for opponents to use against South Carolina itself twenty years later, had they cared to unearth them.

As in the period of peacetime commercial restrictions, South Carolina suffered economically during the war. The average price of sea island cotton at Charleston in 1812 was 17.5 cents, the lowest average for any year between 1800 and 1833. The highest average for any of the war years was the 25.3 cents of 1814, not a good price for the long fiber.

Rice exports in 1813 sank almost as low as in the disastrous year of 1807, but the hurricane of 1813 may have cut rice production. To help relieve the distress, the South Carolina legislature set up the Bank of the State of South Carolina and authorized it to lend money to businessmen and planters. Thus bolstered, the people of the state came through the conflict in fair spirits. Despite its hardships, South Carolina remained patriotic and nationalistic.[15]

The protective tariff of 1816 was largely the work of Congressmen John C. Calhoun and William Lowndes and was defended by Calhoun, even though his own constituency was largely agricultural, on the ground that the young country needed to develop industries in order to become self sufficient in time of war. Not only the tariff but other nationalistic measures as well were supported by South Carolina's representatives in the postwar years. A majority of them favored the establishment of the Second Bank of the United States and the bill providing for national internal improvements.

A South Carolina judge in 1819 condemned the notion that a state had the right to defeat the operation of an act of the general government. In 1820 John C. Calhoun warned against sectionalism and the disunion which could result from pressing too far. A year later a South Carolina Congressman strongly asserted the supremacy of the national government and attacked the "ultra doctrines respecting consolidation and state sovereignty."[16]

While South Carolina politicians were still relishing the vision of a united and powerful nation, the economic trend in their own state and elsewhere held portents that would rob the vision of its brightness. The reverses accompanying the commercial and military campaigns against Great Britain have already been mentioned. But these had no long term significance.

The invention of the cotton gin in the last decade of the eighteenth century enormously boosted cotton cultivation as a profitable enterprise. Efficient removal of the seed from the fiber made cotton far more readily usable for weaving cloth. As the demand for the staple rose, South Carolina devoted more and more of her resources and energy to its production. The state's harvest rose from about 1,500,000 pounds in 1791 to 20,000,000 pounds in 1801, to 40,000,-000 in 1811, to 50,000,000 in 1821, to 65,500,000 in 1834. Rice cultivation also became more profitable after Jonathan Lucas about 1787 erected on the Santee River the first water driven mill for pounding the husks from the grain.[17] In 1805, because of European war, rice brought a higher price than at any time during the first half of the eighteenth century. But rice planting was limited by the availability of land suitable for the South Carolina cultivation method of flooding the fields. The yield, in the absence of machine cultivation procedures, reached the optimum fairly early in the century. Thus cotton came to be ascendant, with the low-country growing the long staple, higher priced sea island variety.

To obtain the labor needed for expanding cotton and rice production, South Carolina in December, 1803, re-opened the slave trade for the four remaining years before Congress under the Constitution could forbid it. Acting on a pretext provided by Governor James B. Richardson when he said in his annual message that the laws against the traffic could not be enforced, the legislature not only opened the ports of the state to the African slave trade but also repealed the law against trading with other areas, except for a restriction on the importation of slaves from the West Indies, South America, and other states unless they were certified to be of good moral character.[18]

During four years of frantic importation, 202 vessels registered in four American states and three foreign countries brought into Charleston harbor a total of 39,075 African slaves. Britain led in the activity, with seventy ships bringing in 19,649 human chattels. Rhode Island came next, with fifty-nine ships moving in cargoes totaling 8,238 bondmen. Sixty-one Charleston vessels participated in the trade and brought in 7,723 slaves. The rest of the four-year total of human freight was accounted for by vessels owned in France and Sweden and in various other American ports.[19]

Representative of the ships, through which South Carolina took its last legal fling in the international slave business, was the 160-ton brig, *Tartar*. She was owned by Frederick Travell, a native of Switzerland but a resident of Charleston. Her master, Captain James Taylor, was born in Boston but lived in Charleston, as did most of the crew. The ship's doctor was a Frenchman. The *Tartar* cleared Charleston on November 22, 1806, bound for Pongo River, just north of Sierra Leone. Her cargo, for trade on the African coast, included tobacco, brandy, claret, tar, flour, five bales of dry goods, and a box of white hats. The captain was authorized to do some trading for his own profit. But he was instructed that all slaves taken aboard must be clearly marked with the owner's initials or the captain's, so that if there were any losses through death the loser could be properly determined. The brig arrived at her destination on January 24, 1807.[20]

The revived slave trade brought more than 15,000 involuntary immigrants into Charleston in the single year of 1807[21]—an influx equivalent to about three-fourths of the city's entire population. Such a stream of shackled human beings moving through the community at an average of more than a thousand a month could hardly have failed to make a memorable impression on its inhabitants, slave and free alike—an impression that was not likely to be heartwarming to one like Denmark Vesey. Though later generations of South Carolinians sought to put the blame for this traffic on outsiders, they overlooked the fact that their state was the only one to authorize the trade during this period.

When Congress, to counteract the action of South Carolina moved to levy a tax on each slave imported into the United States, the state's representatives in Washington resented the effort. While most of them said they had opposed the reopening of the slave trade, they fought the proposed tax as an unwarranted interference with their state. Consideration of the tax was postponed in the hope that South

Carolina would renew its prohibition, and further attempts to pass the federal bill in 1805 failed. In response to the governor's appeals to place curbs on the traffic, the state House of Representatives passed restrictive bills in 1805 and 1806. But each time the measure was lost in the Senate. South Carolina continued to serve as a trading center until 1808 when a congressional prohibition went into effect.

During the state legislative debate over whether South Carolina should close the floodgates before the Constitution's allowable cutoff date of 1808, some of the lawmakers took offense over condemnation of the trade as immoral and un-christian. Their sentiment provided a clue as to the motive that was uppermost in the minds of many in the state. The editor of the Charleston *Courier* spoke of the need for more laborers. But besides the need of supplying a larger work force for cotton and rice planting, there was the hope of turning a profit in selling slaves. Servile labor was being moved westward into Georgia, Alabama, and Mississippi as cotton cultivation expanded there. And South Carolina had the only ports of entry to receive the last big shipments of Africans. Many of the slave ships simply touched at South Carolina wharves to legitimize their imports, then sailed on what were technically coasting voyages to Gulf ports where prices were higher.

After 1808 considerable numbers of slaves were brought into South Carolina from Northern states. An 1816 esti-mate placed the annual imports into the state from Mary-land and Virginia alone at 30,000. In 1816 the legislature sought to stem the flow, but the act was so ineffective that it was repealed in 1818.[22] In 1821 the governor felt constrained to comment on the tide of imported slaves. As with bondmen shipped in from abroad, many of those imported from the North were sent to the frontier. In the West former residents of South Carolina would be in a position to capitalize on the black cargoes being funneled in through their native state.

Beginning in 1810, the shifts in South Carolina's popu-lation were symptomatic of the rise of the West as a land of opportunity and of the accentuation within the state of the cotton-slave economy. During the first three decades of the nineteenth-century South Carolina's population rose at a fairly steady rate. But, like the other South Atlantic states (with the exception of Georgia), South Carolina during this period was registering a rate of increase considerably less than that of the nation as a whole. What was happening was that South Carolina was supplying emigrants to plant the virgin soil of the Gulf and Southwestern states and take advantage of the expanding market for cotton.

In each decade between 1810 and 1840 South Carolina lost increasingly larger contingents of her population through outward migration. For the thirty-year period the outward movement came close to a quarter of a million people, with two-thirds of this number being white, mostly members of the small farmer class who hoped for a better life in a new land. Some big planters moved too, along with their slaves; but not until the depression of 1819 were there noticeable signs of emigration by the planter class. The state's net loss in white emigrants from 1810 to 1840 was equivalent to the entire white population of South Carolina in 1790.

Meanwhile the population ratio of the state was shifting from 56.8 per cent white in 1800 to 56.4 per cent Negro in 1840. The change in favor of Negroes, the first in more than thirty years, showed up in the 1820 census when South Carolina's population stood at 265,301 black and 237,440 white. Since the racial composition of the coastal districts was not changing appreciably during this period, the rise in the state's proportion of Negroes was an unmistakable signal of the spread of the slave system to the middle and upper portions of the state. As the white yeomanry moved out, the slave economy was moving in and dictating that more and more the political spokesmen for the state, including those from the upcountry like Calhoun, should speak for the plantation oligarchy.

As cotton cultivation spread and increased in output in South Corolina, it smothered a budding program of manufacturing. During the last quarter of the eighteenth century a number of spinning and weaving enterprises had been started, several near Charleston. In the early years of the new century such products as rope, paper, clocks, gunpowder, and castor oil were being produced in the state, with Charleston as the site of a variety of ventures. Cottonseed oil was being processed in Columbia. The value of manufacturing was being debated in Charleston in 1800. Charles Pinckney wrote approvingly of manufacturing in 1811 in a letter to Jefferson. Calhoun spoke in 1816 of the need to develop manufacturing enterprises in the interest of national self-sufficiency.

But opposition was latent and began to mount. In 1808 a promoter of industrial development deplored the hostile attitude of the influential men of Charleston. Their view was aided by the extraordinary profits which cotton planting brought in the early years of the century. It was enhanced by a widespread sentiment attaching prestige to planting and regarding business activity as afflicted with crassness. New England mill workers were frequently referred to in a scornful manner. By 1810 most of the little mills had disappeared. By 1825 manufacturing in South Carolina had noticeably declined.

South Carolina had the raw material (cotton) and the water power for mills to process it. Moreover, slaves could have been transformed into capital to finance the development of industry. The result could have been a more rounded economy with manufacturing and diversified agriculture. But South Carolina chose the course of enslavement to cotton, with an economy geared to exporting the fiber and importing almost all other necessities.

In 1821 South Carolina, with an annual harvest of fifty million pounds, was producing more cotton than any other state in the nation. Not until 1826 was its output surpassed by the larger state of Georgia, and not until 1834 did the harvests of Alabama and Mississippi exceed that of South Carolina.[23] This intensive concentration on a single crop was not only wearing out the land but was channeling the energies and thoughts of the people. Their attention became engrossed in an all-out defense of the system of chattel slavery which was deemed necessary to the production of the fiber. Seeing in the institution the source of their economic well-being, South Carolinians hotly challenged the right of other sections to interfere in any way, the rationale being that the state's domestic security would be endangered.[24] Calhoun, who had once condemned the slave trade as an "odious traffic," said in 1820 that slavery was "the best guarantee to equality among the whites. It produced an unvarying level among them . . . did not admit of inequalities by which one white man could domineer over another."[25]

Neither Calhoun, with all his brilliance, nor the other political leaders of the state, had the insight to profit by what economists said about the disadvantages of slavery, some of them speaking long before South Carolina's attitude on the system had hardened. On one point there was almost universal agreement—that the slave's output per man hour was lower (for obvious want of incentive) than the free laborer. Adam Smith, in his great work, *The Wealth of Nations*, published in 1776, had said that the cost of slave labor was "the dearest of any."[26] J. B. Say, writing in 1803, noted some advantages in the system but added that slavery caused violence and brutality to usurp the place of intelligence and hampered the progress of invention.[27]

Dr. Thomas Cooper, president of the South Carolina College and a strong partisan of the state, summed up the many economic drawbacks of slavery. Though he wrote in 1827, his conclusions should have been apparent earlier to any keen observer of the system. He noted the cost, without any corresponding return, of rearing young slaves to the age of self-support. He thought the cost of maintaining the working slave was higher in proportion to the rate of productivity than would be the cost of free labor. "Slave labour," he asserted, "is undoubtedly the dearest kind of labor."[28]

About the same time as Cooper wrote, James Raymond, a Marylander, contended that slavery hampered economy by preventing seasonal changes in the size of the work force, by requiring planters to support their operatives in lean years as well as fat, and by hindering the accumulation of wealth by the laborers.[29] Added to all the other disadvantages was the endless problem of control.

Among the few advantages from an economic standpoint were the relative ease of shifting the labor force from one region to another and an assured regularity of work through the reduction to a minimum of turnover in employment. To these, contemporary observers often added the mistaken notion that white men could not labor in the hot fields of the South, whereas Negroes could. This was one rationalization for a system under which the employer could exert absolute control over the labor force and drive it to harder work than he might care to engage in himself.

Led on by big profits that were realized in some of the years of high cotton prices, slave-owners continued to invest available capital in the purchase of more slaves to produce more cotton for the continued purpose of buying more slaves to produce more cotton. Thus the system became ever more deeply rooted and its proponents ever more attached to it economically and emotionally.

South Carolina's preoccupation with cotton led to what seemed to be an inevitable reckoning. The crucial year was 1819, which marked not only a period of depression but also the beginning of a long-range economic change. After that year the state was never again to set the economic records it was once to register in comparison with the other members of the Union. In 1801 South Carolina's exports had ranked third among the states of the nation, and in 1816 they were second only to New York's. In 1818 the price of middling upland cotton began a steep decline from the 1817 record of 34 cents a pound, a price the fiber was not to reach again in the anti-bellum period. The trend was the same with the higher priced sea island variety, grown near Charleston. The 1818 price of 63.2 cents at Charleston was to be the peak. By 1823 it had plummeted to 24.5 cents. [30] Meanwhile Charleston, which by 1820 had dropped to sixth place among the cities of the United States, had begun to decline in importance as a port until by 1822 it was surpassed by New Orleans, a much younger port.[31]

While there were to be periods of relative prosperity after 1819, they were never to achieve the boom levels of some years of the pre-1819 era, a period that might be called the golden age of the plantation in South Carolina. It was an age that furnished a vision which South Carolina slave-holders sought constantly to refurbish with more slaves and more cotton. But despite steadily rising cotton production up to the time of the Civil War, the goal of pre-eminence through the labor of fettered employees turned out to be only a dream.

It was in the second decade of the nineteenth century that the leadership of the South passed from Virginia to South Carolina. For a brief period, under the aegis of Calhoun, this leadership was exerted in favor of strong nationalism. But within a few years South Carolina was in the forefront of a swing toward sectionalism. Calhoun and others, instead of seeking to stem or direct the trend, went along with the stream. At a time when a major portion of the country was moving into a libertarian tide of history, South Carolina was setting in motion a current of reaction. The force of the current was soon sufficient to command the support of most of the South. Yet even as the mainstream of reaction was gathering power it was creating division— division within the nation and division within the South. In the South the opponents of the trend toward neo-feudalism were left with little hope of making headway using the devices of democracy. The politically polarized nation and the politically polarized South would soon be moving toward a violent contest.

# EDDIES
# OF REVOLUTION

● During the same decades that certain economic and political events were turning South Carolina toward insularity and reaction, other events were exerting a counter force. The Palmetto State's shift away from the main course of national history was effected by a political leadership largely controlled by slave-owning planters; the bulk of the white population for the most part subservient to this group, went along. Yet even while the mainstream of reaction was propelling the destiny of the state in one direction, eddies of revolution were seeping through to the silent masses who had no voice in that destiny. They were thereby made to feel that they had some link with the destiny of the world beyond the borders of South Carolina. The difference between the new revolutionary currents and those of the pre-1800 generation was that in the earlier period libertarian sentiments were overt and were sympathized with to some extent by the state's ruling group, whereas such doctrines became more and more suspect in South Carolina as the influence of the Revolutionary War receded into the past.

The first year of the new century was marked by several events that were auspicious for people in bondage. Though their significance at the time was only symbolic and could be little appreciated, they eventually came to be meaningful to those yearning for freedom. It was in 1800 that Denmark Vesey obtained his liberty. It was in 1800 that Toussaint L'Overture, now recognized by Napoleon as virtual monarch of part of the French empire, was consolidating the hold of Negroes on the island of St. Domingue. It was in 1800 that Gabriel plotted rebellion in Virginia. It was in 1800 that Jefferson was elected President of the United

States in a bloodless revolution that saw proponents of oligarchy overthrown by proponents of democracy.

In Charleston Captain Joseph Vesey, from the vantage point of a local election manager, observed the events that brought Jefferson to power. Denmark Vesey, until a few months previously a member of the captain's household, was still in a position to visit the old mariner and absorb something of the political campaign.

Jefferson, the new leader of the nation, was a man who had expressed some highly unorthodox views on Negroes and slavery. As early as 1774 he had seen the abolition of slavery as the "greatest object" of the colonies. He included a condemnation of the slave trade in the original draft of the Declaration of Independence. In his Notes on Virginia, he alluded to the chance of Negro rebellion, observing that, "considering numbers, nature, and natural means only, a revolution of the wheel of fortune, an exchange of situation is among possible events." He added—significantly for those who might take the Bible as a text—that supernatural interference might give no comfort to the targets of an insurrectionary effort. "The Almighty," said Jefferson, "has no attribute which can take side with us in such a contest."[1]

Let it not be supposed that libertarian doctrines such as Jefferson's escaped the notice of Negroes. In the Federalist period Negroes in Charleston were actually urged by Republicans to reveal undemocratic intrigues of their owners.[2] The subjugated race was not as oblivious to political events and personalities as slave-owners liked to pretend when they spoke of the naivete and savagery of their chattels in order to justify their own scheme of things. The masters attempted to keep channels of communication between free and slave society closed on political and social matters, but they didn't always succeed. Denmark Vesey, and other Negroes in Charleston, read newspapers and could understand the import of their dispatches even though they were phrased in guarded language.[3] Discussion was open enough so that in 1800 a Charleston supporter of Jefferson could answer an attack on the philosopher of the Revolution in a letter to the *City Gazette*.[4]

As early as 1789 a free Negro in Baltimore had written an anonymous anti-slavery pamphlet in which he invoked Jefferson's words in the Declaration of Independence. In 1791 Jefferson had engaged in a sympathetic correspondence with a free Negro (possibly the author of the anti-slavery tract). While there is little knowledge of the dissemination of specific documents to and through the slave community, there is evidence that Negroes were cognizant of political ideas voiced in them. Denmark Vesey spoke of the rights and privileges to which members of his race were entitled.[5]

Regardless of how carefully Negroes were watched to prevent them from utilizing written means of communication, little could be done to cut off oral transmission of thoughts and information. A communication belt for such transmission was provided by travel—by the movement of masters and slaves from one part of the country to another and back and by the shipment of slaves from one region to another. South Carolina itself had a steady influx of slave immigrants from the North. No matter how discreet white overlords tried to be, their conversations undoubtedly let drop significant bits of information within the hearing of black house servants. The South's apprehensiveness about word-of-mouth "infection" was signified by its strictures against certain kinds of travel by free Negroes and slaves and by its often-expressed concern lest some knowing Negro traveler talk too much. John Randolph of Virginia once warned that free Negroes "acted as channels of communication, not only between different slaves, but between slaves of different districts."[6] Whenever there was a period of tension the concern became acute.

Such a period came in 1800 as a result of Gabriel's abortive uprising in Virginia. Gabriel, a twenty-four-year-old giant of a man, began planning his strike for freedom in the spring of 1800. With the aid of an unknown number of recruits, he assembled crude swords, bayonets, and bullets.

He and his fellow revolutionists expected to launch their rebellion by mass slave attack on Richmond on August 30. But their design was betrayed by two slaves. And stormy weather and high water hampered the rendezvous. About a thousand slaves who did assemble disbanded in the face of the massive preparations that had been made by the forewarned whites. Governor James Monroe had posted cannon at the state capitol, had called more than 650 well armed men into service and notified every militia commander in the state. In the ensuing days scores of Negroes were arrested and some thirty-five hanged.

Meanwhile slave-owners near and far, noting or hearing about the zeal and mettle of the rebels, became thoroughly alarmed. The insurrectionists were aware of the difficulties between France and the United States at the time and hoped for French assistance. And one of them reportedly recalled the revolutionary spirit of George Washington.

Monroe wrote to Lieutenant Governor John Drayton of South Carolina about Gabriel's conspiracy. A Charleston paper gave notice of it in a vague report which mentioned the execution of several of the rebels. More details could eventually have reached Charleston via the slave grapevine after the Virginia press finally broke its silence to report that the rebellion had been crushed and its leaders punished. While the breaking of the news in this fashion was undoubtedly intended to serve as a deterrent, it could not fail at the same time to inform Negro readers that the insurrectionary attempt had been made and to imply certain lessons for the planners of any future effort.

Because of the secrecy and the censorship commonly associated with Negro revolts, it is hard to tell how many there were or how many become known to slaves in other localities. But one authority has estimated that between 1800, the year of Denmark Vesey's liberation, and 1821, there were at least fifty-three uprisings plotted in the United States, six of them in South Carolina.[7] Potential insurgents were given a chance to find out about several of the South Carolina events by the publication of items about them in the

press. And at least two of the conspiracies in the state
(at Camden and Columbia) evoked enough public reaction
to become generally known in the communities where they
occurred.

An alarm at Columbia just before Christmas of 1804
led to the alerting of the militia and unusually diligent patrolling. Cannon were placed in front of the State House. At
Camden in 1816 an uprising was planned for the Fourth of
July. Employing espionage to uncover the ramifications of the
plan, the authorities arrested many Negroes and eventually
hanged six. While the conspiracy was being investigated, a
resident of Camden wrote: "This is really a dreaful situation
to be in—I think it is time for us to leave the country where
we cannot go to bed in safety."[8]

Such expressions of fear were not uncommon. During
the summer of 1812 a Charleston resident had put the matter
in stark terms: "Consider, I beseech you, that the coast of
S. Carolina and Georgia is principally inhabited by a black
population, which it is not to be denied, the whites are not
able to control . . . A regiment of militia has been sent us
from the interior for our protection, but they have mutinied
. . . tho' the mutiny is arrested for the moment, the spirit
of it is by no means quelled."[9]

Two years later slave-holders were alarmed when a
British admiral, blockading the coast, offered slaves a chance
to emigrate and become free settlers in British territory.

As one of many steps taken through the years to discourage slave conspiracies or uprisings, South Carolina in
1805 had enacted a law making aid for such schemes by free
people, Negro or white, a capital offense.

In slave-holders' minds, the problem of runaway slaves
was closely related to feared revolts. Runaways not only
represented a loss of property, but they were considered a
menace when, as sometimes happened, they formed themselves into independent camps in remote areas. Thus established, they were exhibits of insubordination, havens for
other fugitives, bases for marauding expeditions against

nearby plantations, and sometimes sources of leadership for planned uprisings.[10]

That these camps of runaway slaves—sometimes called maroons—caused no little uneasiness in South Carolina is indicated by the amount of official attention they commanded. Governors reported on efforts to subdue the rebel strongholds. Sometimes they were the targets of organized military expeditions. The daily advertisements for runaways suggested the potential for building up such refugee communities. As the camps became more populous and bolder in their guerrilla activities, they drew upon themselves the periodic counterattacks that occurred in South Carolina from colonial times forward.[11]

In 1816 Governor David R. Williams, after dispatching a body of troops against a community of runaways near Ashepoo, reported to the legislature that their force had become "alarming, not less from its numbers than from its arms and ammunition." Three years later an outlaw community in Williamsburg County was attacked, three Negroes were killed and others captured; one of the attacking white men was wounded. In a similar clash near Georgetown in 1821 one slave-holder was killed and three outlaws captured.

The recurring expeditions against the maroon camps sometimes drew notices in the press where interested observers such as Denmark Vesey could read about them.[12] The frequent newspaper references to runaways, including descriptions of their capabilities, of course, gave a clue to the potential any rebel leader might draw on in making recruitments. (At least one of Vesey's followers was identified as a runaway.)[13] Sometimes the advertisements, still running many months after the flight, indicated that the fugitives had enjoyed a considerable period of freedom if not ultimate escape. The fact that the escaped slave could read and write and thus could pen his own pass was also noted from time to time. Readers were often informed that the runaway was "plausible," in order to put them on guard against being talked out of making a capture.[14]

Methods of apprehending fugitives were frequently far from humane. With rewards of considerable value sometimes being offered for the seizure of the runaway dead or alive, the slave-catchers might employ bloodhounds and have no compunction about killing the quarry if he put up resistance. In some communities slave-hunters offered their services for a fee.

Many escaping slaves lost their lives fighting their pursuers or as a result of exposure.[15] Since fugitives were ordinarily viewed as outlaws, the few restraints that the law imposed for the protection of slaves were of little value to them. Even if they were not killed or injured in being captured, they were likely to get a severe whipping at the time of return to their owners. Sometimes runaways found themselves the property of new owners as a result of flight. They might be "sold running" or "sold in the woods," which meant that their masters had transferred title to another at a reduced price, with the new owner taking the chance of recovering his property. Despite all the barriers that stood in the way, some slaves made good their escape to the North or to Canada or, before 1819, to Spanish Florida. The Underground Railroad came into being about 1804 but was not operating as a co-ordinated organization until 1818.

Fleeing slaves could usually count on the co-operation of their fellows in their effort to escape. Free Negroes also lent aid by concealing the fugitives or otherwise helping them on their way. The runaways used whatever havens they could find. On the east side of Goose Creek near where it entered the Cooper River above Charleston was an abandoned house that was believed to be a hiding place for fugitive slaves. Their confederates reportedly sought to give them freedom from observation by encouraging the notion among Negroes that the house was haunted.[16] Not all slaves could be relied on to maintain secrecy, since there was great risk of discovery and of punishment for aiding escaping bondmen.

South Carolina's basic slave law of 1740 made it the

duty of any person capturing a runaway to return him to his master immediately or to turn him over to the sheriff within four days. Upon claiming the slave, the owner was required to pay the expenses incurred in his capture and confinement. If the fugitive was still unclaimed after eighteen months, he was to be sold at public auction to defray the cost of his upkeep; and if there was any balance above this, it was to go into the public treasury.

From 1740 onward free Negroes were penalized for aiding slaves to escape. In 1821 the South Carolina law against harboring runaways was made more strict, with free Negroes found guilty of the offense being made subject to any punishment the court saw fit to impose short of disfigurement or execution. White persons convicted of the same crime might be fined $1,000 or imprisoned for a year.[17]

The right of owners to reclaim fugitive slaves who had fled to another state was recognized in the federal constitution (Article IV, Section 2). And though the constitutional provision did not specify what agency, state or federal, was charged with its execution, Congress had in 1793 proceeded to put the responsibility for returning runaways upon both federal and state courts, empowering them to issue warrants for the runaways' return on proof of identity. For years slave hunters, under this law, had a free hand. But Northern states, prompted by growing anti-slavery feeling, began in the 1820's to enact "personal liberty laws" to provide certain safeguards for alleged fugitives and to protect Negroes from kidnapping.[18]

By the year 1800 relations between South Carolina and the Negro-dominated island of St. Domingue had become comparatively routine. There were periodic notices in the Charleston press of ship sailings to Cap Francais.[19] Toussaint L'Ouverture gave public notice of the official actions of his regime in a letter to the *City Gazette*.[20] The same paper carried accounts of diplomatic deliberations in St. Domingue.[21]

Under a calm surface, however, feeling in South Carolina concerning the French dominion was far from unruffled.

Former French residents of the island, now living in Charleston, were a daily reminder of what happened there. The Negroes whom the refugees had brought with them, and many of whom had been freed or sold to South Carolinians,[22] were an even more pointed reminder of events in St. Domingue.

South Carolina had been severely shaken by the momentous uprising of slaves so near the shores of the United States. And in the years since the initial black blow for freedom, occurrences on the island were not calculated to ease the fears of white slave-holders. They knew that in 1793, at the invitation of Léger Félicité Sonthonax, an emissary of the revolutionary regime in Paris, a massive wave of rural slaves had overrun the port city of Cap Francais with ease, had pushed a French army into the sea and left the city in ruins. In the intervening years rebellious slaves, under the leadership of Toussaint, had consolidated their grip on St. Dominigue and had established a semi-independent nation with Toussaint as governor-general.

The distrust which Charleston entertained for the black regime of St. Domingue had been reflected in the city's action in 1797 in forcing a visiting mulatto general from the island to put up bond, as required by South Carolina law of out-of-state Negroes. The bond had been remitted only after the French consul pointed out that the visitor was on an official mission for the French government and had been wounded while fighting for the American cause at the siege of Savannah. Suspicion and fear were also evident in South Carolina's curb on slave importations from the West Indies. Congress in 1803—in an effort to aid South Carolina and other states to enforce this restriction and to calm the general panic over the possible influence of St. Domingue Negroes—passed an act providing for the forfeiture of any ship (and punishment of the captain) which brought into port any person whose admission was barred by state law.

Apprehensions over possible subversive activities by the former slaves of St. Domingue were heightened by the Negroes' link with revolutionary France. A number of prominent Americans, including John Rutledge and Robert Goodloe Harper of South Carolina, expressed concern that the island rebels, independently or at the behest of France, were stirring up trouble. Rutledge wrote: "There have been emissaries amongst us in the Southern States, they have begun their war upon us . . . [the slaves] have been tampered with . . ."[23] While these alarms were probably exaggerated, they were no doubt genuinely felt by their authors who, in turn, succeeded in communicating their ideas to fellow citizens and perhaps unintentionally to Negroes as well.

General fear of France in the United States was behind American and British diplomacy directed at St. Domingue at the turn of the century. But one element of that fear was the notion that France might use Negro troops from the island to liberate the slaves in the United States and in the British West Indies and then annex the latter. Britain and the United States came to the support of Toussaint, believing that St. Domingue, politically independent of France but economically dependent on the Anglo-American axis, would be less dangerous to their slave-holdings. In 1799 Toussaint signed an agreement with the two powers under which American and English ships were given exclusive trading privileges with St. Domingue and the black leader pledged that no persons dangerous to the slave regions of the United States or the British Empire would leave his domain. In spite of proddings from France to aid in an attack on Jamaica and possibly the southern part of the United States, Toussaint kept his part of the bargain.

Even Southern members of Congress visualized an independent St. Domingue with less fear than a free Negro dominion allied with the martial French nation. Thomas Pinckney of South Carolina put it thus: "should the independence of the island take place, the event would be more advantageous to the Southern States, than if it remained under the domain of France. . . . If our dispute with France should not be accommodated they could invade this country only from that quarter."[24] But Pinckney's advocacy of independence did not go so far as to favor recognition for a

Negro regime. This, he felt, might encourage the Negro slaves of the United States to seek to emulate the Negroes of St. Domingue.

With the signing of the treaty of Mortfontaine on August 1, 1800, came the end of the quasi-war between the United States and France, as well as America's peculiar relationship with Toussaint. Thomas Jefferson approved of this shift in policy upon assuming the presidency in 1801. But Jefferson had hardly been inaugurated when he heard reports of the retrocession of Louisiana from Spain to France and of Napoleon's plans to reduce Toussaint and to occupy New Orleans.

Napoleon's ambitions were to be thwarted in the jungles of the Caribbean. France's costly and ineffective military operations against the blacks of St. Domingue in 1802-1803 played a part in Napoleon's decision to pull out of the New World. Defeated by yellow fever and the black soldiers of Dessalines, Christophe, and Petion, the French withdrew from St. Domingue. And having lost the island, Napoleon decided to sell Louisiana to the United States. In 1804 Dessalines proclaimed Haiti (the high place) independent. From that time onward the black nation was viewed as an incendiary flame by white slave-holders and as a beacon of freedom by their Negro bondmen. Years later Denmark Vesey and his followers were to reveal that Haiti was figuratively quite visible from South Carolina.

While the slave masters of South Carolina were trying to wall off unsettling insurrectionary currents from outside the state, the insidious (to them) influence of domestic opponents of slavery continued—though, by the first decade of the new century, the libertarian fire of the Revolutionary epoch had begun to cool. Quakers, who did not lose their anti-slavery zeal, found espousal of their views increasingly difficult. About the turn of the century a movement was begun among Quakers to get them to leave areas where slavery existed. In South Carolina the leader of this crusade was Zachariah Dicks, who was born in Pennsylvania and

moved to North Carolina about 1754. He visited South
Carolina between 1800 and 1804 and warned the Friends
to quit the land of slavery, telling them that if they didn't
their fate would be the same as that of the slaughtered Santo
Domingans. Convinced of the sinfulness of slavery by Dicks
and his predecessors, including that compelling teacher, John
Woolman, Quakers resolved to leave the slave states. About
1,200 members of their faith are known to have left South
Carolina between 1805 and 1819 for points in Ohio and
Indiana.[25]

Two of the most vocal and active anti-slavery advocates
that South Carolina ever produced were strongly influenced
by the Quakers. They came from the unusual Grimké family
of Charleston. Sarah Grimké, who was born in the South
Carolina city in 1792, said later that she held a lifelong
detestation of slavery and that it was "a millstone" about
her neck. Sarah's younger sister, Angelina, who was equally
vehement against the institution after the two young women
had moved to Philadelphia, was not so quick to perceive
the evil as Sarah. Sarah early in life ignored the law of South
Carolina by teaching a Negro maid to read. She cried when
a servant woman was whipped. The Grimké sisters were to
reveal the intensity of their feelings when they referred to
slavery as a "system of oppression and cruelty, heathenism
and robbery."[26]

Another South Carolina foe of slavery during this
period was Lewis DuPre, like the Grimkés of French Hu-
guenot extraction. DuPre in 1810 issued two emancipation
pamphlets. A few years later a writer, using the pen name
"Montesquieu," lamented in the press about hordes of
slaves being brought into South Carolina from Maryland and
Virginia. Slavery, he said, whatever form it might assume,
could never be justified, though it might be tolerated. He
declared that even a mind warped from virtue could not
but condemn it, for it was productive of indolence and
cruelty. The wealthiest citizens, Montesquieu complained,
bought vast tracts of land and sought to make them profitable by the easiest and quickest way, "butchering" the soil

and with the proceeds acquiring more land and more Negroes and so on in an endless round. "In the meantime," he concluded, "South Carolina is the victim."

In 1820 Mrs. Elizabeth Yates of Charleston wrote to a Massachusetts senator, denouncing slavery and saying she hoped Congress would rouse the nation on the subject, though not by reproaches which she said only stiffened Southern opposition. She and her husband planned to free their slaves (worth $25,000), and they rejoiced that students at the South Carolina College almost unanimously recognized the evil of the system.[27]

Some indication of the anti-slavery sentiment in the South is suggested by the fact that, of 130 abolition societies established before 1827 by Benjamin Lundy, more than 100, with four-fifths of the total membership, were in that region.[28] While it should be noted that a majority of these southern societies were in the non-plantation country of western North Carolina and eastern Tennessee,[29] their doctrines no doubt found some outlets into slave territory.

Talk in the South of the perniciousness of slavery prompted laws and violent verbal reactions which in themselves called attention to the subject in dispute. From the first Quakers had been sneered at for meddling in a business with which they had nothing to do. As the years passed the acrimonious comments became less reserved. Anyone who circulated inflammatory literature was dealt with severely. In 1809 several hundred pamphlets of an insurrectionary character were reported to have been brought into Charleston by the Negro steward of the ship *Minerva*. A Charleston citizen, a passenger on the vessel on her passage from New York, reported the circumstances to the intendant of the city. That official boarded the ship along with the city marshal, but they arrived too late to seize the pamphlets. Several of them were found, however, and the steward was allowed to avoid trial upon his agreement to leave the state never to return.[30]

Despite such zealous efforts to keep offensive publications out of the wrong hands, anti-slavery pamphlets from the North and from abroad were at times distributed among Negroes in Charleston.[31] Denmark Vesey got possession of some and not only absorbed them for his own information but also read them to others.[32]

In South Carolina in 1820 the state law against incendiary publications was strengthened to offset growing protests against slavery. White persons convicted of, directly or indirectly, bringing into the state or circulating any written or printed paper intended to disturb the peace in relation to slaves were made subject to a fine of $1,000 and imprisonment for a year. Free persons of color convicted of the same offense were, for the first offense, to be fined $1,000 and jailed for the second offense, given a whipping of up to fifty lashes and banished from the state; for returning from banishment, to be put to death "without benefit of clergy."[33] The nature of these sanctions was publicized in the Charleston *Courier,* thus warning potential offenders but also informing them by implication that certain doctrines feared by the whites were being spread in print. Denmark Vesey and his friends read newspapers avidly.[34]

In addition to the inspiration slaves might draw from the writing and speaking in their behalf in the South, they might also be encouraged by acts for freedom beyond the borders of the region—acts which they found out about only indirectly and belatedly. While the South was beginning to institutionalize slavery more solidly than it had ever been, states in the North were passing anti-slavery laws. By 1804 all the Northern states had adopted measures for the gradual emancipation of all Negroes. Word of these acts would sooner or later reach slave ears and motivate new yearning. Calhoun anticipated this result when he observed that Negroes must never know of any exertions in their behalf since they would surely meet them halfway.

The halls of Congress provided a setting for early and continued exertions in behalf of Negroes. The debate struck verbal sparks which served not only to signal Negroes as to who were their friends but also to let them know the temper of their captors and their flinty opposition to change. If the net effect was to dim hope of peaceful manumission, it was also to suggest the alternative of a more radical approach. When Congress in 1790 had seemed on the point of rejecting a memorial to curb the slave trade, a speaker got up and declared that if anything could induce the slave to rebel, it must be a stroke like this, impressing on him all the horrors of despair.

So the debate continued periodically, with proponents of restricting the human traffic making little headway. The frame of mind of the slave-holders was revealed by Congressman William Loughton Smith of South Carolina when he said that objections to the slave trade sprang from a "misguided and misinformed humanity."[35] As the date when Congress could constitutionally prohibit the slave trade neared, the oratory was fanned into new flame. In his annual message of December 2, 1806, President Jefferson wrote:

> I congratulate you, fellow-citizens, on the approach of the period at which you may interpose your authority constitutionally to withdraw the citizens of the United States from participation in those violations of human rights which have been so long continued on the unoffending inhabitants of Africa, and which the morality, the reputation, and the best interests of our country have long been eager to proscribe.[36]

This language about "human rights" and the bill which followed stirred some Southerners to heated protest. Congressman Peter Early of Georgia said: "A large majority of the people in the Southern states do not . . . believe it immoral to hold human flesh in bondage."[37] So volatile were Southern feelings that the change of three words in the proposed legislation set off an explosion. One version of the Senate measure had provided that neither the importer, nor any purchaser under him, should "have or gain" any title to the persons illegally imported. When the quoted passage was revised to say "hold," Senator Smith of South Carolina exclaimed that he considered this word "hold" (presumably because it undermined the title of third party purchasers) as leading to the destruction and massacre of all the whites in the Southern states.

The event in Congress which was to serve as a clarion call to white and black alike and which made a burning impression on Denmark Vesey was the debate over the admission of Missouri, whether as a free or a slave state. This was the immediate issue, but the far larger question was the power of Congress to prohibit slavery in the vast territory west of the Mississippi. The question had momentous implications. Jefferson called the Missouri debate "a fire bell in the night." While it was going on he confessed that his long-felt hopes for gradual emancipation were fading. John Quincy Adams perceived the debate as the death knell of the Union and added that he took it for granted that the airing of the question then was "a title page to a great, tragic volume."

Congressman James Tallmadge of New York opened the issue in 1819 by proposing to amend a bill for the admission of Missouri so as to bar further introduction of slaves in the state and require that all children subsequently born there of slave parents should be free at the age of twenty-five. Tallmadge said he was mindful of the safety of the white population of the old South and of the servile war which might result from the intercourse between slaves and free blacks there, hence he would not advocate the prohibition of slavery (evil as it was) in a territory such as Alabama; but Missouri was different. The New York congressman said he would not be put off by a Southern imprecation that he had "kindled a fire" which could only be extinguished with "seas of blood." His purpose, he declared, was fixed and was to set bounds to "a slavery the most cruel and debasing the world has ever witnessed." His cause was "freedom of man," the redemption of "unregenerated human beings."

The legislator from New York ignited a national clamor. Those on Tallmadge's side were accused of endeavoring to excite a servile war, and they answered by invoking the principles of liberty. The preamble of the Declaration of

Independence was quoted. South Carolina came in for criticism for holding slave life cheap. There were threats of disunion from both sides. The issue was taken up in newspapers, in state legislatures, and in popular mass meetings. With such widespread discussion of slavery versus liberty taking place, it was bound to come to the attention of Negroes. Vesey read about the debate and told acquaintances of it.[38] What was said on the floors of Congress was not always adequately reported, and word spread among the slaves that Congress had actually freed them.[39] In addressing audiences, Vesey was to make use of the Missouri debates as a text for freedom.[40] Even if emancipation generally was not explicitly called for, he could argue logically that some of the oratory supported the justness of an effort to win liberty.

Curiously, Senator Rufus King of New York, one of the milder debaters, became Vesey's hero in Congress—probably because material on King's activity happened to fall into the black carpenter's hands. King's speeches were reported in the press and circulated in pamphlet form.[41] While King may have been less fiery than some of his allies, he offered a powerful constitutional argument for his view. John Quincy Adams said "the great slave-holders in the House gnawed their lips and clenched their fists as they heard him."[42] King did not equivocate. He said in an 1819 speech that enlightened men everywhere regretted the existence of slavery and sought means of limiting it. He observed that when the manual labor of the country is performed by slaves, labor dishonors the hands of free men.[43]

Showing more spirit in an 1820 address, King declaimed against one man making a slave of another or a body of individuals making slaves of others. He declared that all laws or compacts imposing such a condition upon any human being were absolutely void because they were contrary to the law of nature, which was the law of God and beyond all human control.[44] A few days after this speech, Linn Banks wrote to Senator James Barbour of Richmond that he had no doubt that the language ascribed to Mr. King would "sound the tocsin of freedom to every negro of the South, and we may live to see the tragical events of Santo Domingo repeated in our own land."

Banks' words proved at least partially prophetic. Vesey saw in King's oratory a sign that he was the black man's friend in Congress. He told listeners that the Senator from New York had sworn undying enmity against slavery and would continue to speak and write against the system until the Southern states consented to emancipate their chattels because slavery was a disgrace to the country.[45]

The Missouri debate was an event which, to white political leaders, may have seemed isolated. But to Negro aspirants to freedom it was only one climactic occurrence in a series of events, all of which were seized upon for hope and inspiration. In their yearning they paid special attention to whatever talk or action seemed to promise delivery from bondage—the revolts of slaves either nearby or far away, the struggle for independence in St. Domingue, the escape efforts of runaways, the pleas of local and national anti-slavery advocates, and the slow translation of their petitions into law in some parts of the nation.

# PREPARING
# THE GROUND

● By 1822 Denmark Vesey had lived in the city of Charleston for nearly forty years. Whatever other homes he had known were now buried deep in the recesses of memory. For twenty-two years of his life in Charleston he had been a free man. He enjoyed the kind of liberty which, from a white point of view, was enough to fulfill any reasonable yearning by one with a black skin. He could occupy himself as he pleased and go and come as he pleased without excessive restriction. For all white Charleston knew, Denmark Vesey's cup was full. He kept busy at his carpentry. There were only about a dozen free Negroes in the same field.[1] He had accumulated property valued at $8,000.[2] He had won the respect of the white community. At fifty-five, and looking older than his years, he seemed to be beyond the age of ambition.

But as far as Denmark Vesey was concerned, all was not right with the world. While his status might have satisfied all the criteria a white observer might prescribe for a black man's happiness, there were some things a casual white observer (in Charleston at least) wouldn't understand. Vesey did not enjoy the kind of freedom that would lend dignity to his spirit. While all may have seemed serene on the surface, the Vesey residence at 20 Bull Street[3] did not embrace all the conditions for a satisfying home life. Though Vesey himself was "free," all of his children were slaves[4] and thus did not have the same freedom of movement as their father. Vesey, during at least some of his married life, was forced to visit his spouse, a slave, at a place other than his own residence.[5] On these occasions he was cast in the role of a supplicant for the favor of his consort's owner.

His enforced role as father and husband of slaves did not comport well with Vesey's idea of a self-respecting status. Schooled by long experience as a slave himself and acquainted through his reading with many expressed aspirations for freedom, Vesey had his own opinions as to what the liberties and the rights and privileges of Negroes should be. His notions did not conform to the white views that mere liberation from bondage was the ultimate reward for a black man and that freed slaves should be grateful for small blessings. He was annoyed by the obsequious forms which anyone with dark skin was expected to observe.

As one who traveled widely and who followed the news of the day, Denmark Vesey might have been expected to entertain interests that extended beyond a simple concern with his personal status. He began to visualize the degradation of Negroes as an affront to their race and he wanted to do something about it. His own superior attainments sometimes caused him to exhibit impatience with those of his race who did not see beyond the narrow conventions and rigid rules of slave society as it existed in Charleston. He deplored the conditions under which Negroes lived, occasionally even in the presence of whites. He rebuked his fellows for being less discerning and more servile than he. He urged them on to efforts to help themselves.

Behind Vesey's public protestations was more than a mere display of bravado. His complaints could serve a twofold purpose: both to test whether there was any sympathy among whites and to build confidence among Negroes in his courage and his capacity to lead and speak for them.

For several years before he articulated any specific objectives, Vesey seized upon suitable events to voice dissatisfaction with the status of slaves in South Carolina. One such event was the city's repressive action in 1818 against the independent African Church which had been formed by Negroes and conducted in their own building in Hampstead, a suburb of Charleston. Fearful of unsupervised meetings of

Negroes, white authorities had arrested a large number of African Church members and had punished their leaders.[6] This incursion against one of the rare exercises of Negro autonomy inevitably created resentment.

Undoubtedly those Negro religious services that were unpoliced provided a forum for doctrines subversive of the status quo. The Bible itself provided some convenient texts which, with appropriate interpretation, could be adapted to the cause of Negro freedom:

> Masters, give unto your servants that which is just and equal; knowing that ye also have a Master in heaven. (*Colossians 4:1*)

Or, for more militant preaching, there was another suitable text:

> . . . and the children of Israel sighed by reason of the bondage, and they cried, and their cry came up unto God by reason of the bondage.
> And God heard their groaning, and God remembered his covenant with Abraham, with Isaac, and with Jacob. (*Exodus 2:23-24*)

The advantage of religious meetings, Vesey realized, was that they were held for an approved purpose, and that purpose could provide protective coloration for unapproved talk. Such meetings, where large numbers were gathered together, not only provided a convenient mode of indoctrination in the iniquities of slavery, but also provided a persuasive vehicle. For what lesson could be more convincing than one taken from the Bible, presented, as it was, as the word of God which even the whites were bound to obey?

Whenever an occasion presented itself, Vesey used the Bible and the religious forum to convince Negroes of the injustice of enforced servitude. Long before Abolitionism, with its scriptural overtones, became a movement to reckon with, Vesey was invoking the Bible in the interest of an even more aggressive movement. For some years before he took any steps to implement a plan of action, he sought to mentally condition prospective followers. In encounters on the street, in shops, in gatherings at the African Church, and in other secret meetings[7] he employed whatever literature he could find to convey a revolutionary message.

By December of 1821 Vesey was beginning to talk about direct action. His expressions of dissatisfaction began to hint at an objective. Negroes in Charleston, he said, were living such an abominable life and their situation was so bad that he did not know how they could endure it. The time was at hand when they should not be slaves of damn white rascals any longer but should fight for liberty.[8] After all, he observed, the ability of Negroes to fight had been proved at the Battle of New Orleans (in 1814) where black men had been in the line and had helped to hold the city.[9]

With the voicing of such sentiments, the die was cast. Once such a daring goal as a fight for freedom was communicated to other Negroes without attracting the lightning of white retribution, it became easier to take the next steps —to choose lieutenants for the enterprise and to begin making concrete plans. By the winter of 1821-22 Vesey, having demonstrated his boldness and his gift for argument, had acquired a reputation with and considerable influence over Negroes of Charleston. Some black acquaintances feared him, some admired him, all respected him.[10] As a man of obvious intelligence and ability, as a domineering personality who scorned any sign of weakness among his fellows, as a Negro who was recognized as a man of capacity even among whites, Vesey naturally could sway Negroes of lesser stature. This was to help him in enlisting recruits.

Before assembling an army of followers, however, Vesey had to select able lieutenants. He chose well, with a view not only to the character of his aides but to the strategic usefulness of their connections in the community. His first two deputies were Ned and Rolla Bennett, confidential servants of Thomas Bennett, the governor of South Carolina. Since Governor Bennett lived at 19 Lynch Street (now Ashley Avenue) at the corner where it intersected with Bull,[11] his residence—the same, of course, as the residence of Ned and Rolla—was scarcely two blocks from where Denmark Vesey lived (on Bull at Smith). The proximity of the conspirators' homes lent convenience to their plotting, as did the fact that they were trusted black men. Rolla, according the governor, was entrusted with the protection of the latter's family when he (the master) was away from home. He was said to be bold, convincing in demeanor, and a man of uncommon self-possession. Ned, also a trusted slave of the governor, was looked upon as a man of firm nerves and general good conduct.

Rolla and Ned were quick to assent to Vesey's plan. His means of persuasion was to tell them that Negroes were by right free but that their white owners would not grant what was rightfully theirs; therefore the only recourse was to rise up and fight the whites.

To help convince his intended company commanders, Vesey also read to them from the newspapers accounts of events in St. Domingue, anti-slavery pamphlets, and the congressional remarks of Senator Rufus King of New York who, he said, was the black man's friend and who was determined to speak against slavery until the South's bondmen were emancipated. This approach was effective with Jack Purcell,[12] his next lieutenant, who was to prove a zealous promoter.[13]

Peter Poyas, the fourth sub-leader to be recruited, was perhaps the most noteworthy of all. He was a first-rate ship carpenter, a man who could write well and who was regarded by his master, James Poyas, as trustworthy and a slave of great value. As a plotter of revolt, he was to prove intrepid and resolute, foresighted and resourceful, eager to be on with the project and yet cautious in planning. Once having committed himself, however, he was true to his word and loyal to his associates.[14] Since James Poyas lived at 49 King Street, operated a shipyard at 35 South Bay, and also had a place on Cooper River,[15] Peter had opportunities to move about the city and into the country.

The next officer to be recruited by Vesey was Gullah

Jack, slave of Paul Pritchard who, like Peter's owner, operated a shipyard. Pritchard lived at 6 Hasell Street and conducted his business at Gadsden's Wharf. Gullah Jack, who was to be one of Vesey's most effective lieutenants, joined the enterprise sometime after Christmas of 1821. He was a little man with bushy black whiskers, an animated manner, and the swiftly changing countenance of a consummate actor. His value to the enterprise was his great sway over the superstitious slaves who regarded him as a conjurer with the power to both charm and curse. He worked through a Gullah Society which met regularly and whose members were bound to Jack by a shrewd combination of magic and discipline.

Monday, a slave of John Gell, was the last member of the group of five principal officers engaged by Vesey. A man in the prime of life, Monday was regarded by white men who observed him as intelligent, steady, and dependable. Though he was an Ebo in origin, a member of one of the tribes of the lower Niger, he had by 1822 been in the United States fifteen or twenty years. His master being the operator of a livery stable—at 127 Church Street—Monday was a harness maker, and an excellent one. He pursued his craft in a shop on Meeting Street. Since his time and a share of his earnings were at his own disposal, his status was above the common level of slavery.

Having enlisted the support of able lieutenants, Vesey at intervals called meetings at his own home, at Monday Gell's shop, and at Bulkley's farm on Charleston Neck, for the purpose of exchanging opinions, collecting and giving information, and in general advancing a plan for a massive uprising of slaves. Vesey's house was the most logical and convenient place to rendezvous—first, because it was in the heart of the city, and second because, being the abode of a free Negro, meetings held there could more easily escape observation.

Conspirators often crowded thirty at a time into Vesey's quarters and were addressed by the leader. Vesey would rise before the gathering and read from the Bible of how the children of Israel were delivered out of Egypt from bondage. Thus introducing the justification for his own message, he would exhort the assembled men to rise against the whites and fight for their own liberation. He declared that Negroes were living an abominable life, that their church had been shut up so that they could not use it, that their rights and privileges were denied them. He assured them that if they were as unanimous and courageous as the people at St. Domingue they could overcome their oppressors.

Vesey eagerly kept up with events in the Negro republic of Haiti. When news came about Haitian President Jean Pierre Boyer's battle with the Spaniards, Vesey savored it, called it to the attention of his followers, and said he too could carry his men to victory in battle. He set about to establish liaison with Boyer by writing him a surreptitious letter, addressing it ostensibly to the uncle of the cook on board a schooner bound for Haiti, and directing that the addressee deliver it to the Haitian president.

At the meetings of revolutionists Jack Glenn, a painter, was often given the assignment of reading the Bible. He also passed a hat around among his fellows. These collections were taken up to pay for the making of weapons and to hire horses for slaves who were to be sent secretly into the country to bring down plantation workers on the appointed day. The couriers were to pass the word at prayer meetings.

Sometimes new recruits were introduced to the enterprise by being escorted into gatherings at Vesey's. A large book stood open as if ready to receive their names for the record. If they exhibited any faint-heartedness, they were promptly informed that refusal to go along meant death. This was the standard threat against those who would not join. Yet, despite all the pressure that was exerted on some, there were other Negroes whom the leaders ruled unacceptable as recruits even if they were willing. The leaders drew the line against drunks and babblers.

Enlistment activities for the planned insurrection covered not only Charleston but a wide territory around it, extending, some said, as far east as Georgetown, as far north as St. John's Parish, well inside Berkeley County, as far west as the Combahee River. Vesey himself reportedly traveled from the Santee River on the east to the Euhaws on the west in behalf of his project. By March, 1822, he was devoting full time to recruitment. Places outside Charleston where various emissaries reported making efforts were Goose Creek and Dorchester, Hibben's Ferry, St. John's Parish and Santee.[16]

Eventually Vesey's army grew to formidable strength—some 9,000 men by some counts, though its real size was never really known. Since a special effort was made to exclude servants as untrustworthy and to enlist those who were hired out or worked out and thus had certain hours at their own disposal, Vesey's men tended to fall into certain occupational categories: carters, draymen, sawyers, porters, laborers, stevedores, mechanics, lumber workers, and field workers. Many of them fell naturally into coherent units, linked by occupation or language or some other drawing power. There was a company of French Negroes (slaves of former Santo Domingans), a Gullah Society, a company of men who worked on the Bay, bands of slaves from neighboring plantations. A few free Negroes were numbered among the enlistees, indicating that Vesey was not the only member of his class who was willing to risk all on what white overlords might regard as a fool's goal.

Having banded together for rebellion, the conspirators needed weapons, horses, and any other equipment that might help them obtain a quick advantage over their heavily armed foes. Some arms would be needed at the outset; others could be seized in the initial assault. Tom Russell and Jim Bennett, slave blacksmiths, could fashion weapons. Robert Robertson, another Negro blacksmith, was assigned specifically to make pike heads and bayonets with sockets ready to be mounted on poles. Vesey reported at one meeting of his men that 100 pikes were ready. Two or three hundred bayonets were said eventually to be on hand. A bundle of ten-foot poles suitable for pike heads and bayonets was concealed under the house at Buckley's farm by Polydore Faber.

Daggers too, being easy to conceal, would be useful, and a blacksmith was put to work on these. Perault Strohecker at one rendezvous let it be known that 300 or 400 were in readiness. A quantity of slow match (fuse) was stolen from the Arsenal by Lot Forrester who often worked there for his employer; it was later hidden at Gibb's and Harper's Wharf. Bacchus Hammet was made responsible for securing powder; after lifting a keg from his master's store, he carried it to Vesey's. Monday Gell's shop was used for temporarily storing powder, and some was also secreted in a cache three miles outside of the city. John Vincent, who had a mold, was set to work making musket balls. A quantity of these were concealed under water at one of the docks. Another conspirator offered to make cartridges. Lot Forrester said he had combustibles ready for setting fire.

Having undertaken to lay up a supply of arms in quantity, some of the would-be insurgents set about to equip themselves individually. Vesey got possession of a pistol, and Peter Poyas and Monday Gell acquired swords and Rolla Bennett, a crude dagger. Pharo Thompson had a scythe converted into a sword. Adam Yates became the owner of a long knife, and John Horry, Bacchus Hammet, and Charles Drayton got possession of swords.

To make sure that mounts were available, stable boys at public livery stables were assigned the job of commandeering horses. Draymen, carters, and butcher boys were to seize their own mounts. And those insurgents whose masters owned horses were to take posession of them at the proper time. Canoes and boats of various kinds were easily accessible at the river banks for transporting country slaves to the city.

Not overlooking the possibility of camouflage, Vesey employed a man to make a number of wigs and false whiskers, using white men's hair. Even dark lanterns for use in entering stores at night and securing arms were thought of.

The conspirators had marked well the places where they could armor themselves for the attack: an unguarded wooden store on King Street Road, where were deposited 200 or 300 muskets and bayonets belonging to the Neck Company of militia; Duquercron's store on the same road, containing about 500 muskets and bayonets for sale; Schrirer's store on Queen Street and various gunsmiths' shops where militia company arms were deposited so that they might be kept in order; finally the Arsenal on Meeting Street opposite St. Michael's Church, in which were deposited a greater store of arms than anywhere else in the state.

With preparations approaching a state of readiness, Vesey set July 14, the second Sunday of the month, for the attack. This would be a time when the number of white inhabitants in Charleston would be much reduced, with many having departed to spend the summer on Sullivan's Island, in upper parts of the state, or in the North. Sunday was also a day when great numbers of Negroes could visit the city without being suspected of an ulterior purpose. Mid-July would be a time when the Charleston heavens would be darkest, the moon's last quarter having occurred on the 11th and the new moon not due until the 18th.[17] On the night of the assault, leaders were to make sure they would have picked men on hand by concealing them beforehand on their own premises.

At the hour of midnight Vesey's army would begin to move, with strikes occurring simultaneously at several key points. Leading a party assembling on South Bay and including a force from James Island, Peter Poyas would march up Meeting Street, seize the Arsenal and Guardhouse across from St. Michael's Church, and secure its arms. Meanwhile, a body detached from this force would be on the alert to prevent citizens from assembling at the alarm points.

A second force, consisting partly of slaves from the

country and partly of those from the Neck, was to assemble on the Neck under Ned Bennett and take control of the United States Arsenal there.

A third company, under Rolla Bennett, would gather at Bennett's Mills, kill the governor and the intendant, and march through the city, leaving a guard at Canon's Bridge to prevent inhabitants of Cannonsborough from entering town.

A fourth party, made up partly of country Negroes and partly of city Negroes, would rendezvous at Gadsden's Wharf and proceed from there to attack the upper Guardhouse.

A fifth force, consisting of country slaves and some from the Neck area, would assemble at Bulkley's Farm, seize the powder magazine three-and-a-half miles from town, and then march into the city.

A sixth company under Gullah Jack would meet at Boundary Street at the head of King Street and seize the arms in Duquercron's store and those belonging to the Neck militia company in another nearby store.

A seventh and final force would gather at Vesey's and, under his command, march down to the main Guardhouse ready to meet any eventuality on the way. Meanwhile, scattered units would be riding through the streets killing all white persons they met and preventing them from giving an alarm or reaching a rendezvous.

Once the insurgents had taken a large supply of arms for their enterprise, they would fire the city and begin a general massacre which would include not only whites but those blacks who did not join. "He that is not with me," declared Vesey, "is against me." (Luke 11-23)

For the sake of the insurgents' own safety, Denmark Vesey ordered that they were to spare neither women nor children nor ministers; indeed, they were to leave not one white skin alive; this was the plan that was followed in St. Domingue.

From the Bible he backed up the command: "And they utterly destroyed all that was in the city, both man and woman, young and old, and ox, and sheep, and ass, with the edge of the sword." (Joshua 6:21)

Overriding the protests of some of the squeamish, he asserted that it was no sin for the revolutionists to exterminate their enemies, for the Lord commanded it:

> Behold, the day of the Lord cometh, and thy spoil shall be divided in the midst of thee.
>
> For I will gather all nations against Jerusalem to battle; and the city shall be taken, and the houses rifled, and the women ravished; and half of the city shall go forth into captivity . . .
>
> Then shall the Lord go forth, and fight against those nations, as when he fought in the day of battle. (*Zechariah 14:1-3*)

While Vesey hailed the faithful to the standard of the Bible, Gullah Jack employed his own peculiar methods for boosting morale. On the morning of the attack, his troops were to eat nothing but parched corn and ground nuts. And to protect themselves from being wounded, they were to hold in their mouths crab claws which Jack gave out for the purpose.

Lest the rebels trust not in the sufficiency of their own resources and numbers, Vesey assured them that they would soon have allies in the form of armies from St. Domingue and Africa. Peter Poyas foresaw aid eventually from the English. But in any event, he saw no need to fear, for once the standard of liberation was raised, slaves from the country would converge on the city and it would become an impregnable stronghold. "Let us assemble a sufficient number to commence the work with spirit and we'll not want men, they'll fall in behind us fast enough."

Thus was laid the blueprint for black rebellion. What came after Charleston was theirs? That might depend on how the battle went. There were goods in the stores, money in the banks, and ships in the harbor. A sizeable army could sail to St. Domingue which had promised, Vesey said, to receive the rebels.[18]

Was a scheme for the conquest of Charleston by slaves

entirely visionary? Why should it be? The carnage might be frightful, the destruction ruinous. But why should the aim of slave triumph be impossible of attainment? Slaves only thirty years before had risen in wrath and taken the French colony of St. Domingue, and the slaves at Charleston held that event as their example for emulation. That the odds were higher need not deter them from the attempt. They were not reckoning in terms of an equal contest. And they left to the future the possibility of reconquest from beyond the borders of the state.

# THE HOUR
# FOR REVOLT

● At the southwest corner of Meeting and Broad Streets stood the guardhouse, the entire first floor of which was occupied by the guard—100 men under the command of a captain and three lieutenants. From this post regularly were sounded reveille and tatoo, signals which told the colored population when its members were expected to be in their habitations. At night a sentinel stood at the north door of the guardhouse and another in the steeple of St. Michaels across the street. From the steeple the voice of the sentry could be heard proclaiming the time every quarter of an hour throughout the night. The same ritual was repeated from time to time at other sentry posts in different parts of the city,[1] the cries serving not only to announce the time but to reassure the inhabitants that all was well.

The Charleston of the 1820's, despite a growing provincialism, was a city that could lay claim to a diversity of cultural interests. It was the home of Robert Mills, architect and designer of the Washington monument; Charles Fraser, the artist; Dr. John Edwards Holbrook, herpetologist; Dr. John Bachman, ornithologist. There were in the city at the time four library societies, four free schools, and a great many benevolent and charitable organizations. There were four daily newspapers: the *City Gazette*, the *Courier*, the *Southern Patriot*, and the *Charleston Mercury*. Papers from various parts of the Union were available in public reading rooms, and Walker's shop stocked periodicals and a variety of books in English literature.

On the northeast corner of Meeting and Broad Streets stood the City Hall where the City Council met and where city court, presided over by a recorder, was convened on the first Monday of January, April, July, and November. On the northwest corner of Meeting and Broad was the court house, a place where justice followed the forms and traditions long ingrained on Charleston attorneys by the Middle Temple.

Charleston now had Episcopalians, Methodists, Presbyterians, Roman Catholics, Baptists, Congregationalists, Quakers, French Protestants, German Protestants, Unitarians, and Jews—all with places of worship in accordance with their numbers. Most of them had setled into routines of worship that were untroubled by the moral barbs of slave society.

Besides overseas shipping, there were ten steamboats plying between Charleston and Savannah, Augusta, Columbia, Cheraw, and Georgetown. Wagons being the chief means of overland transportation, there were extensive wagon yards along the upper part of King Street. Cotton was shipped from the interior by wagon and was sold outright or bartered for goods. It was then resold to shippers on the Bay, making fortunes in the process for the King Street merchants. Some planters, however, realizing the disadvantages of this kind of trading, stored their cotton in warehouses on the wharves and employed factors to sell it for them at a favorable time.[2]

Enough wealth was being produced at this time so that some Charleston women at social events could wear outfits costing $2,000 to $3,000—elaborate white muslin dresses trimmed in pink or blue and covered with nettings of silver or gold thread. Close-fitting jackets of pink or white were worn over the dresses. And on their heads the women wore tiaras of diamonds and other jewels.

Charleston, according to the census of 1820, had 25,781 inhabitants: 11,654 of them free whites; 12,652 of them slaves, and 1,475 of them free colored persons.[3] The city now ranked sixth among the urban centers of the United States, having dropped from fifth place since the last decennial count. There were 1,200 to 1,500 mechanics, black and white, with the former, among whom was Denmark Vesey, earning a half to two-thirds as much as their white counterparts. Prime field slaves were averaging $650 on the Charleston market in 1822.[4]

Saturday, May 25, 1822, was a day like many others in the late spring at Charleston. The afternoon was a time of slack work and the weather invited leisurely sauntering on the waterfront. Peter, slave of Colonel John C. Prioleau, went to the fish market to see about a purchase and then, having finished his business, strolled down to Fitzsimmons Wharf (near what is now the Custom House) below the fish market. From this point he could see a small schooner, the *Sally* from Cap Haitien, anchored in the harbor. At her masthead fluttered a flag with the number 96 on it.[5]

As Peter stood watching, he was joined by another slave with whom he was not well acquainted but who he thought was one of the bondmen of Messrs. J. and D. Paul who did business as grocers at the southwest corner of Broad and Church. Peter's companion remarked that he had often seen a flag with the number 76 on it but never one with 96 before. Having thus drawn Peter into conversation, he proceeded to ask whether Peter knew something serious was about to happen. When Peter said he didn't know anything was brewing, the Pauls' man assured him that there was. The slaves of Charleston were determined to right themselves, said he. When asked what he meant, he explained that the slaves were resolved to shake off their bondage, that many had joined for the purpose, that if Peter would go with him he would take him to the man who had the list of revolutionists and who would put Peter's name on it. Colonel Prioleau's slave was astonished and shocked. He informed the other that he would have nothing to do with the proposed rising and abruptly left him, lest he become suspect from having been seen talking with one later proved to be a plotter.

The conversation on the wharf represented a fateful turn of events for Denmark Vesey. In entrusting Peter with his momentous information, the Pauls' slave had violated one of the cardinal rules laid down by Peter Poyas: "Take care you don't mention it to those waiting men who receive presents of old coats, etc., from their masters, or they'll betray us; I will speak to them."

Sorely troubled by his terrible secret, Peter told one of the Prioleau sons about it (Colonel Prioleau was away from home). Then he decided to seek the advice of William Pencil, a free Negro of his acquaintance. Pencil, a tin plate worker, lived at 81 Meeting Street, not far from the Prioleau residence at 50 Meeting. Upon hearing the explosive intelligence, Pencil advised Peter earnestly to lose no time in communicating his information to his master.[6]

Since Colonel Prioleau was out of the city, Peter informed Mrs. Prioleau and her son of what he had heard. Despite the startling nature of the reported intelligence, they took no formal action but waited for the return of the colonel on the morning of Thursday, May 30. After hearing their report, Colonial Prioleau promptly questioned Peter, then notified the intendant of Charleston, James Hamilton, of Peter's experience and said he (Colonial Prioleau) had strong reason to believe that an insurrection of slaves was in the making.

It was then three in the afternoon. By decision of the intendant, the City Council was summoned to meet at five that same afternoon and Governor Thomas Bennett was also invited, the purpose being to give the authorities a chance to hear Peter's narrative. Meanwhile, Colonel Prioleau had secured enough identifying information from Peter to conclude that his accoster had been one of the slaves of the Pauls. He therefore interceded with these men to have all of their male slaves committed to the guardhouse until Peter's informant could be identified.

With the Council and the governor listening, Peter repeated his story at five o'clock. By this time William Paul had been singled out as the man who had talked to Peter. (He had by chance been arrested at Vesey's) William, as soon as Peter was dismissed, was brought before the authorities to be interrogated. Without giving him a hint of what information they had about him, his examiners sought to get him to relate the events of the previous Saturday afternoon. After a great deal of verbal sparring, William acknowledged that he had spoken to Peter about the singular flag flying from the schooner. But when confronted with the incriminating question, he flatly denied having referred to an intended uprising of slaves. The authorities nevertheless considered his manner guilty and ordered him remanded to the guardhouse for the night and to solitary confinement in the black hole of the workhouse beginning the following morning.

William was quizzed during the night by the captain of the guard and again on the morning of May 31 by the warden of the guardhouse. After all of this grilling, accompanied by no one knows what other means of persuasion, he finally admitted all of the reported conversation on the wharf and said Peter Poyas and Mingo Harth had told him of the plot and that Mingo had the muster roll of the insurgents. Despite his disclosures, William was consigned to solitary confinement in the black hole of the workhouse in the hope that this would still further loosen his tongue.

On the basis of the information supplied by William Paul, Peter Poyas and Mingo Harth were arrested and their trunks searched. They behaved, however, with great composure and coolness and actually treated the charge against them with levity. Nothing suspicious was found in their belongings except for an enigmatic letter in Peter's chest. It read:

> Dear Sir,—With pleasure I give you an answer. I will endeavour to do it. Hoping that God will be in the midst to help his own. Be particular and make a sure remark. Fear not, the Lord God that delivered Daniel is able to deliver us. All that I inform agreed. I am gone to Beach Hill.
>
> *(Signed)* Abraham Poyas[7]

Failing to detect a conspiratorial implication in the letter and being impressed by the calm conduct of Poyas and Harth, the wardens released the two but set a secret watch upon them.

Meanwhile, William Paul was kept in solitary confinement. After about a week of it, fearing that he would soon be led forth to the scaffold, he admitted that he had known about a plot for some time, that it was very extensive, envisaged a massacre of the whites, and was led by a man who carried a charm which made him invulnerable. William's information was secured about June 8, and immediately the authorities intensified their efforts to obtain confirmation of it. But as several more days passed nothing more could be learned. In fact, the investigators were thrown off the track when Ned Bennett, who had been named by William, came forward voluntarily and asked to be examined if he were the object of suspicion.

At the same time that the official inquiry was running into a blind alley, however, a private pursuit of information was paying off. A citizen of Charleston, Major John Wilson —having heard about the suspected plot and having the utmost confidence in George, a slave belonging to his mother —told George about the rumors of an intended insurrection and asked the slave to see what he could find out. George was deemed a good prospective spy because he was a class leader for Negroes in the Methodist church where much of the conspirational activity was thought to exist.[8]

George Wilson was a blacksmith, a dark mulatto man of large frame and striking appearance. He could read and write and bore a reputation for excellent character among blacks and whites alike.[9] George sought information among members of the church class and on Friday, June 14, one of his friends came to him with startling intelligence. Reporting promptly to Major Wilson, George told him that a revolt among the slaves of Charleston was indeed being contemplated and that not a moment should be lost in informing the authorities, since the outbreak was scheduled to begin at midnight on Sunday, June 16. (Upon the arrest of Peter Poyas, Vesey—fearing that the plan would be frustrated if its execution were delayed until July 14 as originally scheduled—had advanced the date to June 16.)

Thoroughly alarmed by the report from George, Major Wilson on Friday evening hurried to the home of Intendant

James Hamilton with his news. By nine o'clock, within an hour after Wilson's arrival, Hamilton had informed Governor Bennett of the latest developments. And by ten o'clock Hamilton's residence at Cumming and Bull Streets,[10] only two blocks from Vesey's house, was a scene of humming activity. Summoned by the governor, the commanding officers of the city militia regiments hurried to the intendant's home to confer on the approaching emergency of Sunday night.[11] The assembled officials decided to keep the slaves under surveillance, and Governor Bennett that same night ordered an increase in the military guard. The governor said the force to be organized must be large enough not only to defeat the expected attack but to bolster the confidence of the citizens.

On Saturday morning Governor Bennett ordered the quartermaster general of militia to place in the Charleston Arsenal 20,000 ball cartridges and to have ready for delivery 300 muskets. These were to be in addition to the arms and ammunition already in the hands of the militia and were to be for the use of special detachments called into service to suppress the uprising. Muskets and cartridges were to be given a fresh inspection to make sure they were in working order. To hedge against a possible attack on the poorly constructed United States Arsenal, some of the arms were removed from that installation to a place of greater security. Guards were placed at all the other military depots and troops were sent to every assailable point in the city.

Civil and military officials met again on Saturday afternoon to decide on further protective measures. Units ordered to rendezvous for duty at 10 p.m. Sunday were Captain Chattel's corps of hussars, Captain Miller's light infantry, Captain Martindale's Neck Rangers, the Charleston Riflemen, and the city guard.[12] All of them were organized as a regiment and, by order of the governor, placed under the command of Colonel Robert Y. Hayne. The number of watchmen at the two or three signal stations were ordered doubled.[13] Sixteen hundred rounds of ball cartridges had already been issued to the guard.

While state and city authorities were mobilizing to meet the expected assault, the conspirators themselves were not idle. On Saturday afternoon Peter Poyas, Ned Bennett, and other leaders met at Vesey's. Also present at the meeting was Frank Ferguson, slave of James Ferguson, who had a residence at 5 Liberty Street in Charleston[14] and a plantation on the west bank of the Cooper River twenty-six miles away.[15] Frank Ferguson reported to Vesey that he had just returned from a visit to his owner's plantation in St. John's Parish and that, while there, he had induced John O. and Pompey to lead the slaves of that vicinity down to Charleston when they received word.[16] Vesey asked Jesse Blackwood, another slave who was present at the extraordinary meeting, whether he would undertake to go into the country and give the word to John O. and Pompey. After receiving some instructions from Frank, Jesse agreed, and Vesey handed him $2 to hire a horse.

On Sunday morning Jesse set out on his mission. A light-skinned Negro who might at a distance have been mistaken for white, he successfully passed two patrol units on his way out of Charleston but was turned back by a third. That afternoon Jesse reported his failure to Vesey, who expressed disappointment because the enterprise depended on the country people.[17] While Jesse's effort was blocked, twenty or thirty of Vesey's country followers did reach the city in a canoe and the insurrection leader was informed of their arrival. With the critical hour rapidly approaching, Vesey and several of his lieutenants held another meeting at four on Sunday afternoon. By this time it had become quite evident to the Negro revolutionists that the authorities had been alerted, that massive military preparations had been made, and that surprise, which was essential to success, was impossible. Therefore Vesey sent word to such supporters as had gathered to disperse and wait for further orders.[18]

Yet as the night descended and the prospect of a strike for freedom became gloomier, the conspirators did not entirely give up preparations. Bacchus, slave of Benjamin Hammet, managed to gain possession of a pistol belonging to his owner and carried this weapon as well as a sword to the house of Denmark Vesey that Sunday evening.

By this time knowledge of the anticipated insurrection was general among citizens.[19] There was great excitement among the whites that evening. The streets were filled until a late hour with persons who were uncertain whether it was safe to retire.[20] Even children were allowed to remain up.[21] At the appointed hour of 10 p.m. the extra military units took up their stations, although their size had been ordered reduced somewhat as a result of the noticeable lack of activity among the slaves.[22] A night of sleepless anxiety in the white community followed.[23] Unknown to the aroused white citizenry, however, the basis for immediate alarm had been quietly removed. Vesey and the other insurrection leaders had decided that midnight of June 16 was not the right time to rise for liberty.

The City Council of Charleston convened on Monday, June 17, to consider extraordinary steps to safeguard the city. From among its members the Council appointed a committee of vigilance and safety to aid the intendant in executing the laws and to co-operate with him during the recess of the Council "in all those measures necessary for exploring the causes and character of the existing disturbance, and bringing to light and punishment the suspected and guilty." This group began its investigation on the night of the 17th, and during the following twenty-four hours ten slaves were arrested. Vesey was not among them.[24] In addition to Peter and Mungo Poyas, slaves of James Poyas, this first group of suspects included four slaves of the governor. They were Ned, Rolla, Batteau, and Mathias Bennett.

On June 18 Intendant Hamilton sought out Lionel H. Kennedy and Thomas Parker, members of the Charleston bar, informed them that several Negroes were in confinement charged with an attempt to "excite an insurrection," and requested them to organize a court for the trial of the accused. Meanwhile, the Council had agreed on the names of five freeholders who would have the "publick approbation," and the names of these men were thus passed on to Messrs. Kennedy and Parker, the intended presiding magistrates. With Kennedy and Parker approving, Nathaniel Heyward, a planter, J. R. Pringle, collector of customs, James Legare, a planter, R. J. Turnbull, lawyer and planter, and Colonel William Drayton, city recorder, were summoned to assemble the next day and begin hearing the evidence against the prisoners.[25]

After the court had been organized, the intendant related how the plot had been detected, outlined the preliminary measures adopted, and presented a list of names of all the Negroes then in custody, the charges on which they had been arrested, and the witnesses against them. Before beginning any trial, the tribunal informally heard the testimony to ascertain how extensive the conspiracy was. Being convinced of the existence of a revolutionary plot, the magistrates and freeholders prepared for the trial of the accused.

Though the court began sitting on June 19 and arrests and hearings continued for two months, little headway was made at first in determining which Negroes were involved in the plot. So true were most of the conspirators to their pledge of secrecy that the authorities were impeded in their search for evidence and for culprits. Vesey reportedly burned books and papers relating to the insurrection as soon as the plan was discovered, and Peter Poyas and Monday Gell were believed to have destroyed their records too. In fact, all but one of the leaders so firmly maintained their silence through it all that Charleston officials were afraid many of the plotters were escaping detection. During the first ten days after the formation of the committee of the vigilance, only twenty-five Negroes were arrested, and of these all but eight were eventually released. Not until June 27 did the investigators find a break in the united front of insurrectionists (an event which will be described later). Meanwhile, they were being frustrated by the iron influence of such slave captains as Peter Poyas.

One of the first to be arrested, Peter Poyas was taken to jail and chained to the floor of a cell in the company of another alleged conspirator. Men in authority came and, according to a white witness, sought by promises, threats, and finally tortures to extract the names of accomplices. Weakened by the torment and hoping for mercy, Peter's companion showed signs of yielding. Peter raised himself from a prone position and, resting on one elbow, looked at his cell mate. "Die like a man," he said sternly. The injunction was effective.

Some of the lesser revolutionists were not as circumspect. On June 20 the authorities, by now suspecting Denmark Vesey as the chief of the conspiracy, began searching for him. The frantic hunt continued for three days from one end of the city to the other. It was feared that the leader of the insurrection had made good his escape. Finally, on the night of June 22, with a storm in progress and the search continuing despite the fury of wind and rain, members of the city guard pushed into the home of one of Denmark Vesey's wives and there seized the man who for more than a week had held Charleston in a grip of fear and excitement unequaled since the approach of a conquering British army during the Revolution. Captain Dove of the guard, who made the arrest, was, along with a colleague, officially lauded for having prevented Vesey's possible departure by ship the next day.

While the general public of Charleston was barred from the proceedings of the special court, the city was nevertheless deeply agitated. Though the press and city officials were guarded in their revelations, word of the prosecutions got out, and popular feelings ran high. Private citizens wrote letters communicating their intense fears to relatives and friends in other cities. One prominent citizen wrote to Langdon Cheves in Philadelphia that he wished his wife and daughter could be in the Pennsylvania city rather than in Charleston, the scene of such violent designs and harsh repercussions. "This plot," he warned, ". . . will be constantly in agitation if we do not get rid of the poison that has been too deeply and I fear successfully introduced into this place."[26]

# REBELS
# ON TRIAL

● The workhouse in Charleston, where punishment was meted out to slaves, rose forbiddingly on the south side of Magazine Street. Next to it on the west was the jail.¹ This dingy area, four blocks from the dignified square where white offenders were tried, was the scene of feverish activity during the summer of 1822. The accused conspirators were put on trial in a small room in the same building in which they were confined.² The general public was barred from the courtroom, and no Negro unconnected with the proceedings was allowed to go within two blocks of the building. To enforce the secrecy of the trials and to guard against a later uprising or a possible attempt by the insurrectionists to rescue their leaders, a cordon of troops was thrown around the place where the special court sat. The soldiers were assigned to duty day and night.³

The main rationale for the sealing off of the trials was the usual one: the need for quarantining the "infected" rebels to prevent their insurrectionary germs from spreading to uncontaminated slaves. In obedience to the rationale, the Charleston press was extremely circumspect in its initial reporting of events. But nothing could stop excited verbal communication among citizens, and the people became highly alarmed and anxious over what they heard. Slaves were abused in the street, and some were imprisoned for wearing sackcloth.

In South Carolina the law under which alleged Negro subversives were tried was a peculiar product of the slave system,⁴ having been written to protect the rights of masters, not the rights of their chattels or their former chattels.⁵ The law provided, for example, that masters were to be compensated, at least in part, for executed slaves (except those convicted of murder or taken in actual rebellion). This was to discourage owners from concealing offenses of slaves in order to save their property. The law also made a distinction between a homicide committed by a slave in defense of a master and other kinds of homicides. When free Negroes were involved in offenses, they were tried not under the same law as free white men but under the laws enacted for the regulation of slaves. Free Negroes were considered the potential allies of slaves and natural enemies of the white community.

The law under which Denmark Vesey and his followers went to trial was a formidable weapon of suppression. It gave to any two justices of the peace and any three to five freeholders absolute power of life and death over accused Negroes. Such courts were to be convened not more than three days after the apprehension of the accused.[6] Cases were to be disposed of "in the most summary and expeditious manner." The unsworn testimony of slaves was to be admitted. And lest any oversight in the writing of a warrant or record be construed in such a way as to upset a trial, the law specifically provided that such proceedings should not "be reversed, avoided or in any ways impeached by reason of any default in form." If the judges decided in any proceeding which began as a non capital case that the accused might "deserve death," all they had to do was to reconvene the court with added judges and proceed to "final judgment and execution." Three out of five judges could convict, and their judgment was final. For any slave or slaves convicted of raising or attempting to raise an insurrection, and for his or their "accomplices, aiders and abettors," the penalty was death. In cases in which several slaves were involved, the court was empowered to reduce the punishment, provided that at least one of the offenders should be executed as an example to other would-be insurrectionists.

Perceiving that the requirements of the statute fell far short of the usual safeguards of justice, the court itself decided that in the proceedings against Vesey and his associates it would lay down certain rules left within its discretion. In stipulating these rules, the court noted that the procedures under which it was ordered to operate by the local statute departed "in many essential features, from the principles of the common law, and some of the settled rules of evidence." Then it went on to declare that no slave should be tried except in the presence of his owner or counsel, that notice should be given in every case at least one day before trial, that convictions of a capital nature would not be based on the testimony of a single witness unsupported by additional evidence "or by circumstances," that witnesses should confront the accused and each other except where a pledge to withhold their identity was given to witnesses, that free Negroes might be represented by counsel upon request, that the accused might examine any witnesses they thought proper to make statements or offer defenses in their own behalf.[7]

While these rules appear to have provided for a good deal more fairness in the Vesey trials than the statute called for, they did not give in practice what they seem to have promised. For one thing, a number of witnesses were induced to testify under a pledge of secrecy; therefore the accused could not confront them.[8] Moreover, prisoners were held incommunicado and it is highly unlikely that there was any real consultation between defendants and their counsel. Defense counsel made no spirited presentations in behalf of the accused. Hearsay testimony was admitted without objection by counsel. When offered the opportunity on occasion to put up a defense, counsel took no advantage of it.[9] There was, of course, no jury which would have to agree unanimously on any guilty verdict.

Behind the guarded walls of the workhouse, the unequal legal drama proceeded. Defendants were brought before the court one at a time, with little time being lost between arrest and presentation before the bar of slave justice.[10] There was, of course, no requirement of indictment by a grand jury. Witnesses, who were themselves under arrest, were kept ready in a room next to the trial chamber. A member of the city guard stood over them to see that there was no collusion.

Among the first of the alleged conspirators to be brought to trial were Rolla, Batteau, and Ned Bennett, slaves of the governor, and Peter Poyas, the man who, next to Denmark Vesey, exerted the most profound sway over the Negro insurrectionists. Evidence was introduced to show their participation in the planning of a massacre of whites. The prosecution's case was difficult to refute. It is significant that of the five witnesses who testified against Rolla, four (one of whom was George Wilson)[11] gave their evidence anonymously and the fifth was a slave-owner.[12] Only two witnesses appeared against Batteau and the identity of both was concealed from the accused. Two of the four witnesses against Ned were anonymous. One of Peter's chief accusers was anonymous.

Despite the virtual hopelessness of their situation, these initial defendants, by acknowledgment of the court, showed no fear at their trials. Rolla's judges credited him with "great presence and composure of mind." And Ned, the judges noted, was "stern and immovable." Peter's behavior throughout, said the court later, "indicated the reverse" of fear. When the court pronounced the sentence of death on these slave leaders, they received the news stoically. Peter, with no tone of supplication in his voice, asked simply: "I suppose you'll let me see my wife and family before I die." (The judges never deemed it of interest to report whether this request was granted.) White officialdom was confounded when Peter, upon being asked whether he really had wished to see the murder of the master who had treated him so kindly, responded only with a cryptic smile.

With tension in the atmosphere mounting daily, the trials went forward. Denmark Vesey was brought before the court on June 23, the day after his arrest.[13] Now for the first time in an official confrontation the topmost leader of the blacks faced the leaders of the white community among whom he had stirred such consternation. The seven men who sat in judgment had the passions of an aroused citizenry behind them. The authorities were in no mood to be indulgent; their property and their very lives had hung in the balance. Now all the protective resources of the city were mobilized. The judges held the legal and physical instruments of absolute power over the accused. Yet Vesey did not enter the chamber in a beseeching manner. He presented himself before his judges as if the law and the facts were on his side.

As the trial of Denmark Vesey progressed, some of the forms of fairness were present. Colonel George Warren Cross appeared as his counsel.[14] Four of the five witnesses appearing against the accused were identified. After being examined by the court, they were cross-examined by Cross. The defendant himself was then permitted to question the witnesses.

First to testify against Vesey was William Paul, the slave whose indiscretion had led to the series of events culminating in the tense scene in the workhouse. William pointed to Vesey as the chief of the conspiracy and said he had often heard the carpenter voice his hatred of the whites and speak of the prospective uprising. Vesey, he asserted, studied the Bible a great deal and sought to prove from it that slavery was wrong.

Next to be heard, but not in Vesey's presence, was a witness who was an acquaintance of George Wilson, the Negro blacksmith whose co-operation with the authorities had done much to lay bare the plan for insurrection. This witness testified how Vesey had told him that Congress had freed the slaves but that they would never be delivered out of bondage unless they raised a hand to help themselves. Vesey, according to the witness, then related the fable of Hercules and the waggoner whose wagon was stalled: the waggoner prayed, whereupon Hercules exclaimed: "You fool, put your shoulder to the wheel, whip up the horses, and your wagon will be pulled out." To help the slaves in their battle, a large army would come from St. Domingue, Vesey was reported to have said.[15]

Frank Ferguson, a slave, offered the most detailed

evidence. He reported how Vesey had declared that Negroes were living under such abominable conditions that he didn't see how they could endure it, that they ought to rise up and throw off the yoke. He told of attending meetings at Vesey's and of details of the plan that were worked out there. Adding to what Frank had said, Adam Ferguson, a fellow slave, gave his own account of meetings at Vesey's in which arrangements were made for a messenger to go into the country and bring down plantation hands.[16]

The final witness was Benjamin Ford, a white boy of fifteen or sixteen. He told of how Vesey had frequented his family's shop, which was near the Negro carpenter's house, of how Vesey boldly spoke out against the hardships under which the blacks were forced to exist and against the strict and unfair laws, of how Vesey would dwell on the subject of religion and observe that it did not condone such treatment as the Carolinians visited upon the Negroes. Everyone had his time, Vesey said, and his (Vesey's) would come one day.

While all of this was being related, Vesey listened intently, sitting immovable, with his arms folded and his eyes fixed on the floor. When the examination and cross-examination were over without defense counsel apparently being able (or perhaps even trying) to shake the witnesses' stories,[17] Vesey asked and was given permission to examine the witnesses himself. He addressed them in an imperious manner, exhibiting surprise that they would dare to give false testimony against him; he bore down on them as to the accuracy of their reported encounters. But, according to the court, he was unable to tear apart the web of incriminating evidence. He then—using a tactic familiar to defense attorneys—reportedly addressed the court at length, arguing that the charge against him had to be false, that a man in his situation would have no inducement to revolt. The judges, however, remained unconvinced.

On Friday, June 28, Lionel H. Kennedy, the presiding magistrate, pronounced on Denmark Vesey the sentence of death. The words of the sentence, in all of their orotund righteousness, bespoke the attitude of the community:

Denmark Vesey—The Court, on mature consideration, have pronounced you Guilty—You have enjoyed the advantage of able Counsel, and were also heard in your own defence, in which you endeavored, with great art and plausibility, to impress a belief of your innocence. After the most patient deliberation, however, the Court were not only satisfied of your guilt, but that you were the author, and original instigator of this diabolical plot. Your professed design was to trample on all laws, human and divine; to riot in blood, outrage, rapine . . . and conflagration, and to introduce anarchy and confusion in their most horrid forms. Your life has become, therefore, a just and necessary sacrifice, at the shrine of indignant Justice. It is difficult to imagine what *infatuation* could have prompted you to attempt an enterprise so wild and visionary. You were a free man; were comparatively wealthy; and enjoyed every comfort, compatible with your situation. You had, therefore, much to risk, and little to gain. From your age and experience you *ought* to have known, that success was impracticable.

A moment's reflection must have convinced you, that the ruin of *your race*, would have been the probable result, and that years' would have rolled away, before they could have recovered that confidence, which, they once enjoyed in this community. The only reparation in your power, is a full disclosure of the truth. In addition to treason, you have committed the grossest impiety, in attempting to pervert the sacred words of God into a sanction for crimes of the blackest hue. It is evident, that you are totally insensible of the divine influence of that Gospel, "all whose paths are peace." It was to reconcile us to our destinies on earth, and to enable us to discharge with fidelity, all the duties of life, that those holy precepts were imparted by Heaven to fallen man.

If you had searched them with sincerity, you would have discovered instructions, immediately applicable to the deluded victims of your artful wiles—*"Servants' (says Saint Paul) obey in all things your masters', according to the flesh, not with eye-service, as men-pleasers, but in singleness of heart, fearing God."* And again *"Servants' (says Saint Peter) be subject to your masters' with all fear, not only to the good and gentle, but also to the forward."*

On such texts comment is unnecessary.

Your "lamp of life" is nearly extinguished; your race is

run; and you must shortly pass "from time to eternity." Let me then conjure you to devote the remnant of your existence in solemn preparation for the awful doom that awaits you. Your situation is deplorable, but not destitute of spiritual consolation. To that Almighty Being alone, whose Holy Ordinance, you have trampled in the dust, can you now look for mercy, and although "your sins be as scarlet," the tears of sincere penitence may obtain forgiveness at the "Throne of Grace." You cannot have forgotten the history of the malefactor on the Cross, who, like yourself, was the wretched and deluded victim of offended justice. His conscience was awakened in the pangs of dissolution, and yet there is reason to believe, that his spirit was received into the realms of bliss. May *you* imitate his example, and may *your* last moments prove like his![18]

As these words of lordly condemnation were intoned, white observers thought they saw tears trickle down the face of the leader of the insurrection. Though the authorities hoped they represented a sign of garrulous repentance, Denmark Vesey never confessed anything. If tears there were, they were probably tears of the wrecked hopes of a man who had grown old in the expectation that he might one day be able to change his world of chains.

On the day following the sentencing of Denmark Vesey, four Charleston dailies all broke their silence. They announced to the world in general, and undoubtedly to the slave community in particular, that not only Vesey but also five of his lieutenants had been found guilty and condemned to death. The convicted insurrectionists were to die on the gallows on Tuesday, July 2, between the hours of six and eight in the morning.[19]

Despite the court's and the newspapers' manifestation of outraged innocence, all was not well with the conscience of the community. On the morning of June 21, a week before the convictions, Charleston had been struck by a legal thunderbolt. In the columns of the conservative Charleston *Courier* had appeared an unsigned "Communication" questioning by implication the fairness of slave trials.[20] It could only have been placed there by someone with considerable influence. The author of the statement, entitled "Melancholy Effect of Popular Excitement," was soon revealed to be William Johnson, a justice of the United States Supreme Court who was a native and resident of Charleston.

Without mentioning the Vesey proceedings but with obvious reference to them, Johnson told of an occurrence in the Edgefield District in the upper part of the state a few years earlier. As a result of what they took to be a sign of an impending disturbance among slaves, the governors of South Carolina and Georgia had mobilized the militia and sent armed units to patrol the two-state area adjacent to Augusta, Georgia. Though at least one prominent citizen of the area was convinced that the excitement was based on a false alarm, he could not prevail on the authorities to call off the preparations. Consequently "the whole country on the designated night was kept in agitated motion."

One night, Johnson related, the trumpeter of the Augusta cavalry was on his way from the opposite side of the district to report for duty. He and a fellow militiaman were spending the night in the attic of a roadside house and were amusing themselves over a pint of whisky when they happened to notice the continual passing and repassing outside of the mounted militia. The half-intoxicated trumpeter decided to see what effect a blast of his horn might have on the troops. The impact was electrical. Thinking that the sound was the signal for the uprising, the cavalrymen galloped off in all directions in search of the offender.

The only person they could find, said Johnson, was "a single poor half-witted Negro," who was taken crossing a field on his way home "without instrument of war or of music." Though the man denied giving the alarming blast, he was not believed. The militiamen first whipped him severely to extort a confession and then, after binding his eyes, commanded him to prepare for instant death from a saber which a horseman beside him was in the act of sharpening. Thus under fear for his life, the prisoner recalled that a man named Billy, the slave of Captain Key, had one of those long tubes used by boatmen on the river. He declared that Billy had sounded the horn but without any illegal intent.

An armed force was immediately dispatched to search for Billy. The detachment found him "quietly sleeping" but nearby was the incriminating horn. So Billy was hurried away to be tried for his life.

Then Johnson, in a passage that could hardly have failed to arouse the Vesey tribunal, went on:

> The Court of Magistrates and Freeholders was selected from men of the first respectability in the neighborhood; and yet it is a fact, although no evidence was given whatever as to a motive for sounding the horn, and the horn was actually found covered and even filled with cobwebs, they condemned that man to die the next day!—and, what will scarcely be believed, they actually received evidence of his having been once charged with stealing a pig, to substantiate the charge upon which he then stood on trial.

Billy's owner, Johnson related, was thunderstruck at the sentence and, failing himself to get a more deliberate hearing of the case, he prevailed on a number of his friends, including a judge, to appeal to the slave court. Though the citizens pleaded with the court against the injustice and precipitateness of the sentence, the magistrates and freeholders would not yield. The presiding magistrate, said Johnson, actually conceived his dignity to be attacked and threatened impeachment against the judge, though that individual had only interfered (in Johnson's words) "to prevent a legal murder."

"Billy," Johnson's statement concluded, "was hung amidst crowds of execrating spectators;—and such appeared to be the popular demand for a victim, that it is not certain a pardon could have saved him."[21]

Though the Supreme Court justice had simply sought to put the community on guard against rumor-mongering and hysteria, his well-intended effort seemed to have the opposite effect. Members of the Vesey court immediately took umbrage and a behind-the-scenes battle was soon in progress between Johnson and the magistrates and free-holders, who insisted that the justice issue an apology. Meanwhile, the public was vehemently siding with the slave court[22] and exhibiting irritation against Johnson.[23]

The high indignation of the Charleston authorities broke into the open on June 29, the same day as the publication of the news of the insurrectionists' conviction and their pending execution. On that day the members of the Vesey court had published in the *Courier* a communication bristling with injured pride, accusing Johnson of insinuating that the court, "under the influence of popular prejudice, was capable of committing perjury and murder," and insisting that the publication of this defense was made necessary by Johnson's refusal to make good on a promise to issue an explanation saying he had not meant to reflect on the honor of the court. The court's communication was preceded by an apologetic note from the editor for having published Johnson's statement in the first place.[24]

Johnson, having meanwhile been informed of the court's reply, had placed in the same issue of the *Courier* a letter asking the public to suspend judgment of him and pledging to satisfy all the world that the slave judges had published "one of the most groundless and unprovoked attacks ever made upon the feelings of an individual."[25]

Within the next week the Supreme Court justice published a sixteen-page pamphlet to explain his position. He said that at the time he had first written he had not even been aware of the establishment of the court and had actually doubted that such a court would be necessary. He went on to say he had thus meant no reflection on the character and reputation of the judges, who were men of "unqualified respectability." He revealed that the initially promised disclaimer had not been forthcoming because he had submitted several drafts, only to have them returned with requests for withdrawal or suggestions for alteration. When finally a city constable had appeared with a per-emptory demand from the court for satisfaction, Johnson had refused to be browbeaten.

The pamphlet pointed out that the original publication had only been intended to illustrate the danger of spreading false rumors and to quiet the alarms of the weaker sex. The author observed that it was incomprehensible to him how the court could have discovered defamation in a "mere reported case, an historical fact."

Johnson made clear that he shared the interests of the community, noting that all his relatives lived there and that he depended on his native city for protection. But he declared stoutly that no true freeman could tolerate the highhanded behavior of the court, and he took the case of the "humblest citizen" and made it his own.[26]

In this case the Supreme Court justice seemed to be taking the side not just of the humblest citizen but the humblest people in the community, the slaves. At such a time, with the community in a state of extreme agitation and fear, Charleston was not willing to listen. John Potter of Charleston no doubt revealed the general insensitivity of the citizenry concerning the forms of justice about which Johnson spoke when, with evident satisfaction, he informed a friend in Philadelphia that "six wretches are to pay the forfeit of their worthless lives, on Tuesday." The plot was "deeply laid," asserted Potter, and the investigation had proved a "scene of . . . murder to be intended, unparalleled, even exceeding if possible, the Demons of St. Domingo!!!"[27]

Two days after the publication of the court's reply to Johnson, excitement was running as high as ever. The magistrates and freeholders having threatened to resign, letters from citizens appeared in Charleston papers referring to the state of popular anxiety, assuring the court of the public's confidence in its integrity and pleading with the members to stay on the job.[28] To one was appended a note by the editor stating that, if necessary, thousands of citizens would sign the request.[29]

The protest by Johnson involved more than met the eye. While Johnson was undoubtedly concerned with justice for the accused insurrectionists, he was himself a lifelong slave-holder and at no time advocated abolition. Though he considered slavery an evil, he defended the institution as necessary in the South. When he chided the community for what he thought was its undue excitement, his concern for fair procedures was, therefore, probably mixed with a concern for property. It is significant that during the period of the public furor over Johnson's communication to the *Courier*, Governor Bennett, Johnson's brother-in-law, had sought to influence the court in behalf of his own (Bennett's) slaves then on trial. The court for a time refused even to let the governor communicate with the prisoners. A citizen who suspected the involvement of his own slaves, and who on June 28 visited the governor to report his suspicions, said later that the chief executive expressed regret over having a misunderstanding with the court. But the governor declined to take action to arrest his visitor's slaves. He said it would be a great pity if those poor wretches should suffer on slight evidence.

In a letter to the court, dated July 1, the governor observed that the evidence against Batteau Bennett was slight and requested the tribunal to review the case "with a view to the mitigation of his punishment." The court did take up the case again but refused to be budged from its original decision condemning Batteau to death.

Other citizens were not so confident as the governor of the reliability of the slaves. John Potter wrote wrathfully of his belief that the governor himself was to be the first victim of Rolla Bennett and exclaimed that his (Potter's) blood boiled at the thought that the governor's daughter was to be Rolla's reward.[30]

The incipient split in the community leadership between Johnson and Bennett and a few others, on the one hand, and between most of the officials and prominent citizens on the other, was symptomatic of a phenomenon that would grow and sharpen with the years. While Governor Bennett's sympathy with Johnson's position on the unfairness of the Vesey trials was not immediately apparent, his regard for due process was later to come into clear focus. Johnson's and Bennett's outlook on the slave trials seemed to go hand in hand with their orientation in politics. Johnson was a Jeffersonian Democrat with a feeling for people of humble origins, and at the same time he held a nationalistic point of view that was not to be warped by the slavery question. Though Johnson eventually achieved considerable business interests, he had been born into a modest blacksmith's home where his father had evidenced sympathy with Christopher Gadsden's revolutionary preaching.

Governor Bennett, the son of a builder-architect, was, like Johnson, a man of means. He owned lumber interests and a brick yard on Cooper River where he spent some of his time.[31] But he too had the common touch. He had been raised to power by the white artisan class. Like Johnson, he was to remain nationalist in outlook and to entertain moderate views on slavery despite the steadily rising temper of Charleston on the issue.

Arrayed against Bennett and Johnson and the few allies who would join them were to be most of the authorities who had to do with suppressing the Vesey rebellion. James Hamilton, whose zeal in rounding up the suspected insurrectionists was perhaps unequalled among the officials, was the author of one of the most heated attacks on Johnson in the Charleston press.[32] So determined was he to root out the conspiracy that he at one point secreted himself in the house of a Negro in order to apprehend a suspect.[33] Writing later of the insurrectionists, Hamilton declared, "there is nothing they are bad enough to do, that we are not powerful enough to punish." Beginning with his activity in the Vesey affair, Hamilton played an increasingly intense part as a defender of slavery and a proponent of states rights.

One of Hamilton's most ardent fellow officials was Colonel Robert Y. Hayne, commander of the troops during the frightening night of June 16, attorney general of the state, and later to be one of the judges of the Vesey insurgents. In response to a request from Governor Bennett, Hayne, as attorney general, was to issue an opinion in support of the legality of the Vesey proceedings. Though Hayne had originally been elevated to political power by the artisan class, he in time came to be closely identified with states rights and the interests of the big slave-holders. He was elected to the United States Senate in 1822 with Calhoun's support.

Another of the leading actors in the Vesey drama was Robert J. Turnbull. A large slave-holder himself, he was a member of the court which tried the insurrection leaders. He was a fiery defender of slavery and, as an eager states rights advocate, would come into conflict with Johnson.

With such single-minded leaders as Hamilton, Hayne, and Turnbull in control of both the community and the instruments of justice, the fateful day of July 2 approached. The intercession by the governor and the Supreme Court justice had had no effect. There were reports of a planned intercession by the insurgents themselves in a last-ditch effort to rescue their chiefs: at reveille on the morning of the scheduled day of execution, a general attack would be launched by the insurgents as the nightly guards were being discharged from duty. The rescue attempt did not materialize, however, and it was later thought to have been thwarted by the arrest of additional slave leaders.

On the morning of the appointed day, July 2, the *City Gazette* carried a notice of the scheduled hanging of Denmark Vesey and five of his confederates: Rolla, Batteau and Ned Bennett, Peter Poyas, and Jesse Blackwood.[34] Immense crowds of whites and blacks gathered at the scene. The gallows was located on Blake's Lands, near Charleston. As the convicted insurgents were being detached from their cell irons [35] and brought forth, the onlookers waited expectantly. Nothing now seemed capable of stopping fear and vengeance from exacting their toll. But if the doomed men realized they were caught in a vortex of merciless hysteria, they never let it shake their wills. To the end most of them were true to the code expressed by Peter Poyas: "Do not open your lips! Die silent, as you shall see me do."[36]

The executions were carried out. To make sure that the price of entertaining revolt was well advertised, the Charleston papers published notices of the hanging of the free

black man and the five slaves who had been found guilty
of planning to overthrow the constituted civil and slave
authority.[37]

Meanwhile, Charleston was preparing to pay tribute
to the overthrow of British authority nearly fifty years
before. On June 29, the same day that the news of Vesey's
conviction had been published, the *Courier* printed general
orders for the troops who were to participate in the Fourth
of July parade. Unit commanders were reminded, however,
that they must not let their men's enthusiasm for the blessings
of "Rational Liberty" interfere with military dignity.[38]

At six o'clock on the morning of July 4 the brigade
was formed on Broad Street at Meeting with the head of the
column facing east. The troops consisting of cavalry, infantry, and artillery, marched along Broad Street to East Bay,
turned right on East Bay, where they were reviewed by
the governor, and proceeded to the Battery, where a national
salute was fired by the cavalry and a *feu de joie* by the
infantry.[39] These military exercises were followed during the
day by church services and meetings of the Revolution and
Cincinnati societies and of the '76 Association. After the
service at St. Philip's Church, R. B. Gilchrist read Washington's Farewell Address. And in St. Michael's, R. Elfe read
the Declaration of Independence: ". . . all men are created
equal . . . they are endowed by their creator with certain
unalienable rights . . ." During the day at least five orations
to liberty were delivered before religious, military, and civic
assemblages in the city.[40]

A few days after these fulsome celebrations of freedom,
the Charleston *Courier* exhibited annoyance because the London *Morning Chronicle* found something incongruous in the
*Courier's* publishing of an advertisement for a runaway
slave in the same issue in which it defended Greek freedom. Showing a typical slave-holder's inability to conceive
of freedom having any meaning for the servile class, the
*Courier* gave the *Chronicle* what it considered a coup de
grace in the argument simply by quoting Edmund Burke

as to why Southern colonials were more jealous of their freedom than others.[41]

While white Charleston might take time out for gala observances, July remained a gloomy period for Negroes in the South Carolina city. New arrests took place almost every day. The court of magistrates and freeholders stayed in session, hearing cases and turning out sentences.

Even after Vesey and some of the other leaders were in their graves, the insurgents, under the leadership of Gullah Jack, the conjurer, were planning an attack, according to the authorities. But on July 5 Gullah Jack was located and taken into custody, even though he had shaven off his beard to avoid detection. At Jack's trial members of the court were struck by the way in which he played the fool; some of his judges could not believe that he was a culprit. As the trial progressed, however, and the third of six witnesses was being heard, Jack dropped his feigned ignorance. His countenance changed swiftly and he showed clearly by his hard looks and vehement gestures that he understood and resented the evidence being given against him. On July 9 Jack and four others were condemned to death. On the pronouncement of the sentence Jack pleaded with the court for an extra two weeks, even an extra week of life. He continued to entreat until he was taken from the courtroom to his cell. Three days later Gullah Jack and another insurrectionist were hanged from a gallows on "The Lines," an area corresponding to Calhoun Street today.[42] The authorities reported that Jack "gave up his spirit without firmness or composure."

The conviction[43] and execution of Gullah Jack got dutiful attention in the press.[44] On the same day that this second set of insurgents met their doom, "A Citizen," through the columns of the *Southern Patriot*, thanked the intendant for his "zealous discharge" of his duties and the court for its "unwearied labors" and its "calm and discriminating investigation."[45]

It was on July 10, the day after the sentencing of

Gullah Jack and four fellow defendants, that one of the most important developments in the entire investigation occurred. The four condemned to die along with Jack were John Horry, Charles Drayton, Monday Gell, and Harry Haig. But Drayton, Gell, and Haig, by making extensive disclosures to the authorities, were to save themselves from the gallows. Drayton began it by reporting details of the insurrection plan and the names of reputed conspirators to Intendant Hamilton during a confrontation in his cell. In the next few days additional names and further information were revealed by Gell[46] and Haig. As a result of the revelations of these three and of Perault Strohecker, who was picked up on July 10, dozens of slaves were arrested in the course of three or four days.[47] The court was supplied with new material for its mill. In one period of seven days thirty-two Negroes were convicted.[48]

During this period while the investigation was at its height, Governor Bennett, though he was one of the most level-headed of the officials, revealed that he himself was not free of anxiety. In a letter to Secretary of War John C. Calhoun, dated July 15, Bennett reported the public alarm over the Vesey affair and the resulting acute awareness of the unready state of the federal forces at Charleston. Fort Johnson, which contained 140 barrels of gun powder, was garrisoned by only five men and was separated from the mainland simply by a narrow creek fordable at low tide. The governer, therefore, favored the removal of the powder from this accessible storage point. And, more important, he urged an increase in the number of U.S. troops at Charleston.[49] Calhoun responded by ordering the transfer of a company of artillery from St. Augustine to Charleston[50] and by instructing Major James Bankhead to co-operate with Governor Bennett in "such measures as may be deemed advisable in quelling the disturbances at Charleston."[51] News of Calhoun's order was published on July 30,[52] and on August 15 the troop reinforcements landed at Fort Moultrie at the mouth of Charleston harbor.[53]

Meanwhile, at the end of July, in a second letter to Calhoun, the governor had said the arrival of the additional forces would help to allay the public apprehension. He then suggested the erection of a magazine on the island of Castle Pinkney to which the Fort Johnson powder might be transferred, and concluded with an expression of regret that the reinforcements could not have numbered three companies instead of one. Such a force, said the governor, would not only have helped more to "tranquillize the public mind" but would also have produced a "sapient" effect on that "class of persons" which was causing the disturbance.[54] Clearly the chief executive of South Carolina was not taking the threat from insurrection lightly.[55]

As the trials had gone on, further convictions were regularly reported in the papers.[56] With the approach of July 26, the community was on notice that an unusual spectacle was in the offing. Twenty-two men had been condemned to be executed on that day. A long gallows was erected on "The Lines." The whole city turned out for the occasion that Friday morning. In the confusion at the execution ground, a small slave boy was trampled to death by horses.[57] From a third story window of his home nearby on King Street, a twelve-year-old white boy, witnessed the hangings. It was, he recalled later, "a sight calculated to strike terror into the heart of every slave." This, indeed, was the purpose of the officials. Commenting on the executions, the *City Gazette* noted with satisfaction that the "twenty-two culprits [had] expatiated, on the gallows, the crime" of plotting "a scheme of wildness and wickedness, enough to make us smile at the folly, did we not shudder at the indiscriminate mischief of the plan and its objects."[58] Other papers too saw that the executions were publicized as a warning to would-be rebels.[59]

Though four more slaves were sentenced to be hanged on July 30, the court which tried Denmark Vesey ended its activities on the day of the mass execution, July 26.[60] The special tribunal had sat for five and a half weeks and, along with the committee of vigilance, had considered charges against 117 Negroes, of whom thirty-eight were released for lack of evidence and seventy-nine were put on trial. Of the seventy-nine accused who were tried, fifty-nine were convicted and twenty acquitted. But of the twenty who were found not guilty, eleven were deemed to be so dangerous that they must nevertheless be transported out of the state. In the end this court sent thirty-four men to the gallows and caused thirty-five to be condemned to exile[61] (usually sold into slavery elsewhere),[62] separated forever from relatives and friends.

Even in death the bodies of the condemned slaves were still treated as property, subject to disposal by the authorities and not by their families. The corpses of the executed men were, on request, consigned to surgeons for dissection.[63]

As the court concluded its work, Charleston newspapers paid the respects of the community to the law enforcement authorities.[64] The *City Gazette* observed that the intendant had combined the character of the magistrate with the "ardor of a patriot" and added that he and the members of the committee of vigilance and of the whole City Council would not sleep in the remembrance of citizens. It noted that the members of the court had laid aside their private concerns and dedicated their time and talents to the service of the community "in one of the most awful and delicate junctures" that had occurred "since the settlement of Charleston." It voiced the hope that the axe had been "laid to the root of the evil" which threatened the whole state.[65]

The "evil," however, was not yet extinguished. William Garner, a slave now suspected as a leader, had gone to Columbia on a ticket supplied by his mistress before information had been lodged against him.[66] His feared escape had stirred the authorities to feverish action. Governor Bennett on July 19 had issued a proclamation offering a $200 reward for Garner's capture.[67] Intendant Hamilton had written a letter to Intendant D. McCord of Columbia and that official on receipt of the letter on July 23, had acted immediately.[68] His emissary had located Garner in Granby and had lodged him in Columbia until a guard could be procured to send him to Charleston.[69]

On August 1 a new court of magistrates and free-holders was organized to try Garner and such other slaves as might be brought before it.[70] Its membership was made up of Jacob Axson and Charles M. Furman, magistrates, and Thomas Rhett Smith, Joel R. Poinsett, Robert Y. Hayne, Thomas Roper, and John Gordon, freeholders. The trial of William Garner opened on August 3, the day after his arrival in Charleston.[71] On the basis of testimony that Garner was to be the leader of a party of horsemen and had agreed to enlist men among the draymen, he was convicted and sentenced to be hanged on August 9. This was the last death sentence to be imposed as a result of the insurrection fright, the second court having decided that enough offenders had been executed to furnish an example to the slave community.

Thirteen other cases were heard by the second court. Seven more of the defendants were convicted and were sentenced to transportation outside the limits of the United States. Six of the accused were acquitted. The second tribunal concluded its assignment on August 8 and adjourned.[72]

Though the trials of the Negroes ended early in August, there was to be an unusual sequel. At the Court of Sessions in Charleston on October 7, 1822, four white men were tried on indictments charging them with a misdemeanor in "inciting slaves to insurrection." The authorities were certain that these men had nothing to do with organizing the plot but that, once rumors of it were abroad, they and other white men of "lowest" character were prepared to engage in "any enterprise of blood and ruin" from which plunder might be gained. While officials were convinced that other desperate white men were involved, there was difficulty in proving their participation because of the incompetency of slaves to give evidence against white persons. To supply proof, white witnesses who had overheard the accused conversing with Negroes had to be rounded up. The four white defendants were all convicted and sentenced to short prison terms and fines and required to give security for their good behavior on release.[73] In reporting one of the cases, the authorities observed that the sentence, unless modified by pardon, would amount to imprisonment for life, since the circumstances of the prisoner would prevent his paying the fine or giving security.

With these cases, the courtroom phase of the Vesey affair came to a close. Altogether seventy-one men, sixty-seven of them Negroes, had been convicted. Thirty-five men, all Negroes, had paid with their lives for the offense of instigating revolt or adhering to the plan for it.[74] Forty-two Negroes (including eleven who had actually been acquitted)[75] were condemned to banishment; one was jailed and finally whipped and released. Manifestly the price which the law exacted for subversion was higher for some members of the community than for others. For one segment it was death or banishment; for another segment, distinguished solely by skin color, it was imprisonment.[76]

But the score in the Vesey insurrection was not settled without dispute. Governor Bennett had continued to hold misgivings about the way the court was conducting business. He commuted the punishment of three slaves to banishment after the court had sentenced them to death. Twice, at the request of the court, he had ordered delays in the execution of Monday Gell, Charles Drayton, and Harry Haig in order to allow time for more testimony to be drawn from them.[77] But the governor balked when the court recommended that he pardon the three state's witnesses on condition that they be sent out of the United States. The rationale of the judges was that Monday, Charles, and Harry had enabled the court not only to detect the general plan of the conspiracy but to convict a number of the principal offenders, that the three had co-operated under the impression that their lives would be spared, that it would be politic to let Negroes know that even their principal advisers could not be confided in. In refusing to act on the recommendation, however, the governor advised the magistrates and freeholders that they themselves had the power to commute the penalty to banishment, which they did. Governor Bennett subsequently observed that the court had earlier used other witnesses and had nevertheless allowed them to be executed.

This disagreement over pardoning, plus the earlier differences with the court, undoubtedly intensified the feelings between the chief executive on the one hand and the Vesey judges and the community on the other. Irritation with the governor had also cropped out in connection with the effort to apprehend William Garner, some citizens suspecting that Bennett was not doing his utmost to help.[78]

In September the governor was the target of veiled press criticism for reducing the punishment of an old slave, Peter Cooper, from death to twenty lashes on his bare back. The *City Gazette* said the community would want to know the reason for the final escape of a culprit who had "contemplated the worst of crimes."[79] Bennett explained later that the pardoned slave was very infirm, that his connection with the conspiracy was equivocal, and that the reprieved man's master had been requested to send him from the state and had agreed to do so.[80]

At the root of the division between Governor Bennett and other officials was the way in which they analyzed the danger of the contemplated insurrection. The governor never doubted that there had been a plan for revolt, but he felt that, once it was discovered and counter measures taken, the hazard was minimized. He recoiled against overly harsh treatment of the would-be insurrectionists. He was influenced in part perhaps by a regard for due process (as held by his brother-in-law, William Johnson) but also influenced by a probable feeling that the necessity for severe repressive action would reflect on his administration as governor. City officials, on the other hand, having been frightened into immediate and drastic moves, felt a need to justify their actions.

The difference in attitude, apparent almost from the beginning, had come into sharper focus as the end of the trials approached. In late July the court and city officials let

it be known that an account of the proceedings would be
published which would show the extensive nature of the plot
and overwhelm those "who at first thought" there was "no
cause for alarm."[81] But before this planned publication by
the city was ready, Governor Bennett had published his own
version of events. Written on August 10, two days after the
second court completed its work, the governor's account
described how the conspiracy was promoted, how it was un-
covered, and what steps were taken to punish the participants. The theme of his narrative was that rumor had magni-
fied the extent of the conspiracy and that, therefore, a
recitation of the facts was needed not only to quiet the
general anxiety and alarm but also to protect the reputation
of the state abroad and to prevent "a rapid deterioration of
property."[82]

Within less than two weeks after the governor's publication, the city had its own history of the insurrection off
the press. It was a forty-eight-page pamphlet by Intendant
James Hamilton, and it got far more attention in the Charleston press[83] than Governor Bennett's effort. Written at the
request of the City Council, the Hamilton account emphasized that all insurrectionary activity had been crushed by the
conscientious work of the authorities, but it made no attempt
to downgrade the significance of the plan for insurrection.[84]
So popular was the Hamilton narrative that the printer
promised in an advertisement that "the greatest expedition"
would be used "to supply the pressing demand."[85] In the
next few months four editions of this pamphlet were published, the first and fourth in Charleston and the second and
third in Boston.[86] The public was so eager for more information, however, that a 202-page report on the Vesey insurrection was prepared by the presiding magistrates of the
first court. It was ready for distribution in early November.[87]

Once the crisis was passed and more information was
revealed, the public had begun to express itself in vigorous
terms. Self-satisfaction and outrage were both evident in the
reactions. The *City Gazette* had promised that the Hamilton

narrative would show all the people of the Union that the vigilance of the people of South Carolina made it impossible for them to be taken by surprise and that the diligence of the court made certain that, although a few guilty slaves might have escaped, not a single innocent slave had suffered.[88] Denmark Vesey's "devilish plan" was said to have been prompted by the "Prince of Darkness."[89] The conspirators were accused of using religion as a "perfidious cover" for their schemes.[90]

Outside the borders of the state, however, the reaction to the Vesey affair was not so uniformly smug. Though there was some support for the way in which the revolt had been suppressed,[91] there was also a good deal of questioning. News of the insurrectionary design and of the punitive actions of the Charleston authorities was widely published. An item on the execution of the insurrection leaders appeared in *Niles Weekly Register* (Baltimore) on July 13,[92] and further information on the events in Charleston was published in the papers of Richmond, Virginia; Little Rock, Arkansas; Philadelphia, New York, Hartford, Boston, and London.[93] In New York the *Daily Advertiser* labeled the mass hanging of 22 of the defendants a "Bloody Sacrifice."[94] And in Philadelphia the *Franklin Gazette* spoke of the insurrectionists in terms of patriots and martyrs "striking for liberty."[95] These comments roused furious rebuttals in the Charleston press. The depressed condition of Negroes in Philadelphia, New York, and Boston was noted; despite these conditions, (according to Charleston correspondents) Northern spokesmen had had the effrontery to create trouble for Charleston by the "poison" doctrines they spread through the Missouri debates.[96]

Citizens of South Carolina did not allow the criticism from outside the state to interfere with their vision of themselves as a chosen people. The Charleston *Courier* suggested that the City Council appoint a day of thanksgiving to be observed in all the churches, where the people would give praise to God "for his preserving care" and for defeating the "evil and secret malevolence" of those who had conspired against them. [97] The Baptist Convention of South Carolina urged the governor to appoint a day of thanksgiving, for it was nothing less than a special intervention of Divine Goodness which had delivered the city and state from the conspirators.[98]

This proposal set the tone for the outlook of a people who were becoming ever more convinced of the righteousness of their particular cause and who were less and less willing to listen to differing opinions either inside or outside the state.

The law of South Carolina before the year was over was again to measure the cost of insurrection-plotting and to make sure that, in the final balancing, the scales were tipped in favor of the slave owner. In the Charleston *Mercury* of November 19, 1822, appeared a notice addressed to owners whose slaves had been executed in connection with the late attempted insurrection. They were called upon to meet that evening at the Carolina Coffee House to draft a memorial to the legislature.[99] The next month the General Assembly of South Carolina revealed its sympathy for these property owners in a bill providing that those whose slaves had been put to death should receive $122.44 for each chattel so disposed of.[100] A bill was also introduced to reimburse owners of banished slaves at the rate of $122 each, on condition that such compensated owners assign their property in these slaves to the state.[101] Speaking for the City Council of Charleston, Intendant Hamilton presented a memorial asking the legislature to reimburse the city for expenses incurred in connection with the investigation of the uprising.[102]

In considering the people entitled to recompense, the legislators did not forget "such persons" as had given "important information, tending to the discovery and suppression of a very dangerous plot. . . ." The owners of Peter Prioleau and George Wilson were authorized to emancipate these men, for which they were to be reimbursed for the appraised value of the slave up to $1,000. Once freed, Peter and George were to be paid $50 a year for life and to be exempt from all taxes. If the owners refused to emancipate the slaves who had disclosed the plot, or if the slaves should decline to accept freedom, each servitor was to receive $100 annually. William Pencil, the free Negro who advised Peter, and Scott, a free black man who had helped implicate one of the white defendants, were also to be rewarded—Pencil in the amount of $1,000, and Scott, $500.[103] George and Peter were later emancipated in accordance with the provisions of the legislation.

Thus were the figures totted, the score on freedom versus slavery settled. The legislature seemed to be speaking for the state when it compensated the suffering slave-holders. In the settlement, however, there was no reflection of the losses—in lives and hopes—suffered by suppressed and unrepresented Negroes. South Carolina had no one in authority with the insight to say, as Jefferson did after Gabriel's insurrection in Virginia: "The other states and the world at large will forever condemn us if we indulge a principle of revenge or go one step beyond absolute necessity. They cannot lose sight of the rights of the two parties and the object of the unsuccessful one."[104]

# THE HARVEST
# OF FEARS

● In South Carolina the Vesey conspiracy produced a social trauma, the symptoms of which were observable in acute form for months and in milder form for years. The near panic[1] which struck Charleston in mid-June was still evident in August.[2] In December a Charleston correspondent wrote: "a more painful degree of anxiety has never before been experienced here."[3] "Never," said an outside commentator in later years, was "an entire people more thoroughly alarmed."[4]

Adding to the tension was the necessity for being discreet in communication. One citizen admitted that he dared not discuss the implications of the affair even in his own family.[5] The Charleston papers, as has already been noted, were careful as to what information they published and, in commenting on the event, used various strategems to camoflauge their meaning, referring darkly, for example to "the late attempt to excite a *bellum servile* in this city."[6] When longer pamphlet accounts of the insurrection attempt were published, families kept them locked away from the eyes of slaves and in many cases finally burned them to keep them from being seen.[7]

The nervousness of the slave-holding community following the Vesey affair was indicated by its treatment of Negro offenders or supposed Negro offenders who were involved in unrelated incidents. During July and August of 1822 mail drivers were several times attacked by Negroes in the country southeast of Charleston.[8] In ordinary times the response would have been wrathful enough. But at the height of the fright over Vesey, it was fierce. In one case, though there was no injury of the driver or theft of mail, three of the four accused slaves were promptly hanged.[9]

Some of those implicated in the mail attacks were runaway slaves, and runaways were particularly feared. They were believed to be the instigators of insurrection.[10] A white posse staged an attack on runaways near Pineville, South Carolina in 1823. In the clash a woman and child were killed. One of the runaways was decapitated and his head stuck on a pole and publicly exposed as a "warning to vicious slaves."[11] As part of a general campaign against subversive influences among Negroes, the Seminole Indians in 1823 were induced to sign a treaty promising to return all runaway slaves and other fugitives entering their territory.[12]

The case of Morris Brown and Henry Drayton illustrates the fear, distrust and suspicion that gripped Charleston. Brown, a free Negro shoemaker,[13] was bishop of the African Church and had been a trusted figure in the community. Drayton, also a free black man, was a leader in the African Church. Not long before June 16, the date selected for the Vesey uprising, Brown and Drayton had gone on a trip to the North. When they voluntarily returned some weeks later, they were hauled before a magistrate and charged with violating the act of 1820[14] which forbade the immigration of free Negroes into South Carolina or even the return to the state of free Negroes formerly in residence there, except under certain conditions.

Brown and Drayton seemed to fit under the exceptions.[15] But they were now in a suspect class. The African Church had been identified as the seat of the Vesey conspiracy by many of the witnesses. Moreover, Brown and Drayton had been reported in testimony to have known of the plan, and Brown was said to have given it his blessing. This evidently was enough for Magistrate John D. White. He ordered defendants Brown and Drayton to leave the state within fifteen days. [16] It made no difference that Monday Gell, one of the principal witnesses, had asserted that the two church leaders had not been informed and knew nothing of the insurrectionary design. Nor did it matter that James Hamilton, the chief prosecutor, thought the evidence against Brown was completely false.[17] Some community complainants suspected the two Negro religious leaders; and suspicion seemed sufficient to clinch the case against them.

In September, 1822, Beaufort, a small town down the coast from Charleston, was alarmed by rumors of a plan for a slave outbreak. There were fears, later shown to be unfounded, that the Vesey poison had spread. Nevertheless, a slave court detained a Negro who had been linked with treasonable talk.[18]

Another revealing clue to Charleston's continuing attitude came in October when the city got word about what appeared to be lax surveillance being exerted over one of the convicted insurrectionists who was being taken out of the state. Many of the convicted conspirators were kept in the workhouse at Charleston for months until arrangements could be made for their transportation. In this case, the insurgent had finally been sold to a horse dealer by his master on condition that the new owner remove him from the United States as required by the court.

When it was reported that one of Vesey's men was being taken through the country toward Savannah without being secured in any way, several men from Charleston set off in pursuit of the party. Finding the insurrectionist unguarded and with ample opportunity to escape, the vigilantes seized him and carried him back to Charleston. "It being deemed," said the Charleston *Mercury*, "a highly dangerous precedent, that a felon, convicted of exciting insurrection, should be carried openly and unguarded through the interior of the State, with all the facilities necessary to evade the sentence of the Court, and again expose the community to the contamination of his principles and example." —his arrest was viewed as a measure that would receive the approbation of the citizens. And the incident, it was hoped, would teach a lesson to other owners.[19]

As Charleston began to reflect on what was widely conceded to be a crucial event in its history, dozens of citizens took pen in hand to explain the causes of the threatened uprising and to offer remedies for safeguarding the city against calamity in the future. The venerable General Thomas Pinckney probably spoke for the majority of the community elite as he analyzed the conditions that had brought Charleston to the brink of a massive slave revolt. There were, said General Pinckney, (1) the example of St. Domingue and probably the encouragement received from that island; (2) the "indiscreet zeal in favor of universal liberty" which was voiced by many citizens of the North and echoed by the black population of that area; (3) the "idleness, dissipation and improper indulgencies" permitted among all classes of Negroes in Charleston; (4) the ease with which Negro mechanics, draymen, fishermen, butchers, porters, and hucksters could obtain money; and (5) the disparity in numbers between the white and black inhabitants of the city. Of the indulgencies referred to by Pinckney, the one he viewed as the most dangerous was the teaching of reading and writing, since the first skill brought into play "the powerful operation of the Press," and the second furnished the slaves with "an instrument to carry into execution the mischievous suggestions" of the printed word.[20] Pinckney warned that the city must be viligant against "emissaries" and "incendiary publications" from the northern states.[21]

Pinckney's essay on insurrection summarized causes and criticisms that were being repeated endlessly in the Charleston press as thousands of white residents, convinced that they had narrowly escaped destruction, sought guarantees that they would not be subjected to the same risk again. Little or no recognition was given to the basic reason for their insecurity—the severe subjugation of an army of people with the same human feelings and aspirations as their oppressors. And little interest was evinced in removing this basic reason. Instead, the emphasis was on the perversity of men who would take advantage of their masters' indulgence and on the consequent need for further subjugation.[22] State Comptroller-General John S. Cogdell expressed fear that, if the insurrectionary plot was not effectively subdued, a certain "species of property" would "fall in value very much."[23]

In October, 1822, the Charleston Grand Jury addressed itself to the issues posed by the Vesey affair.[24] A little more than three months later another grand jury—headed by Robert J. Turnbull, a member of the court which tried Vesey —was directing its attention to the same problems.[25]

One of the hottest forums for debate over the Vesey revolt, however, was to be on the floor of the legislature as that body met toward the end of the unsettling year of 1822. Citizens began supplying fuel for the debate months before the session opened. In August, less than two weeks after the trials of the insurrectionists were closed, newspapers were receiving urgent communications calling for a public meeting of citizens to consider changes in the laws regulating slaves and free Negroes.[26] Out of such public consideration came one lengthy memorial to the legislators which well illustrated the frightening impact that Vesey had made on the Charleston populace and which proposed remedies representative of those advanced from many sources. The memorialists interspersed their recommendations with an analysis which in some respects showed a keen perception as to why existing conditions might lead to insurrection. Beginning with a customary pious recital of privileges and benefits which had been extended to slaves, and noting that these advantages might have been expected to induce satisfaction and affection, the document went on to observe that instead the Negroes had plotted a calamity comparable to the worst of the West Indian atrocities.

Having thus paid their respects to the pride of the community, however, the petitioners then proceeded to consider in a fairly dispassionate way why free Negroes and slaves of South Carolina could not safely be allowed to live side by side. Not only did the degraded status of free Negroes spur the freedmen themselves to harbor thoughts of revolt, but their residence alongside slaves aroused similar subversive ambitions in the latter. Free Negroes could acquire property, move about at will, procure information on every subject, and unite in associations. And yet they were deprived of all political rights and subjected to the same police regulations as slaves. Moreover, they were conscious that they could not lift themselves by any peaceable and legal methods. They had, said the memorialists, sufficient liberty to appreciate the blessings of freedom and were sufficiently shackled so that they realized they enjoyed few of those blessings. Among slaves, on the other hand, the superior condition of free Negroes was such as to excite extreme discontent. Since the legislature had closed the door to emancipation, slaves were aware that they could never acquire liberty by purchase or faithful service. Thus their "only chance for freedom" lay in insurrection. And such an enterprise was one in which slaves and free Negroes would be impelled to make common cause.

Recalling that Denmark Vesey was a free Negro and citing figures to prove that, if the population trend continued, free persons of color would eventually outnumber the whites, the writers came to a stern conclusion: "expel from our territory every free person of color, that we may extinguish at once every gleam of hope which the slaves may indulge of ever being free . . . that we may proceed to govern them on the only principle that can maintain slavery, the 'principle of fear.' "

Directing their attention to black mechanics and to slaves hired out by their masters (sometimes, of course, the same Negroes were members of both categories), the petitioners found conditions especially conducive to unrest. Hired out slaves were released to a considerable extent from the control of their owners and, being masters of their own time and movement, they were free to schedule meetings and mature plans for revolt. On the other hand, slaves who were kept in their owners' yards were under constant observation and subject to call without notice by their masters: thus they would find it harder to fix a time for assembling and acting in conspiratorial concert.

As for Negro mechanics, even those who were not hired out slaves usually had only given assignments to perform, after which they had time at their disposal for forming combinations and devising schemes. The irregularity of habits and the idleness of mechanics and hired out slaves produced a "restlessness of disposition" which delighted in mischief.

It was significant, according to the petitioning citizens, that the Negroes engaged in the Vesey conspiracy were with very few exceptions mechanics or persons working out. Therefore they proposed that a law be passed limiting the number of slaves to be hired out and confining the exercise of the mechanical arts to white persons, except for those cases in which black mechanics were under the immediate control and inspection of their masters. Such a regulation would cause a large portion of the city's "dangerous" black population to be transported to the country and to be supplanted by white laborers whose feelings would be in harmony with those of the dominant class.

Observing that slaves' apparel had become too expensive to be consistent with their inferior position, the memorialists recommended that the legislature prescribe the mode of dress for persons of color, ordering them to wear only coarse woolens in winter and coarse cottons in summer and outlawing—except for livery servants—the wearing of silks, satins, crepes, lace, and muslins.

The petitioners noted with alarm that the city guard, as organized, was made up of men who were employed in some other occupation during the day and who were therefore unfit to serve as sentinels at night; that most guardsmen were shopkeepers or retailers of spiritous liquors to Negroes and that therefore they were inclined to permit Negroes (their customers) to pass unmolested through the streets after the bell was rung and the watch set. The legislature was called upon to recognize the inadequacy of this protective means against "an enemy in the bosom of the State" prepared, whenever an opportunity presented itself, to rise up and surprise the whites. In lieu of the existing city guard, the lawmakers should establish a regular well disciplined, well officered military force, distinct from the body of citizens generally, and assigned to duty night and day.

Exhibiting again their concern about any circumstances

that might afford Negroes a chance to conspire in secret, the authors of the petition next turned their attention to the fact that black persons were even the owners of plantations where runaway Negroes might find a haven and carry on "their schemes of destruction" without any likelihood of detection. They therefore recommended that a law be enacted preventing persons of color from holding real property, that Negroes be forbidden to live on premises where no white person resided, that slaves be placed under surveillance as much as possible so as to prevent their leaguing together.

The petitioners found one of the most baleful influences on the colored population to be the influx into Carolina from the middle states of slaves, many of them taken from jails and houses of correction after their punishment was commuted to banishment. To stop the mingling of "this degraded and villainous body of Negroes" with Charleston domestics whose minds were thereby contaminated, the legislature was requested to make the bringing of slaves into the state a highly penal offense.

Being aware undoubtedly that under the existing law the white men who were convicted of complicity in the Vesey conspiracy could not be sentenced to death, the memorialists proposed that the statute in force be amended to permit the execution of "all white persons who shall be principals, advisers or abettors in any actual or projected insurrection of the slaves." As the law stood, capital punishment could only be levied against white persons for being concerned with slaves in *actual insurrection* or for aiding them to raise an insurrection by furnishing them with passports or arms or by providing them shelter, protection, or house room while they were pursuing treasonable ends.

As their last recommendation, the petitioners—obviously mindful of the part that revolutionary literature played in the Vesey project—urged the legislators to prescribe several penalties for teaching Negroes to read and write.

With expressions of dread and concern ringing in their ears, members of the General Assembly convened in Columbia in the fall of 1822. Since excitement over Vesey was still high, the season was not one for sober deliberation on proposed remedies for insurrection. Into this heated situation Governor Bennett introduced a hammering message that seemed almost calculated to produce an explosion of tempers.

After a hint[27] in an earlier communication as to what was coming, the governor on November 28 in a blunt Message No. 2 flung a series of challenges to the law-makers on the Vesey affair. He charged that the Charleston City Council's organization of a court of ultimate jurisdiction to try alleged insurrectionists had been a "usurpation of authority, and a violation of the law." Though he acknowledged that the members of the court were men of talent and that the Council had been governed by the purest motives, he nevertheless asserted that the tribunal had been "illegally constituted;" its organization had been directed by the city government rather than left to the duly constituted magistrates.

Not only did Governor Bennett question the legality of the court but he also went on to attack its procedures. He lamented the fact that the court had closed its doors upon the community, shutting out those "accidental rays" that occasionally "illuminate the obscurity" in which "innocence and guilt are indistinguishable." He chided the special tribunal for allowing the accused to be convicted without seeing the faces or hearing the voices of the accusers. He deplored the pronouncement of death sentences upon three of the conspirators who had provided key testimony under the impression that their lives would be spared.[28]

While emphasizing his respect for the court, the governor upbraided it for receiving testimony under a pledge to keep the names of the witnesses secret. He saw no need for such an extraordinary measure, since the state was competent to protect those who gave evidence. He noted the fact that the witnesses had not been molested, except for minor insults, even though their identities had subsequently become known among the slaves.

When the governor communicated his objections to state Attorney General Robert Y. Hayne, that "enlightened jurist," according to Bennett, gave an elaborate opinion in which he sought to remove any embarrassment that might flow from defects in the trial by observing that the defendants had no civil rights which could be traced to sources other than the statutes. Since the statutes guaranteed them few rights, the implication was clear. The court was not obliged to heed the protests of the chief executive which were made (Bennett took pains to stress) only after the cases of his own slaves were adjudicated. Having been thus rebuffed, Governor Bennett related, he yielded to the prevailing sentiment. He had already been frustrated, he reported, by the City Council's failure to act on his suggestion for setting up an initial informal court of inquiry which would uncover the "wicked machinations" of the conspirators while at the same time avoiding the irregularities in which the court of magistrates and freeholders was eventually to indulge.

On his side, the governor, by his own acknowledgment, had refused the request of the magistrate's court to commute the punishment of certain of the defendants who had aided the prosecution. He pointed out that the court itself had the necessary authority.

Noting with a hint of pride that he had already expeditiously handled most of those cases in which transportation of the defendants had been entrusted to the executive authority, Governor Bennett went on to chide the city for its laxity, disclosing that twenty-one of the convicted conspirators were then (five months after the alarm) still in the custody of city officers.

In the course of his communication to the legislature, Governor Bennett revealed in greater detail than before some of the reasons for his differences with the prosecuting authorities. He explained that, despite the doubts of city officials, he had employed executive clemency to spare the lives of several convicted insurgents because the executions had gone so far that they had "ceased to produce a salutary terror" and were so dreadful that "humanity wept." He complained about an order from the City Council interfering with an investigation which he had launched to discover the nature of the plot among the slaves. Then he went on to express doubt that the Vesey project had been as extensive or as well planned or as likely to succeed as the city officials believed it to be. He saw the habitual respect and obedience of the slaves, their "natural indolence" and lack of opportunity for conspiring, as obstacles to any general effort to rise up—even though he acknowledged that the events of 1822 had demonstrated that ideas of insurrection were latent in the minds of Negroes.

Advancing the view that a successful revolt could not occur in South Carolina, the chief executive called upon the legislators to declare unequivocally that they nevertheless wanted magistrates' courts to continue to have absolute control over "valuable property," unlimited by the rules which ordinarily govern judicial inquiry. But he thought it essential that the lawmakers curb the asperities which such procedural latitude was likely to produce in the trial of Negroes. He asserted that when the death sentence was pronounced under a misinterpretation of the law, the governor was required to interpose his authority. He doubted that the law prescribing penalties for insurrectionary activities among slaves was also applicable to free Negroes. Here indeed was an opinion startling in its intimation of doubt as to the validity of Vesey's execution.

Having guaranteed that his message would arouse hostile reactions among many legislators, the governor proceeded to comment on the laws pertaining to slaves. These laws, he pointed out, already provided for the summary and expeditious adjudication of slave offences, for restraints on the conduct of slaves when they were separated from the supervision of their masters, for curbs on slave spending, for restrictions on assemblages without the presence of white persons, for limits on instruction beyond what was necessary for the slave's spiritual welfare.

The trouble, therefore, said the governor, was in maladministration rather than in insufficiency of the law. He recommended making it the duty of state officers to enforce the mandate of the law, establishing a board in each parish with authority to inspect the conduct and dwellings of slaves and the economy of each plantation; requiring plantation owners to have at least one white overseer, with an additional overseer for every fifty workers; prohibiting commercial transactions by slaves except for the vending of their masters' farm produce or fish; barring slaves from engaging in any of the mechanical trades, since this practice impoverished or exiled white artisans; restricting the hiring out of slaves except under specific contracts with white persons; subjecting owners of runaway slaves (after they were absent for more than a week) to the payment of a specified sum to be used to compensate those who apprehended them and making the person of the runaway slave liable for the amount due; forbidding the use of firearms altogether by all persons of color (even though slaves' use of guns might be of convenience and profit to their owners); prescribing a penalty against proprietors of bridges and ferries for allowing slaves to proceed without proper passes.

Finally turning his attention to the growing number of free Negroes in Charleston, the governor observed that it was due to the laws and practices of neighboring states rather than to natural increase or to the ease with which slaves could obtain manumission. He proposed that the lawmakers expel all free colored persons whose presence was traceable to the prohibitory laws of other states or to their own vices. There would then be little danger from those who had accepted their freedom under the guarantees of South Carolina law. (This proposal overlooked the fact that Denmark Vesey would have fallen within the classification of those permitted to stay.)

In his conclusion, Governor Bennett devoted an aside

to the iniquities of slavery—"the evil is entailed"—but wound up on the side of a benignly maintained status quo. Partial or general emancipation, he asserted, was now out of the question. While the welfare of the slaves must be watched over "with kind solicitude," the restraints of the law must be enforced rigorously but without cruelty. In such a course of conduct lay the best answer to the uncharitable rebukes heaped on the state by outsiders who could not understand the motives of a people trapped with a system of chattel slavery.

The governor's message provoked a frenzied reaction in the legislature.[29] When it was read in the House, a profound silence at first fell over the chamber. Then heated debate broke out, with those members of the legislature who had been connected with the Vesey prosecutions feeling that they had been insulted. A suggestion that the message should be printed was greeted with a motion to the effect that the document should remain unpublished as being unsupported by the opinions of the House, as reflecting unworthily on the court, and as containing a view of the recent insurrectionary activities which was not borne out either by the law or the evidence. The motion was approved, and the message tabled.[30]

With the strident reaction to the message being reflected in the press, a correspondent of the Charleston *Mercury* braved the current of criticism and defended the governor and the offending document. [31] His effort did no good. A few days later the House by a vote of eighty to thirty-five, decided to postpone consideration of the message indefinitely.[32] Opposition to the governor among representatives from the upcountry was also strong. Even those who voted against postponement did so in the hope that the message would be referred to a select committee which would clear the court and the Charleston City Council of the imputations against them.[33]

As the governor's third and final message was delivered on December 6 with little prospect for a reconciliation between the chief executive and the legislators in view, one citizen expressed the hope that the indefinite postponement had "put a perpetual sleep to every cause of irritation" and with the election of the governor's successor (by the legislature) due the next day, Bennett would slip into a retirement more tranquil than his administration had been.[34]

Governor Bennett's retirement came in due course. The next Governor, John L. Wilson, was much more in sympathy with Vesey's prosecutors and judges than his predecessor had been. (In 1835 Wilson backed a public resolution endorsing mob burning of abolitionist papers.) But upon Bennett's withdrawal from executive office, another figure on his side of the battle still occupied a place of power. William Johnson of South Carolina held a seat on the United States Supreme Court for life. And he was not a man to subside into silence. Johnson may very well have had a part in writing the jarring Message No. 2 which his brother-in-law, the governor, had sent to the South Carolina Assembly. In any event, Johnson on December 10—while the legislature was embroiled in the Vesey controversy—wrote to Thomas Jefferson expressing many of the same sentiments that Bennett had voiced. He minimized the danger from the slave conspiracy. He scoffed at the claims of the officials who struck down the insurgents. He deplored the effect of their actions on the value of the community's walking property, on the confidence between masters and domestics, and on the equanimity of visitors to Charleston.

The Supreme Court justice attacked the "illegal mode" of the trial of the conspirators and the support of the court's methods by Attorney General Hayne. In a sorrowful and despairing vein he said to his friend at Monticello

> I have now passed my half-century, and begin to feel lonely among the men of the present day. And I am sorry to tell you, particularly so in this place. This last summer has furnished but too much cause for shame and anguish. I have lived to see what I never believed it possible I should see,— courts held with closed doors, and men dying by scores who had never seen the faces nor heard the voices of their accusers.[35]

Johnson's compassionate sentiments were in sharp contrast to the mood of the state legislators from Charleston. James Hamilton had served notice on November 30 that he would ask leave the following week to introduce a bill for the better regulation of free persons of color and Negroes and for other purposes.[36] On December 4, Hamilton, speaking for the Charleston delegation, offered legislation to prohibit the bringing of slaves into the state for sale, barter, or exchange, to provide for the better government of free Negroes and persons of color, and to banish from the state all free Negroes who had come across its borders in the past five years.[37] Acting on another bill of interest to the Charleston law-makers, a joint committee of the two houses recommended the appropriation of $100,000 to build an arsenal and citadel for the protection of the lowcountry city.[38] The citadel bill was passed and also a companion provision to establish a competent force to act as municipal guard for Charleston and its vicinity.[39] (The old Citadel building still stands today on Marion Square in Charleston, a monument to the fear that gripped the city in 1822.)

One after another, the legislature considered and adopted in some form most of the restrictive measures for which Charleston had been agitating since the Vesey trials. New regulations for the government of Negroes provided that:

No free Negro or person of color who left the state would be allowed to return.

Every free male Negro between the ages of fifteen and fifty, who was not a native or had not resided in the state for the preceding five years, would have to pay a tax of $50 a year.

Free Negro employees on any vessel coming into a South Carolina port would be imprisoned until the vessel was ready to depart, with the captain required, under pain of fine and imprisonment, to pay the expenses of detaining his employees and to take them away from the state upon leaving; otherwise they would be deemed "absolute slaves" and sold.

After June 1, 1823, every free Negro over fifteen would have to have a guardian.

No person could hire from any male slave or slaves his or their time; slaves permitted by their owners to hire out their time were made subject to seizure or forfeiture.

Persons aiding insurrection, actual or not, were to be adjudged felons and might be executed.[40]

The same session of the South Carolina Assembly which reacted to Vesey by adopting these rigorous new curbs on the Negro also recognized the insurrection leader's chief antagonist, James Hamilton, by electing him to Congress.[41] Robert Y. Hayne, state attorney general and legal supporter of the Vesey trials, was elected to the United States Senate. The only major anti-insurrection measure to fail was one which would have imposed a tax on slaves brought into the state for sale, barter, or exchange. It lost in the Senate by a vote of sixty-one to fifty-two,[42] presumably because it would have conflicted with the interests of some slave-holders. But the bulk of the delegation from Charleston, where apprehension over insurrection was now so intense, voted for the measure.

Of the various strictures adopted by South Carolina in 1822, the one that was to have the most noticeable impact was the Negro Seamen Act, not necessarily because it was the regulation which caused the most discomfort among the black targets against whom it was aimed but because it created the greatest inconvenience for white employers. Shortly after the passage of the act on December 31, 1822, the sheriff of the Charleston district or his deputies began boarding vessels as soon as they arrived in the harbor and, without presentation of any writ or allegation of crimes, proceeded to seize and forcibly remove all free Negro crew members and to lodge them in jail in the city. There these worldly-wise seamen—a class to which Denmark Vesey once belonged—could not communicate any of their poisonous ideas to the Negroes of Charleston.

Ship captains protested in vain to law enforcement

officials. Captain Jared Bunce of the Georgia packet, a vessel plying regularly between Philadelphia and Charleston, decided to take his protest to the South Carolina courts. When Andrew Fletcher, steward, and David Ayres, cook were hauled away from the packet and imprisoned, Captain Bunce sought a writ of habeas corpus and requested the judge to release the prisoners on the ground that the statute under which they had been arrested and detained was contrary to the Constitution of the United States. Upon being rebuffed by the trial court, the captain appealed to the Supreme Court of South Carolina. But that tribunal refused to interfere with the ruling below that the Negro Seaman Act was not unconstitutional.

Having failed to get his men released through the state courts, Captain Bunce, along with forty other masters of American vessels whose free Negro crew members had also been jailed, petitioned Congress for relief. Their memorial, written on February 7, 1823, reviewed the provisions of the new law and the events that had happened as a result of it, and charged that the statute violated the United States Constitution in that it destroyed "the liberty of freemen" and improperly regulated commerce by interfering with the freedom of navigation and the employment of seamen. The petitioners, therefore, asked that the government of the United States intervene in their behalf and take such measures as were necessary to free their Negro mariners from "unlawful imprisonment" and their vessels from "an enormous and unncessary expense and detention." The petition was referred to the judiciary committee of the House on February 19,[43] but no action was forthcoming.

During the same period in which the masters of American ships were being harassed by the sheriff at Charleston, the mate and four seamen of a British ship from Nassau were seized and taken to jail. After their eventual release, secured through the payment of the expenses of their imprisonment, the incident was reported to Stratford Canning, the British minister in Washington. That official sent Secretary of State John Quincy Adams a note vigorously protesting South Carolina's law and the "most grievous and extraordinary" treatment accorded His Majesty's subjects under it and requesting that the United States government move "to prevent the recurrence of any such outrage in future."[44]

Adams did not reply immediately to the British diplomat. First the Secretary of State sought out Joel R. Poinsett and James Hamilton of the South Carolina congressional delegation. Both of these men, incidentally, had been connected with the Vesey trials—Hamilton, as the leader of the prosecution and Poinsett as a judge of the second court. When apprised of Canning's note, Hamilton was reported to have responded that its language was "objectionable and not sufficiently respectful when applied to the proceedings of an Independent State.." He offered Adams little encouragement for his effort to appease the British government. Poinsett, however, was more sympathetic with the secretary's problem. He gave assurances sufficient to enable Adams on June 17 to reply to Canning, saying the United States government had taken steps to remove the cause of complaint— measures which he felt would prevent similar difficulties in the future. Whatever Poinsett or others at his behest did, South Carolina authorities for several months showed no disposition to enforce the law. Among those working behind the scenes to restrain impetuous action by South Carolina was Judge William Johnson, an intimate of Poinsett's. When American ship masters and the British consul had appealed to him for protection, he had advised them to respectfully seek relief from state officials first. This deferential approach apparently paid off temporarily.

In the meantime, however, the South Carolina Association had been formed by alarmed members of the white community to see to it that regulations against Negroes were enforced. Prodded by members of this organization, Sheriff Francis G. Deliesseline of the Charleston District in August went aboard the British vessel *Homer* and took off and imprisoned a free Negro named Henry Elkison, a Jamaican by birth and a British subject.[45] The British consul at Charleston conferred with Justice Johnson, showed him a copy of Adams' letter of June 17, and said he considered this a pledge of relief which Johnson's court was obligated to redeem. Johnson was sympathetic, and the case of Elkison was brought before him as he sat as a judge of the United States circuit court in Charleston. The attorneys who appeared to defend the Negro Seamen Act were I. E. Holmes and B. F. Hunt, representing the South Carolina Association.

In the courtroom Elkison's counsel asked Johnson to order the British seaman's release. He attacked the validity of the Negro Seamen Act, saying it interfered with the power of Congress to regulate commerce and was in direct conflict with an 1815 commercial convention between the United States and Great Britain under which the two governments had agreed to extend to each other's nationals a "reciprocal liberty of commerce." By the terms of the treaty, which the petitioner cited, the inhabitants of the two countries were to "have liberty freely and securely to come with their ships and cargoes" and to "remain and reside" in each other's ports.[46]

Rising to meet this assault on the new law, B. F. Hunt first denied that the federal court had jurisdiction to act. He then went on to argue that the act was not in conflict with the law of nations, the Constitution of the United States, or the treaty with Great Britain. He asserted that any sovereign state had the right to prohibit the entry of foreigners, and this implied a right to set the terms under which those who were admitted might remain. All that South Carolina had done, he declared, was "to require free persons of color . . . to take up their abode in a very airy and healthy part of the city" until the vessels in which they had arrived should depart. Explaining that the law was founded upon the right of self-preservation, Hunt characterized it as "a mere police regulation" in the nature of a quarantine law, and it mattered not whether the threat against which it was aimed came in the form of disease or bloodshed.

Using a form of argument that was to be stressed years later by the South Carolina nullificationists, Hunt asserted that South Carolina was a sovereign state prior to and at the time she entered the federal compact and that, as such, her right to enact laws with regard to her slave population was one which she had not surrendered to the national government.

Answering the complainant's argument as to the commercial convention, Hunt claimed that the law was not in conflict with the treaty because the latter's provision for liberty of trade was made subject to the laws of the two countries respectively. But even if the state act and the international agreement did clash, he added, the state was not bound by the latter because the treaty-making power of the United States was limited by other provisions of the Constitution and could not be used to impair rights which had been reserved to the states under Article Ten.

On August 7, 1823, before an audience of hundreds in his courtroom, Johnson responded to the challenge. As a judge, his function was not to execute the laws of the United States. But his function was to interpret and defend the Constitution. He did not propose to keep silent on the significance of the Negro Seamen Act for the federal system, even though he felt he could not grant immediate relief to the petitioner. On the matter of his own jurisdiction, the judge decided that he could not grant the writ of habeas corpus, since Congress had not authorized federal courts to issue that writ to state officers.[47] But he was certain that Elkison might obtain relief through a writ de homine replegiando issuable against a vendee of the sheriff if a seaman's counsel should decide to seek that remedy at the proper stage.

Having thus disposed of the jurisdictional question, Johnson went on to deliver an opinion that left Charleston stunned. He declared the Negro Seaman Act "unconstitutional and void" and added that every arrest under it subjected "the parties making it to an action of trespass." The judge's conclusion was based on two grounds: that the law (1) violated the commerce clause of the United States Constitution and (2) violated the treaty with Great Britain.

In examining the effect of the act on commerce, Johnson

noted that its direct aim was to bar from Carolina ports all ships employing free Negro seamen regardless of nationality. If "the color of his skin" were sufficient ground for excluding a seaman, why not "the color of his eye or his hair?" The law, he said, might as easily apply to Nantucket Indians aboard the ships of Massachusetts. Retaliation might follow and complete the destruction of Charleston's diminishing commerce.

South Carolina's assertion of so broad a power, Johnson found, collided with the "paramount and exclusive right" of the general government to regulate commerce among the sister states and with foreign nations. The Constitution, by implication, denied a concurrent power in the states to regulate commerce. The very words of the grant to Congress, said the judge, "sweep away the whole subject, and leave nothing for the states to act upon." In such a situation direct prohibition is not necessary. Here for the first time a federal judge, a Jeffersonian appointee, was finding the commerce clause a ground for invalidating state legislation, and he was doing it in language even more sweeping than that which his nationalist colleagues on the bench were to adopt later.[48]

In dealing with the relationship between the treaty and the state law, Johnson spent few words. The two nations had agreed to extend to each other's nationals a "reciprocal liberty of commerce." Secretary of State Adams, the judge observed, had assured the British government that South Carolina's interference with its treaty rights would be ended. The treaty-making power was paramount, and therefore the treaty took precedence over the state law.

Having chosen to speak so strongly against the Negro Seamen Act, Johnson was not inclined to let the arguments of the defending counsel go unnoticed. To the argument that the law was a necessary police measure, the judge responded that it had gone too far (just as he had believed earlier that the prosecution of alleged insurrectionists had gone too far). He thought that a suitable statute could have been framed to protect the state without at the same time conflicting with the Constitution and the treaty. He asked why seamen could not simply be confined to their ships if it was dangerous for them to go ashore. Such a restraint, he thought, could be lawfully exercised, since all that commerce required was the right to land, to unload and load cargoes, and to depart. By compelling the sale of stranded Negro seamen into slavery, the South Carolina law, in his opinion, actually defeated its own purpose, since it thus would permanently domesticate potential agitators.

Responding to Hunt's assertion that the state alone was the judge of the necessity of such a police measure, Johnson asked: "Where is this to land us? Is it not asserting the right of each state to throw off the federal Constitution at its will and pleasure? If it can be done as to any particular article, it may be done as to all; and like the old confederation the union becomes a mere rope of sand." William Johnson made clear that he thought too highly of the national charter to see it repudiated:

> In the Constitution of the United States, the most wonderful instrument ever drawn by the hand of man, there is a comprehension and precision that is unparalleled; and I can truly say, that after spending my life studying it, I still daily find in it some new excellence.[49]

Johnson had hardly finished delivering his opinion when it became abundantly evident that his devotion to the union was not shared by fellow Carolinians. Charleston was stirred to fury by the decision. The city's newspapers deemed the opinion so controversial that they balked at printing it, whereupon Johnson himself published it as a pamphlet and sent copies to Jefferson and to John Quincy Adams. The Secretary of State forwarded the judge's communication to President Monroe. Robert Y. Hayne, South Carolina's new U.S. Senator and erstwhile commander of the anti-Vesey military forces, became so incensed when the Johnson decision came up in conversation that his companions found it necessary to change the subject.

Meanwhile letters began appearing in the Charleston press violently attacking Johnson for betraying his native state by delivering the Elkison opinion and publishing it to the world. For two months the verbal assaults kept up, with the assailants resorting to more than a dozen pseudonyms to mask their identity. Seldom if ever (in the opinion of Johnson's biographer) has an American judge been subjected by his fellow townsmen to so sustained and acrid a torrent of criticism and abuse.

Probably the newly-organized South Carolina Association helped to inspire the attacks. It met regularly during the controversy and at one meeting recruited over a hundred new members. Robert J. Turnbull, the secretary of the association and a man who had been one of Vesey's judges, teamed up with Isaac E. Holmes, the organization's solicitor, to produce the longest of the series of hostile letters. Using the pen name "Caroliniensis," they opened their volley in the Charleston *Mercury*, an extreme states rights organ. Soon another attacker, calling himself "Zeno" and using the one-time Federalist Charleston *Courier*, joined the newspaper battle in which the arguments of the courtroom were repeated and expanded. In the scathing words of this 1823 disputation were manifested all of the seeds of nullification and secession that were to sprout in South Carolina in later years.

Johnson's critics exhibited a common fear that the government at Washington might prevent South Carolina from regulating Negroes. "Caroliniensis" declared that the greatest danger to South Carolina lay in "the free and un-interrupted ingress of a colored population into this State, from the North, and elsewhere, with their known habits, feelings and principles, animated and emboldened as they are, by the philanthropy of the day, and by the events, which Europe in its throes and convulsions casts upon mankind."[50] "Citizen by Choice" accused Johnson of opposing the continuance of slavery. "Zeno" thought that the only alternatives that the judge left to South Carolina were to alter the Constitution or to violate it, and he saw no hope of alteration by amendment. The defenders of the Negro Seamen Act evolved arguments that were later to be elaborated by John C. Calhoun: the state had ultimate sovereignty; the federal government was simply an agent of the states; when the agent exceeded his authority, the principal could disregard his acts.[51]

All of this was distressing in the extreme to Johnson. He had already written to Jefferson after the Elkison decision that in Charleston the idea of disunion, "that greatest of Evils," appeared to be losing its terrors, and informing the former President that the same men who once denounced the "self-created" Democratic societies of an earlier day were now heading a formidable one which seemed ready to go to any excess. In answering the state sovereignty argument, Johnson said it reduced the "noble" Constitution to "a mere letter of attorney." Rather than distrusting the national authorities, South Carolina, the judge pleaded, should place confidence in them. He invoked Washington's farewell address in urging that common interests bound the states and sections together.

But Johnson's pleas fell on deaf ears. Though Elkison was in time released, the federal judge's decision in the case was ignored. Negro seamen continued to spend in the jail the days their ships remained in Charleston. Johnson later complained bitterly to Adams over being obliged to see the Constitution "trampled on" by men whom he believed to be "as much influenced by the Pleasure of bringing its Functionaries into contempt by exposing their impotence as by any other consideration whatever."

Meanwhile British authorities were still highly displeased by the continuing harassment of British citizens in Charleston. H. U. Addington, British chargé d'affaires in Washington, reminded Secretary of State Adams of his promise of the previous June and asked him to take "immediate measures" to protect British subjects against the recurrence of acts so "totally at variance with the . . . Convention of 1815." The embarrassed Adams explained verbally to Addington that under the federal system indirect measures were sometimes more efficacious than "official interference." Pointing out that United States citizens had suffered greatly under the South

Carolina law and complained bitterly about it, he expressed the opinion that it was improbable that the state would refuse to grant them relief. He added, however, that if South Carolina should persist in enforcing the provisions of the act, the national government would "attack them with the arms of authority." Impressed by Adams' sincerity and having heard that several British seamen had been released from jail without any assessment of the costs of their keep, Addington let the matter drop.

In December, 1823, the South Carolina legislature, in a conciliatory mood, amended the Negro Seamen Act to eliminate the provision for the enslavement of free Negro seamen in the event that they were not carried away on their ships; instead it required that they leave the state under penalty of whipping if they should return. Free Negroes on war vessels of the United States or of foreign powers were exempted from imprisonment unless they should be found on shore after having been warned to remain on board.[52]

Despite the modification of some provisions of the 1822 law, Negro seamen continued to suffer imprisonment at Charleston. When four crew members of the British ship *Marmion* were jailed and her master was forced to pay the expenses of their detention, the incensed captain lodged a strong complaint in London. Again Adams heard from Addington, this time in the form of a note demanding "redress and reparation" and the repeal of the "obnoxious law" or at least of further modification. This protest brought a conference between Adams and President Monroe and, at the President's request, the Secretary of State sought an opinion on the South Carolina statute from Attorney General William Wirt.

Wirt, a Virginian, did not equivocate. In an opinion dated May 8, 1824 he told Adams that the Constitution of the United States conferred on Congress the exclusive power to regulate commerce and on the general government power to make treaties. Congress had exercised its power by prescribing the terms under which intercourse between the

United States and foreign nations should be carried on; the terms did not specify that vessels entering the ports of the several states should be navigated "wholly by white men." Great Britain, the nation with whom the question at issue arose, was granted by treaty rights of commerce "without any restriction as to the color of the crews" by which it was to be conducted. Despite all this, South Carolina had adopted regulations declaring in effect that what Congress had ordained might "be freely and safely done, shall not be done." and punishing that which the treaty authorized. Therefore, said Wirt, he was of the opinion that the South Carolina law was "void, as being against the constitution, treaties and laws of the United States."[53]

While Wirt's reply was being awaited, Adams, at Monroe's behest, called on the U.S. attorney in Charleston to take action which could lead to a test case in the Supreme Court. Since the American seaman who was to provide the basis for the test was released before the President's instructions were received, some other approach seemed to be indicated. Upon receipt of another complaint from Addington, Secretary Adams, speaking for the President, wrote to Governor John L. Wilson of South Carolina, in July, 1824, enclosed Wirt's opinion as well as copies of his correspondence with British authorities, and expressed the hope that the "inconvenience complained of" would be remedied by the legislature.[54] To keep the British chargé mollified, Adams then wrote him that he expected South Carolina would remove "all grounds of complaint."

If the Secretary of State was serious, he did not reckon with South Carolina's growing spirit of intransigence on matters concerning the Negro. In the interval since the passage of the Negro Seamen Act and Johnson's judicial attack on it, other events had arisen to feed the state's phobia concerning outside interference. The legislature of Georgia in December, 1823, had proposed that the federal Constitution be amended so as to leave "the importation or ingress of any person of color" into a state wholly to the laws of each state. Governor Wilson was immediately sensitive to the implication that the states did not already have this power. In 1824 a memorial by the Ohio legislature in favor of a system of gradual emancipation of the slaves stirred bitter resentment in South Carolina.

With the South Carolina slave-holders' tempers already high as a result of supposed threats from their walking property, a real show of outrage followed the receipt of the Wirt opinion and the request from Adams. Upon the convening of the legislature, Governor Wilson forwarded the letter from the Secretary of State along with the opinion of Attorney General Wirt. In a letter to the Senate, dated Nov. 25, 1824, the governor said flatly that he thought South Carolina had the right to "interdict" the entrance into her ports of persons likely to disturb "the peace and tranquility" just the same as she had the right to bar those afflicted with infectious diseases. The state alone, he added, had the power to determine what was necessary in the interests of self-preservation.[55]

A few days later Wilson's anger had mounted still higher. And in another message to the legislators he called for concerted action among the slave-holding states to meet the crisis precipitated by the President and the Attorney General who, he said, seemed disposed to use the powers of the general government to aid a foreign ministry in its fight against South Carolina. Adopting a defensive argument that was to become increasingly familiar, he said the evils of slavery had been visited upon the South by the "cupidity" of those who had become the "champions of universal emancipation." (There was no acknowledgment of the proposals by the would-be emancipators to compensate slave-owners in the course of undoing the evil.)

There must be, declared the South Carolina governor a "firm determination to resist" and to preserve the state's "sovereignty and independence." If an appeal for the right of self-government was disregarded, he concluded, "there would be more glory in forming a rampart  with our bodies on the confines of our territory, than to be victims of a successful rebellion, or the slaves of a great consolidated government."

After the receipt of this call to arms, the legislature held a spirited debate on the request to stop the incarceration of Negro seamen. Adams (now President-elect) and Wirt were criticized for their failure to champion South Carolina's law. In a display of rebellious fervor, the Senate, by a vote of thirty-six to six, adopted a resolution attacking the signs of "unconstitutional interference" with the state's Negro population and asserting that the state's duty to guard against insurrection was "paramount to all *laws*, all *treaties*, all *constitutions*," and would never be "renounced, compromised, controlled or participated with any power whatever." Though a House resolution rebuffing the appeal of the Secretary of State was milder, South Carolina had categorically rejected the effort of the federal government to assert its constitutional prerogatives of regulating commerce and conducting relations with other nations. Adams in private complained bitterly about the state's defiance of the national government.[56] Even Senator Hayne, though he did not favor yielding on the Negro Seamen Act, thought the legislature had been rather intemperate in its protest.

South Carolina continued to enforce the Negro Seamen Act against both foreign and domestic vessels. All the other Southern seaboard states in time adopted similar resolutions against Negro seamen, with Florida and Alabama apparently patterning theirs after South Carolina's. The British government was reduced to treating with the individual states, by which it sometimes gained concessions. But the United States government seemed impotent in the matter. In 1830 the discovery of an incendiary pamphlet in circulation among Carolina slaves brought more rigorous enforcement of the law against Negro seamen.

By the time of Jackson's administration, Attorney General John M. Berrien, a Georgian and a political ally of Calhoun,[57] had reversed Wirt's opinion. In 1832 Berrien's successor, Roger B. Taney, offered an opinion upholding the South Carolina law as a valid police measure despite its conflict with the treaty with Great Britain. But Taney, a Southern-sympathizer and slave-holder, felt obliged to advise the Secretary of State of the probability that, if the South Carolina Negro seamen law were taken before the Supreme Court, it would be held unconstitutional.[58] However, no such test of the law was to be permitted.

In 1835 South Carolina actually increased the severity of its statute on free black seamen by the reimposition of the provision for their enslavement under certain conditions. Massachusetts in 1844 sent Samuel Hoar as an official representative to South Carolina for the purpose of instituting suit, bringing the question of the law's constitutionality before the Supreme Court and thus protecting the interests of Massachusetts citizens being imprisoned under the act. When Hoar conveyed the purpose of his mission to Governor J. H. Hammond and the chief executive informed the legislature, that body promptly dubbed him "the emissary of a foreign government" and called upon the governor to expel him as a seditious person. Before Hammond could act, however, a mob in Charleston threatened the Massachusetts agent with violence, and he was forced to take refuge on a vessel in the harbor and return to the North. Though Massachusetts denounced the treatment of Hoar and requested Congress to protect her citizens, Congress did nothing.

In matters affecting the possible "infection" of slaves with the ideology of freedom, South Carolina was adamant. The state's demeanor of defiance toward the federal government had begun to harden with events set in motion by Denmark Vesey in 1822. Its aggressive support of the Negro Seamen Act was symbolic of the shift from nationalism to sectionalism and symptomatic of the role slavery played in that shift.

# A FUSE TO
# FORT SUMTER

● Denmark Vesey's call to arms stirred in South Carolina an intensity of feeling that helped to set the state on a determined anti-nationalist course. The Missouri debate had contributed to sectionalism. Other phenomena—relations with Haiti, the abolitionist campaign, and the tariff controversy —also propelled South Carolina away from its one-time nationalist position. But the dominant force underlying the shift was slavery. And no event in the state's experience with slavery up to that time aroused such concern over the explosive potential of the servile population as Vesey's blueprint for revolution.

South Carolina's reaction to the Vesey affair signified the choice of a way of life. The choice was to be confirmed and reinforced by other events, but only after a headstrong commitment to slavery had been adopted. Even Governor Thomas Bennett, who was not the zealot on slavery that some of his contemporaries were, had said after the Vesey commotion that "the evil [slavery] is entailed."[1] This was some years before there was any intensive abolitionist campaign to heat the tempers of slave-holders and cause them to rally behind their system in self-defense. In 1822 the abolitionist movement had hardly begun.

As early as 1820 the economic threat of protective duties had been perceived. But the tariff did not then represent the kind of immediate and personal danger which could goad public sentiment into favoring ironfisted local control of slavery and against a supposedly unsympathetic federal government. Vesey had supplied spurs for South Carolina's horsemen of neo-feudalism.[2]

As time passed, South Carolina's behavior was to show

how solidly the state had welded itself to the slave system. With her commerce declining, with her own soil exhausted from overplanting in a single crop, with her population drifting to the west where fertile new fields were being cultivated in effective competition with the worn out land of the east—South Carolina refused to face the changed conditions. The state ignored warnings against wasting her soil, advice to fight tariff discrimination by adopting varied industry. Instead South Carolina clung to the vision of a one-crop economy based on slaves and supporting an aristocracy of planters in baronial splendor.

It was a chimerical dream and should have been discernable as such. But the Palmetto State was to devote its energies for a generation to defending the delusion. Preoccupied with the wrongs being visited on her by the North, South Carolina insisted on employing ill-adapted political weapons to defend an obsolescent economic order. In the process, the state acquired a persecution complex and became combative and intolerant of dissent, particularly on slavery. As one of the most respected South Carolina historians has put it: "Her thinkers became attorneys in a case, not seekers for essential truth in social and political relations . . . [they] expended vast resources in the defense of an impossible program in which success would have been the greatest calamity."[3] During this period the South Carolina mind—in the phrase of another native authority—became a foetus in a bottle.[4]

While no date can be designated as the one clearly marking South Carolina's turn against the union, it is clear that as late as 1821 there was considerable evidence in the state of nationalistic sentiment and little evidence that the proponents of such views suffered for it. In 1819 President Monroe, accompanied by Calhoun in a tour of the South, had been enthusiastically welcomed in Charleston, as well as in the rest of South Carolina. (This was before the Virginia President had incurred the ire of South Carolina by opposing its Negro Seamen Act.) That same year Judge Abraham Nott of the South Carolina Appellate Court had, without undue repercussion, used the vehicle of a minority opinion to deride the notion that a lower echelon of government could in effect nullify an act of Congress—in this case an enactment on the United States Bank. Judge Nott observed that to give a government the power to legislate and one of its branches the power to defeat its legislative acts "would be like harnessing horses to the hindmost part of the carriage to check the impetuosity of those in front."[5]

In 1820 the state House of Representatives was still acknowledging the supremacy of the general government. The next year George McDuffie, who was to become one of the fiercest of the states' righters, declared that if a law, after its constitutionality had been affirmed by the national judiciary, was still to be resisted by state rulers, then "the Constitution is literally at an end; a revolution of the government is already accomplished; and anarchy waves his horrid sceptre over the broken altars of this happy Union." The general government, he added with assurance, "is not an object of dread." These views were enthusiastically endorsed by none other than James Hamilton.[6] This was the year before the Vesey outbreak.

It was in 1822 that a diplomatic communication fired fears and antipathies already simmering among slave-holders as a result of the Vesey controversy. President Jean-Pierre Boyer of Haiti in that year called upon the United States to be the first power to recognize the second republic of the New World. There had been a phase in the early history of the Negro republic suggesting that such a gesture from the United States might not be entirely unthinkable. In 1799 the Adams administration had actually negotiated a secret agreement with Toussaint L'Ouverture, the leader of the Haitian Negroes, as part of an American effort to check the French in the New World. At one point the American navy even took part in the Haitian civil war by aiding Toussaint against his mulatto opponents. Though America's peculiar relationship with Toussaint was ended when Jefferson became President, the United States government still felt that the Negro nation was less of a menace in the Caribbean than Napoleon.[7]

Though Southern states were alarmed from the beginning over the implications of the Negro rebellion in St. Domingue, they had for a time allowed trading to continue between their ports and the Caribbean isle.[8] As time passed, however, the South became increasingly uncomfortable about maintaining any ties with the Negro republic. Ships trading between Haiti and the United States went mostly to Northern ports. As it became evident that France would not reestablish dominion over its Caribbean colony, representatives of the mercantile interests of the northeast were ready to recognize Haitian independence in order to further their trade. But the planter interests of the South were in no mood to make a deal with the new Negro nation. Their opposition became even more inflexible following the Vesey furor in South Carolina. They knew that Denmark Vesey himself had spent some time on the West Indian island and that there was reportedly communication between Haitians and the South Carolina insurgents. Santo Domingo (as the South Carolinians called it) had been mentioned more than a dozen times during the Vesey trials.[9] When President Boyer's appeal for recognition came, President Monroe (who as governor of Virginia had had an experience with an insurrection) rejected the overture, observing that is was the policy of the United States government to guard against anything which might disturb the tranquility of any portion of the Union.

Four years later the halls of Congress were still far from tranquil on the subject of Haiti. Colombia, which had refused recognition to Haiti, was proposing a uniform American rule of conduct toward the Negro republic. For Senator Hayne, whose experience with insurrectionists had been much more recent and personal than Monroe's, there could be only one way of looking at the question: "With nothing connected with slavery can we treat with other nations. . . . Our policy with regard to Haiti is plain. We never can acknowledge her independence." Hayne even went on to assert that the United States must "protest against the Independence of Haiti," because "you find men of color at the head of her armies, in the legislative halls and executive departments."[10] The South Carolina senator would not even approve American participation in a Panama Congress in 1826 because it would mean association with Haiti. He visualized a possible impingement on the South's peculiar institution. "The very day the unhallowed attempt is made [to interfere with our domestic concerns] by the authorities of the federal government," he declared, "we will consider ourselves as driven from the Union.[11]

With the receipt of a message from the Ohio legislature in 1824, South Carolina got an early taste of a movement that was to progressively embitter its relations with the Union. The idea behind the message, which Ohio was circulating to Congress and to the legislatures of the several states, was simple: Congress would enact a law "with the consent of the slave-holding states," under which all children of slaves, upon reaching the age of twenty-one would become free, provided they consented to be transported to a place of colonization. The approach to implementation was temperate in tone: emancipation was to be "gradual." The evil of slavery was admitted to be "national." And the duties and burdens of removing it were said to be an obligation of the people of all the states.[12]

However unfeasible the Ohio colonization plan may have been (and such a proposal certainly had drawbacks), it was not advanced in a provocative way. But South Carolina would not even consider it. The state Senate adopted a resolution denying that the United States had any right to interfere "in any manner whatever" with the state's slave property. The House informed Ohio that the people of the state would adhere to a system "descended to them from their ancestors, and now inseparably connected with their social and political existence."[13]

In the halls of Congress in 1825 South Carolina's Senator Hayne opposed an emancipation resolution even though it employed a formula dear to the hearts of states' righters. Senator King of New York proposed that a fund, created from the sale of public land, be set up to aid the emancipation and removal of such slaves as *by the law of the states* respectively may be allowed to be emancipated and removed. But Hayne denied that Congress had such power and asserted that the proposed measure would be dangerous to the safety of the states holding slaves. Hayne's biographer notes that the senator had occasion to remember that Senator King in earlier speeches had inspired Vesey.

Confronted with the failure of such mild proposals for emancipation, the antislavery movement in time advanced more uncompromising measures. And as the crusading spirit of the abolitionists mounted, the reaction in the South became more violent. Antislavery Southerners began to find their home atmosphere so hostile to their viewpoint that after 1820 a steady stream of them migrated to the North, where often they guided the attack on the system that had led to their exile. By the middle of the 1820's there were almost no voices for abolution in South Carolina, and those that were lifted spoke in muted tones. The Vesey explosion helped to silence free expression on slavery.[14]

As the resistance of the slave-holders mounted, the abolitionist campaign became more direct in its approach, more refined in technique. Through the means of simple texts and crude pictures, the message was conveyed to unlettered slaves that they were being held in unjust bondage and that thousands of white friends in the North were working for their deliverance. As the antislavery drive gathered momentum, the volume of abolitionist literature rose. Frightened by the possibility that this tinder would ignite a slave revolt, the South reacted with fury.

During the summer of 1835 Charleston displayed the mood of the white South. In July thousands of copies of abolitionist tracts and pictures were brought by ship from New York. Though the material was addressed to respectable citizens, including clergymen of all denominations, the Charleston postmaster immediately impounded it pending

instructions from the Postmaster General. A mob gathered
and was finally persuaded to disperse by the assurance that
the tracts would be delivered only on orders from Washington.
But that night vigilantes took the issue out of the hands of
the authorities. They broke into the post office, seized the
offending matter, and burned it in the street. Charleston was
so aroused that a special citizens' committee of twenty-one
was organized to restore public confidence. For several weeks
the administration of the city was virtually controlled by a
five-man subcommittee headed by Robert Y. Hayne.

Apprised of the episode in Charleston, Postmaster General Amos Kendall called the papers involved "most flagi-
tous" and privately advised Southern postmasters to intercept
all such matter in the future and to deliver it only to those
who would come forward and identify themselves as bona
fide subscribers. But as a long-range solution, Kendall asked
that the Post Office Department be given specific authority
to bar incendiary publications from the mails. The states'
righters, led by John C. Calhoun, wanted no such remedy.
Not only did they doubt that the national government would
protect the South, but they also were afraid that the requested
power might be used as a two-edged sword to bar the
Charleston *Mercury* as well as Garrison's *Liberator*. Their
counter-proposal—in the form of a bill drafted by Calhoun—
was that postmasters should be forbidden to accept for
transmission to any state, or to deliver if received, any
publication prohibited by the laws of the particular state.
The general government was to enforce the law, but each
state was to decide for itself what matter was fit for its
citizens to read.

Calhoun argued that the authority of Congress extended
only to assisting upon request in the enforcement of any
legitimate law. Only the states, he contended, could be trusted
to decide for themselves what papers and pictures were
dangerous to their security. Warning of the tendency of
abolitionist literature to incite servile revolt, Calhoun observed that its long-range effect would be to set one section
against the other and destroy the union. His remedy was that

the South be left alone with its servile population which, after all, was simply an embodiment of a condition that existed in every civilized community where one portion lived on the labor of another.

Calhoun's bill failed. But this did not prevent Southerners from taking the law into their own hands when dealing with abolitionists. In 1836 the American Anti-Slavery Society published a pamphlet, *Appeal to the Christian Women of the South*, by Angelina Grimké, a native of Charleston then living in Philadelphia. The tract was publicly burned by postmasters in the South. Charleston police were ordered to prevent Angelina Grimké from landing or, if she landed, to arrest her. She was threatened with mob violence if she should return to her native city.[15] This was during the administration of Governor George McDuffie who the year before had held that no institution bore more expressly the marks of divine approval than slavery. Instead of being evil, he maintained, it was the cornerstone of the republic; emancipation, however remote and regardless of whether financially compensated for, could not be considered; agitators of abolition should be executed.

McDuffie's views had become the rationale of the state. Some South Carolinians—such as William DeSaussure, William C. Preston, Professor Francis Lieber of the South Carolina College, and Professor Josiah Nott—continued to express disapproval of slavery. But their voices were drowned in the tide of pro-slavery agitation. Robert Barnwell Rhett, a young radical politician, defended slavery as best for both slave and master. In 1837 Chancellor William Harper praised the institution as the buttress of morals. In 1845 James Hammond, addressing himself to the abolitionists, wrote:

> But if your course was wholly different—if you distilled nectar from your lips and discoursed sweetest music, could you reasonably indulge the hope of accomplishing your object by such means? Nay, supposing that we were all convinced, and thought of Slavery precisely as you do, at what era of "moral suasion" do you imagine you could prevail on

us to give up a thousand millions of dollars in the value of our slaves, and a thousand millions of dollars more in the depreciation of our lands, in consequence of the want of laborers to cultivate them?[16]

Meanwhile the abolitionists pressed their campaign with increasing zeal. Among them the Vesey story became well known, and one observer has even suggested that it gave John Brown his idea of how to arm rebel slaves.[17] In the literature of abolition, accounts of Vesey's movement were offered as evidence of the Negro's valiant fight in his own behalf. One account, published in London in 1847, hailed Vesey and his fellow insurgents as "patriots," and, while acknowledging that their plan was "most bloody and savage," asked what else could be expected "under such oppression and tyranny." The author went on to express the certainty that sooner or later Vesey's purpose would be accomplished.[18] Another pamphlet, written by a Negro and published in 1850, dubbed Vesey and his followers as patriots, damned his prosecutors for their despotism and for the "solemn farce" of a trial by which they sought to terrify slaves.[19]

Down to the time of the Civil War the emancipation crusade continued, with one particularly telling shaft being aimed at South Carolina from a Southerner, a resident of neighboring North Carolina. Hinton Rowan Helper, the son of a poor North Carolina farmer, became a nationally known figure in 1857 with the publication of his book, *The Impending Crisis of the South*. The method of the book was to quote census figures to show that in manufacturing products, commerce, and wealth, in schools, libraries, and newspapers the North outdistanced the South, that even in agriculture the North outdid the South. Helper saw slavery as the cause of these disparities. Though his thesis was abolition, his chief concern was with what slavery did to the poor Southern white. His ire against the slave-holders was so deep that he, by implication, encouraged Negroes to massacre them at night.[20]

Aiming his rhetorical arrow to the south, Helper let go:

> Poor South Carolina! Folly is her nightcap; fanaticism
> is her day-dream; fire-eating is her pastime. She has lost her
> better judgment; the dictates of reason and philosophy have
> no influence upon her actions . . . she still clings, with un-
> abated love, to the cause of her shame, her misery and her
> degradation.

Observing that New Jersey's land area, though less than
one-third the acreage of South Carolina's, had an assessed
valuation nearly seven times as great—Helper called on the
"Slavocrats" to glean a ray of wisdom from his figures, to
substitute freedom for slavery, and to raise South Carolina
from its "loathesome sink of iniquity" to the high level of
"one of the most brilliant stars in the great constellation of
States."[21]

All of the advice of this kind, of course, fell on deaf ears.
South Carolina became ever more deeply enmeshed in the
slave system. In 1841 a law had been passed forbidding the
sending of a slave abroad to make him free. By 1850 the
state had 140 Negroes to every 100 whites, a higher ratio
than any other state. Nearly 50 per cent of the white population belonged to slave-owning families (again a higher proportion than any other state), though only 18.78 per cent
of the population belonged to families owning twenty or
more slaves. While there were occasional pleas for the
amelioration of the system of slave justice, courts of magistrates and freeholders continued to exercise, by a majority
vote, life and death power over Negroes.

As South Carolina's economic decline had set in during
the second decade of the nineteenth century, the planters
and politicians of the state refused to face the fundamental
reasons for the distress—the overproduction of cotton,
which pushed the price down, and the state's almost
complete dependence on a wasteful, land-destroying one-
crop economy. They ignored far-sighted advocates of a
shift toward manufacturing. Instead the state's spokesmen looked for causes to blame for South Carolina's
economic adversity. They deplored the emigration of South

Carolinians to other states. This, however, was an effect and not a cause of conditions. They turned to the tariff. With an average rate in 1824 that had almost doubled since 1816, the tariff was a real enough ground for grievance; the cost of commodities which South Carolina purchased went up while the price of cotton was going down. But real as its disadvantages were, the tariff was exaggerated as a basic source of depressed conditions.[22]

Better than anything else, the tariff provided a convenient butt of attack for those who resisted change and regarded slave-based agriculture as the only system suitable for supporting the gentry of South Carolina. It is significant, however, that even the protective tariff system in its early stages, before it was visualized as a threat to slavery, did not provoke the extremism that more clearly recognized dangers to the institution aroused. When slavery was directly at stake, South Carolinians were immediately and vocally anti-nationalist. The same was not true of the tariff issue before it became closely linked to slavery.

In 1820 the state House of Representatives adopted a resolution which deprecated the system of protection as premature and pernicious. But the statement also admitted that Congress possessed the power to enact all laws relating to commerce and deplored the practice of "arraying upon the questions of national policy the states as distinct and independent sovereignties in opposition to, or (what is much the same thing), with a view to exercising control over the general government."[23]

Four years later South Carolina's Robert Y. Hayne rose on the Senate floor and launched a broad attack on the 1824 tariff bill. It was a speech that was moderate in tone, however, and in noticeable contrast to Hayne's frequent sharp words on the slavery issue. While Congressman McDuffie also opposed the tariff of 1824, it is worth noting that in the same year he repudiated the notion that the state governments were "in any respect more worthy of confidence than the general government." In 1824 the state Senate resolved that protective tariffs were unconstitutional, but the House received a committee report denying the right of the legislature to impugn the constitutionality of acts of Congress or decisions of the Supreme Court.[24]

Obviously, where the tariff was concerned, South Carolinians at this time hardly spoke in as unified and uncompromising a voice as they did on slavery. Though the tariff has frequently been given as the cause of the first clash between South Carolina and the union,[25] slavery was actually the first ground for collision and a more fundamental cause of continuing conflict. On an issue that touched slavery, the Negro Seamen Act of 1822, South Carolina openly defied the federal government nine years before the tariff became a pretext for such defiance. Not until the session convening in 1825 did the state's legislature become the forum for a set of really strong anti-tariff resolutions.[26]

As the controversy on the tariff developed, the debate became inextricably tied to slavery. And South Carolina's stance, once the interrelated questions of slavery and the tariff were yoked together, became ever more inflexible. In 1827 a pro-tariff convention in Harrisburg Pennsylvania, memorialized Congress for higher protective duties on a long series of commodities, including cotton goods. The Harrisburg movement prompted a new wave of protests from the South, including a series of articles in the Charleston *Mercury* by Robert J. Turnbull. Signing himself "Brutus," Turnbull not only denounced the protective tariff but carried his recommendations for defending the South to the threshold of armed resistance. His articles, republished the next year in pamphlet form under the title of *The Crisis*, formulated the theory of nullification in all but name and were to become a textbook for disunion. The federal Constitution, said Turnbull, was simply a compact between the states and the federal government merely their agent; between the sovereign states, he contended, there could be no arbiter. In a series of articles in the Charleston *Courier* replying to Turnbull, Justice William Johnson perceived the true meaning of Turnbull's stand. Significantly signing himself "Hamilton," Johnson insisted that Turnbull's doctrine could lead only to sectional discord and war. It was not the tariff principle, asserted Johnson, but the system of slavery that constituted the greatest threat to the union.

Johnson had good reason to be wary of Turnbull. The fiery Turnbull had been one of those who in 1823 had insisted that, with respect to the validity of the Negro Seamen Act (which Johnson had declared unconstitutional), South Carolina had the right to exercise final judgment and to continue to enforce it. Johnson had taken Turnbull to task then. To Turnbull, however, the Southern system, with its foundation of slavery, was unimpeachable. He had sat on the first Vesey court in 1822 and the same year had been a contributor to E. C. Holland's treatise in defense of slavery.[27] He was one of those who supported slavery as a moral good.

Turnbull's 1827 manifesto acted like a bugle call on the South. Taking their cue from him, South Carolinians called mass meetings and sent up memorials against the tariff from 1827 onward. James Hamilton, Turnbull's fellow townsman and political ally, was reputed to be the first speaker to proclaim nullification by name from the stump (October 21, 1828). The tariff act of 1828 stirred violent resentment in South Carolina. One response was the famous "South Carolina Protest," based on an "Exposition" privately drafted by Vice President John C. Calhoun. Though Calhoun brought his own dialectical skill to this delineation of nullification, the theory, now refined by the Vice President, had been anticipated by Turnbull whose earlier *Crisis* articles Calhoun had read eagerly and with approval.[28] In the "Protest," adopted by the legislature, South Carolina made clear that it had cast its lot unreservedly with slavery. Because of the state's climate, situation, and peculiar institutions, the document said, South Carolina "must ever continue to be" wholly dependent upon agriculture; and for the blessings of its system, the state must have slave labor.[29] In 1828 Hamilton declared that South Carolina could not be coerced and that persistence in protection against imports would result in dissolution of the union, all of which was endorsed by McDuffie.

From the strong words of 1828, South Carolina proceeded relentlessly down the path toward action against the national government. In 1830 came the historic Hayne-Webster debate which gave widespread advertisement to the doctrine of nullification. Hayne in that forensic encounter not only gave impetus to disunion but also committed South Carolina more firmly to slavery by expatiating on that system's beneficial influences on individual and national character. In 1831, in his Fort Hill Address, Calhoun for the first time openly identified himself with nullification, defending the doctrine in an appeal that summoned the spirit of Jefferson and spoke of rights and liberties, but which was clearly intended to buttress the economic position of a slave-holding oligarchy rather than to extend Jefferson's objective of freedom for the individual to speak and write and worship as he pleased.[30]

By the spring of 1831 the nullifiers—with James Hamilton, now governor of South Carolina, taking the lead—began laying their strategy for a showdown with the federal government on the tariff. Their plan was to secure in the 1832 elections a majority in the legislature which would favor the calling of a nullification convention. The campaign which followed produced a bitter division in the state between nullifiers and unionists, with the unionists making their strongest showing in the northern districts of the state where slavery was less pervasive. While the nullifiers had a popular vote lead of only 23,000 to 17,000, they won an overwhelming majority of seats in both houses because of the disproportionate representation which the state constitution gave to slave-holding districts.[31]

Having prepared the ground for a challenge to the federal government, Governor Hamilton summoned a special session of the legislature, which called a convention for November 19, 1832, to consider the acts of Congress for protective duties on imports and to devise means of redress. Each district in the state was assigned a number of delegates equal to its representatives in both houses of the legislature. From the upper part of the state came demands that the convention represent only the white people of South Carolina and not "the silent Negro vote" of twelve parishes casting fewer than 150 votes each and three parishes with fewer than fifty votes each. The "silent Negro vote," of course, was reflected in the apportionment of seats partially on the basis of taxable property (including slaves), thus giving the parishes of big slave-holders a legislative voice considerably stronger in relation to their numbers of actual voters than the voices of the less affluent parishes. The Camden *Journal* showed its resentment at this over-representation of slave interests: "The oppression of a tariff, liable to repeal every year, is a trifle to the degrading and overbearing usurpation of these Parish nobility. They ought to be *nullified . . .*"[32] This heretical protest got lost in the general outcry against the general government.

When the convention met, Governor Hamilton was elected its president and a Committee of Twenty-One was appointed to draft an Ordinance of Nullification. Within three days the committee had completed its assignment and, besides the ordinance itself, offered the convention three documents to justify the course South Carolina proposed to take: an Address to the People of South Carolina, drafted by Robert J. Turnbull; an Address to the People of the United States, drafted by George McDuffie; and a Report, prepared by Robert Y. Hayne, which reflected the tone of the proceedings by declaring that South Carolina recognized "no tribunal upon earth above her authority." The Ordinance of Nullification, drafted by Chancellor William Harper, declared the tariffs of 1828 and 1832 to be null and void, prohibited the collection within the state of duties levied under them, prescribed for all civil and military officers of the state an oath to enforce the ordinance and all laws supporting it, provided that no appeal could be taken to the Supreme Court of the United States, and announced that the use of force by the federal government would be looked upon as dissolving the bonds of union between South Carolina and the other states.

The ordinance was adopted by the convention on

November 24, 1832. Meeting in regular session immediately afterward, the legislature enacted the laws necessary to put the ordinance into effect and to organize the state for forceful resistance. Hayne was elected governor; Calhoun was chosen to replace Hayne in the United States Senate, with Hamilton being kept in reserve for military command in the event of armed conflict. The militia was reorganized.

By this time the unionists in the state had been brought face to face with a distressing dilemma. Having been defeated in the elections and in the convention, where their representatives opposed nullification, they were forced to choose between repudiating their convictions or incurring the risk of being declared traitors by their own state. They had already been brought to the point of upholding a protectionist policy in order to defend their position. Meeting in convention on December 1, the unionists were outspoken in opposition to the state's defiant actions and declared their determination, if necessary, to defend their rights by arms.

Meanwhile President Jackson was preparing to enforce the laws, by military means if the need arose. Put on notice by Joel R. Poinsett, the leader of the South Carolina unionists, of the need for firm measures to suppress the insurrection, Jackson ordered the forts in Charleston harbor defended "to the last extremity." To underscore his meaning, he dispatched seven revenue cutters and a ship of war to Charleston, where, upon their arrival, they anchored off the Battery, their guns within point-blank range of the waterfront homes of the city's elite. On December 2 the President wrote to Poinsett that nullification meant "insurrection" and that the other states had a right to put it down. He assured the unionist leader that within forty days he could have 50,000 men in South Carolina.

Eight days later (December 10) Jackson issued his unequivocal proclamation to the people of South Carolina. The power to annul a law, he declared, was "incompatible with the existence of the Union, contradicted expressly by the letter of the Constitution, unauthorized by its spirit, inconsistent with every principle on which it was founded, and

destructive of the great object for which it was formed."
Asserting that disunion by armed force was treason, the
President warned the citizens of his native state that if they
embarked on such a course they would be punished.[33]

The white insurrectionists in South Carolina were not
deterred. Governor Hayne in a counter proclamation called
for a mobilization of 10,000 citizens to repel invasion[34] and
pledged himself to maintain the sovereignty of South Carolina
or perish "beneath its ruins." The legislature, seeing the
"liberties of the people" threatened, resolved to repel "force
by force."[35] Proffers of military service poured in upon the
governor. Meanwhile Poinsett—maintaining contact with
Jackson by courier, since the Charleston post office was in
the hands of the nullifiers—armed his unionist supporters
and drilled them at night.

Anticipating South Carolina's preparations for conflict,
Jackson was determined to be better prepared. In mid-
December he wrote to Martin Van Buren that if the South
Carolina Assembly authorized 12,000 men to resist the law,
he would order 30,000 to execute it. On Christmas day he
wrote the same correspondent that the leaders of nullification would be seized wherever found, regardless of the force
that surrounded them, and delivered "into the hands of the
judicial authority of the United States" to be tried for treason.

Late in December, in keeping with Jackson's previous
commitment to a lower tariff and with a promise implied in
his proclamation, an administration bill was introduced in
the House to reduce drastically the existing protective
duties. As Congress was discussing tariff reduction, the nullifiers held a mass meeting in Charleston on January 21, 1833,
and, pending the outcome of the congressional debate, suspended their ordinance which had been scheduled to take
effect on February 1. Jackson meanwhile was becoming
even more impatient. He had said he would suspend positive
action until he received certified copies of the acts of the
South Carolina legislature giving effect to the ordinance of
nullification. When on January 16 he had still not received
the official copies, he proceeded to ask Congress for authority

to use military force to collect the customs, though he steadfastly maintained that he already had such power. On January 24, with Congress apparently unlikely to agree on the so-called "force bill" by the February 1 deadline, Jackson sent off a hurried personal note to Poinsett informing him that if Congress failed to act, he (Jackson) would nevertheless have 200,000 men in the field in forty days "to quell any and every insurrection that might arise." Soon afterward Jackson received word of the suspension of the belligerent ordinance.

Still defiant, James Hamilton, as president of the nullification body, threatened to reassemble the convention for the purpose of secession if the "force bill" should pass. But Andrew Jackson insisted on passage. In the midst of the parliamentary maneuvering over the administration's "force bill" and tariff reduction legislation, Henry Clay offered a compromise tariff measure. Though Clay's bill actually offered less than the administration bill, it enabled Calhoun, by now Jackson's arch political enemy, to save face. Clay's tariff bill, supported by Calhoun, and Jackson's force bill, which Calhoun said would be resisted to the death, reached the ends of their legislative journeys the same day. Neither Calhoun nor Hamilton carried out their threats. On March 15 South Carolina rescinded the ordinance nullifying the tariff and three days later nullified the force act. It was an empty gesture. The national crisis was over, though South Carolina for nearly two years hovered on the brink of civil war between its nullification and its unionist factions.

The nullification controversy, while it concerned the tariff, helped to reveal the more fundamental issues underlying the national dichotomy. Andrew Jackson, though no abolitionist, saw slavery as the real issue and secession and the formation of a Southern confederacy as the nullifiers' real objective. Nullification, however camouflaged at first, was devised as a political defense of slavery, as was the whole arsenal of so-called state rights. In South Carolina the strongest support for the union came significantly from those areas where slavery was less prevalent.

In the factional line-up in South Carolina, the nullifiers, on the one hand, revealed themselves to be the more parochial in outlook, the more extreme in their defense of slavery—often going to the point of pronouncing it a moral good—and the more inflexible in their political views. The unionists, on the other hand, though not advocates of emancipation, were more moderate in their opinions on slavery and politics.

It is significant that during the showdown on the tariff in 1832-33 those who led South Carolina to the firing line of insurrection were men who had played key roles in suppressing Vesey's insurrection of 1822 and who in the wake of that event had had a dress rehearsal in nullification when they virtually set aside a United States commercial convention with Great Britain and overrode federal protests in their enforcement of the state's Negro Seamen Act. Their success then was enough to embolden them for later efforts.

In 1822 James Hamilton had been the chief prosecutor of Denmark Vesey and had sponsored the new Negro-control measures which the legislature adopted as a result of the Vesey affair. The next year, while in Congress, he was antagonistic to federal efforts to get South Carolina to respect the rights of Great Britain in enforcing the Negro Seamen Act. By 1828 he was publicly advocating nullification of the tariff. In 1832 James Hamilton, as governor, called the special session of the legislature which created the nullification convention. Hamilton then became president of the convention and shortly afterward resigned the governorship in order to be ready to lead his state's military forces against the United States.

In 1822 Robert Y. Hayne had commanded the military forces mobilized to check Vesey, had sat on the second court for the trial of insurgents, and had upheld the legality of the Vesey prosecution. The next year Hayne had been vehement in his criticism of Justice William Johnson for daring to question the validity of the Negro Seamen Act. In his debate with Webster in 1830 Hayne, of course, had become South Carolina's champion of nullification in the

United States Senate. In 1832 Robert Y. Hayne became governor and the leader of the state's drive to upset the protective tariff, by force if necessary.

In 1822 Robert Turnbull had been a member of the court which tried Denmark Vesey. The next year he had violently assailed Justice Johnson for condemning the Negro Seamen Act and had become secretary of the South Carolina Association which was organized to see that the act was enforced. It was Turnbull who in 1827 sounded the tocsin of disunion with his *Crisis* articles in the Charleston *Mercury*. In 1832 Robert J. Turnbull took a leading part in the nullification convention. The next year, when he died, he was dubbed the real father of nullification and the leading states' righters eulogized him as such.

Also among the leading nullifiers of 1832-33 was Nathaniel Heyward. When he died in 1851 he was probably the richest man in South Carolina, his property including sixteen plantations and 1,843 slaves. His annual income had once run as high as $120,000. In 1822 Heyward had sat on the tribunal which tried Denmark Vesey.

Even Calhoun, the leading theoretician and the political general of the nullifiers in the 1830's had had a role in the 1822 controversy. As Secretary of War, he had sent federal troops to relieve South Carolina's anxiety.

In contrast to the nullifiers, the South Carolina unionists, even though some of them had participated in the Vesey proceedings, had been less excited by them, less rigid in their views on the Negro, and less adamant in their commitment to the slave system. In addition to Poinsett, leading unionists of the 1830's included Justice William Johnson, his brother Dr. Joseph Johnson, ex-Governor Thomas Bennett, Benjamin F. Perry, Christopher G. Memminger, and Hugh S. Legare. Justice Johnson and Governor Bennett, of course, had tried to exert a moderating influence in the Vesey excitement. The others displayed their independence of South Carolina orthodoxy later. During the 1844 furor over Samuel Hoar's attempt to obtain a legal test of the Negro Seamen Act, Perry and Memminger were to be the only legislators to vote against resolutions calling Hoar an "emmissary of a foreign government" (Massachusetts) hostile to South Carolina's domestic institutions, an agent who came to the state to subvert its "internal peace." Hugh S. Legare, as Attorney General of the United States, was to offer the official opinion in 1843 that free Negroes enjoyed the same civil rights as white men.

Poinsett, the leading unionist, was a world traveler and, though he accepted slavery, he was sophisticated enough not to be intellectually chained to the system. In 1822 he sat on the court which tried the second set of Vesey conspirators. But the next year he was one of those few South Carolinians (William Johnson was another) who urged respect for the rights of British sailors in the enforcement of the Negro Seamen Act. Poinsett was one of those far-sighted citizens who advised South Carolina to abandon its dependence on cotton alone. It was Poinsett (who died in 1851) who prophetically warned his fellow South Carolinians that secession would "lead to immediate civil war and . . . probably terminate in defeat and humiliation."[36]

South Carolina refused to learn the lessons which the unionists had striven to teach during the dispute over the tariff: that a nation could not exist with its constituent parts taking nullification to its logical conclusion; the federal judiciary, they insisted was the great arbiter between the natonal and state govermnents. Without such an instrument to apply a unifying cement of law, they saw only confusion. One of the unionists, an attorney, summed up the point succinctly when he called nullification "anarchy reduced to system." Even the nullifiers, in their more lucid moments, recognized nullification as a mere step along the road toward dissolution of the union. McDuffie supported nullification as an act of sovereignty but scoffed at it as a constitutional measure.

After 1833 South Carolina moved inexorably, if erratically, down the road to secession. As ardent as some of the nullifiers were for secession during the tariff fight, the time was obviously not then ripe. The state still had a vocal unionist minority and was isolated from the rest of the South. Though there was sympathy in other Southern states, South Carolina in 1832-33 didn't have the declared support of any of them. Virginia urged South Carolina to rescind the ordinance and offered to mediate. Jackson had said at the height of the controversy that he had a tender of volunteers from every state in the union and that the national voice from Maine to Florida had consigned nullification and secession to "contempt and infamy."

Realizing that they were not ready, the dedicated defenders of slavery set out to win support for a cause which some of them acknowledged to involve the prospect of secession and conflict. South Carolina became known as "the Hotspur State." A new generation arose to replace the older one whose rashness had been restrained slightly at least by its links with a time when North and South had worked together to create a nation and had fought against a common external enemy. Members of the new generation symbolized the proposition that Governor Robert Y. Hayne had expressed in 1833 when he said that societies based on slavery were strong for war. The hottest of the South Carolina firebrands was Robert Barnwell Rhett who, soon after the tariff compromise of 1833, was damning it with faint praise, calling for a confederacy of Southern states and asserting that South Carolina had no rights under the United States government "but what she was prepared to assert in the tented field." A people owning slaves, said Rhett, "are mad, or worse than mad, who do not hold their destinies in their own hands."[37]

Francis W. Pickens, another of the rising radicals of the 1830's and a man who was to be South Carolina's first Civil War governor, declared at the time of the tariff dispute: "I am for any extreme, even 'war up to the hilt,' rather than go down to infamy and slavery 'with a government of unlimited powers.' "[38] In a legislative debate in 1833 over a planned "test oath" in which militia officers would be required to swear allegiance to the state, a committee chaired by Pickens brought in a report upholding the need for such military loyalty and pointing to slavery as the ultimate issue. "We have a peculiar and local institution of our own," said the Pickens committee. "The law of State sovereignty is with us the law of State existence."

From 1832 to 1860, said D. D. Wallace, leading authority on the state's history, South Carolina was in effect not so much a part of the country "as a dissatisfied ally, for the last thirteen years of the period only awaiting a favorable opportunity to dissolve the alliance."[39] During the pre-Civil War generation there were times when South Carolina found itself in step with the nation, as when Calhoun assumed the secretaryship of state in order to effect the annexation of Texas as a slave state. But the era was punctuated by events indicating South Carolina's extreme dissatisfaction with the union. The state's leaders talked of nullifying the tariff of 1842. Upon the proposal of the Wilmot Proviso which would have barred slavery from the area acquired from Mexico, South Carolina adopted the attitude that exclusion from the territories would mean dissolution of the union. Dissatisfied with the Clay compromise of 1850 on the admission of new territory, Calhoun just before his death wrote despairingly to J. H. Hammond that the impression was general that "disunion is the only alternative that is left to us." Hammond replied in language that revealed the thoughts that were always uppermost in the minds of leaders of the slave states:

> We must act *now*, and decisively. . . . Long before the North gets this vast accession of strength she will ride over us rough shod, proclaim freedom or something equivalent to it to our slaves and reduce us to the condition of Hayti. . . . If we do not act now, we deliberately consign, not our posterity, but our *children*, to the flames.[40]

South Carolina seriously considered secession between 1850 and 1852. The main factor which held her back was the unwillingness of other Southern states at that time to go along. As the state became more immersed in the slavery controversy with the North, the internal opposition of the unionists all but disappeared. Nevertheless, class dissension over the issue of slavery continued to crop out. Non-slaveholding whites were not inclined to be extremists. In 1851 a correspondent of the Greenville *Southern Patriot* wrote: "Tell the barons of the low country that if they involve the State in war they may defend themselves as well as they can."[41] But the "barons" for all practical purposes, controlled the political machinery of the state. The slave-holders realized their need to remain dominant. And to further consolidate their position, they launched an extraordinary effort to convince the poor white man that he was a beneficiary of slavery and must be its defender. Emancipation, he was told, would Africanize the country and make Negroes his equal in government and in marriage. Between 1855 and 1858 there was agitation in South Carolina for a reopening of the African slave trade so as to make every white man the owner of at least one slave and thus give him a stake in the system of bondage.

In 1859 came John Brown's seizure of the United States arsenal at Harper's Ferry, Virginia, with the objective of supplying arms for the slaves of the surrounding countryside who would then rise up and overthrow their masters. John Brown's raid electrified the South. The South Carolina legislature voted $100,000 for military preparations and sent a delegate to Virginia to express sympathy and to seek her co-operation for secession.

The next year, with a dreaded vision of John Brown still fresh, the Charleston *Mercury* advocated secession if Lincoln should be elected. "If, in our present position of power and unitedness, we have the raid of John Brown . . . what," asked the *Mercury*, "will be the measures of insurrection and incendiarism, which must follow our notorious and abject prostration to Abolition rule at Washington . . . ?"[42]

On November 6, 1860, Abraham Lincoln was elected President and the South, led by South Carolina, took this event as its signal for secession. Soon after the election, the governor of South Carolina summoned a convention. On

December 20, South Carolina's Ordinance of Secession was adopted at St. Andrews Hall in Charleston. Commissioners were dispatched to the other slave states to invite them to join South Carolina in forming a Southern Confederacy.

By an ironic twist of fate, C. G. Memminger, a former unionist and the adopted son of one-time Governor Thomas Bennett, was named chairman of a committee to draft a declaration of the causes of secession.[43] Bennett, too, had been a unionist. Nearly forty years before, at the time of the North-South recriminations over the Vesey affair, he had warned that this "vituperative spirit" might lead "to the dissolution of our happy compact."[44] To his son fell the task of penning the bitter fulfillment of his father's words. Memminger's committee cited the danger to slavery if South Carolina had remained in the union, charged that the Northern states had encouraged and assisted thousands of slaves to leave their homes, and, by emissaries, books, and pictures had incited those slaves who remained to engage in "servile insurrection."[45]

Other slave states soon followed South Carolina out of the union. On April 12, 1861, the fateful order to fire on Fort Sumter was given. The next day, the anniversary of the birth of Thomas Jefferson, the federal fort surrendered to the secessionists after thirty-four hours of bombardment. Lincoln called for volunteers to put down the Southern "insurrection."[46]

For the third time in less than half a century, South Carolina slave-holders were rebelling against the federal government. In 1823 and afterwards they had in effect nullified a solemn treaty of the United States in order to police Negro seamen visiting South Carolina ports. In 1832 they nullified the tariff laws of the United States because they thought the import duties kept their state's economy from being competitive. In 1860 they repudiated their adherence to the Constitution of the United States because they said that instrument's guarantees of equal rights and self government for the states were about to be subverted. With each successive occasion, South Carolina's defiance took a more violent form. But in each case the basic motive was the same: the desire to protect slavery. By 1860 the state's leaders had developed an obsession on the subject. While from the outside their attitude looked like collective paranoia, they themselves regarded their position as righteous. In their Declaration of Causes they appealed to the "Supreme Judge of the world for the rectitude" of their intentions.[47]

Despite all the talk which at times camouflaged South Carolina's motives with the vestments of "rights" and "liberties," the state's leaders were in fact leading an insurrection to safeguard the privilege of keeping thousands of fellow human beings in bondage.[48] The sophistry behind such terms as "state rights," "self government" and "Southern independence" was revealed by the agility with which the defenders of slavery could switch constitutional theories when their fundamental interests dictated it. The same South Carolinians who were for strict constitutional construction in one day were against it in another. The same men who invoked the aid of the federal government to implement their own liberty of action repudiated such aid in behalf of the liberty of others.

At least one South Carolinian of the time appreciated the sober significance for political freedom of South Carolina's secession move. As the secession convention was meeting, Charleston unionist James L. Petigru met J. D. Pope, a young acquaintance who was excited over the proceedings.

"Where's the fire," asked Petigru.

"Mr. Petigru," said Pope, "there is no fire. Those are the joybells ringing in honor of the passage of the Ordinance of Secession."

"I tell you there is a fire," replied Petigru. "They have this day set a blazing torch to the temple of constitutional liberty, and, please God, we shall have no more peace forever."[49]

Petigru's rhetoric was somewhat overdrawn, since the war would end and constitutional liberty would remain enshrined. But he was entirely right in his assessment of what his fellow South Carolinians were doing to the Constitution in their time.

The slave-holders' pretext, of course, was that the Constitution was designed to protect slavery. The founding fathers of 1787, however, had at least exhibited a sensitivity on that subject. They had carefully avoided the use of the word "slave,"[50] realizing that it would have looked incongruous in a document written by men who were on record in favor of the great principles of freedom: free speech, free worship, and fair trial. The men of 1787, including some from South Carolina, had registered their abhorrence of slavery and their desire to be rid of it. The Southern leaders of 1860 displayed no such feeling. The term "slavery" appeared frequently in the constitution of the Confederacy,[51] and this and other Southern state papers of the time staunchly upheld the institution. Jefferson Davis, in a message to the Confederate Congress on April 29, 1861, declared that "the labor of African slaves was and is indispensable" to the South.[52] The maintenance of slavery in turn fostered undemocratic government and a martial spirit antithetical to a climate of freedom.

A martial spirit on both sides, including that of the abolitionists in the North, contributed to the outbreak of civil war. But the fighting fervor of the abolitionists was at least devoted to a morally defensible cause. Also enlisted on the abolitionists' side was the rebellious spirit of Negroes yearning for freedom. The extent to which this spirit contributed fuel to the Civil War—and hence to the ultimate freeing of the slaves—is suggested by the countless times that slave-holders registered their fear of insurrection. Denmark Vesey had played a major role in arousing the fear of South Carolinians. Dread of black revolt was on the lips of South Carolinians as the guns were being readied to fire on Fort Sumter. Mrs. Mary Boykin Chesnut sat in her house in Charleston on April 8, 1861, and recorded in her diary the observation of a friend that, with Yankees in front and Negroes in the rear, the slave-owners expected a servile insurrection.[53] On April 13, as the cannonading of Fort Sumter was in full cry, Mrs. Chesnut wrote:

> Not by one word or look can we detect any change in the demeanor of these Negro servants. . . . You could not tell that they even heard the awful roar going on in the bay, though it has been dinning in their ears night and day. People talk before them as if they were chairs and tables. They make no sign. Are they stolidly stupid? or wiser than we are; silent and strong, biding their time . . . ?[54]

No one can ever know whether the spirit of Denmark Vesey hovered behind the impassive black faces in Charleston. But it is known that during the war the Negro abolitionist Frederick Douglass denounced the slave-holders' "rebellion"[55] and, in urging Negroes to take up the Union's arms in the cause of freedom, called on them to "remember Denmark Vesey."[56] The call was not ignored.

With the onset of 1863 came the Emancipation Proclamation and the partial realization of Vesey's dream of 1822. But the war was to drag on for two more years before the nation's ordeal would be resolved. At the end South Carolina was prostrate, the target of the victors' outraged vengeance. Much of Charleston was in ruins, blackened and forlorn. The issue of slavery had been finally settled at a terrible price, one which South Carolina and the South would be paying for generations to come.

In the aftermath of war, the rights which Vessey had hoped for were promulgated in the Constitution's Thirteenth, Fourteenth, and Fifteenth Amendments. But the laborious process of translating the amended Constitution into a meaningful spirit was a matter for future history.

Viewed in the perspective of time, Vesey emerges as a leader who had a dual impact on the history of American slavery. On the one hand, he helped to crystalize the fears of the slave-holders and to push them into an unyielding defensive stance. On the other hand, he inspired those who fought in the black man's long uphill struggle toward freedom.

When Vesey appeared on the stage, South Carolina had already cast her lot with slavery. The Negro insurrectionist's chief influence was to impel South Carolina toward disunion and into its first overt challenge to the national government, with slavery as the crux of the dispute.

As the sectional chasm deepened, emotions drove each side to a more determined fortification of its supposed vital interests. South Carolina, as the leader of the extremistic defenders of slavery, played a key part in driving the nation toward resort to war as the arbiter. Within South Carolina, Vesey contributed ammunition to the forces of reaction. Outside he helped to arm the fighters for freedom. Out of the irrepressible and tragic conflict between the two sides came the eventual liberation of American slaves and the achievement of what had been Denmark Vesey's seemingly hopeless goal.

# • NOTES

## Preface

1. Higginson, *Travelers and Outlaws*, p. 221.

2. Kennedy and Parker, *Official Report*, p. 59.

3. Quoted in Butcher, *Negro in American Culture*, p. 117.

4. Quoted *ibid.*, pp. 116-117.

5. The South Carolina Archives Department has in its collection a manuscript of about 100 pages which is labeled as copy of the proceedings of the Court of Magistrates and Freeholders that tried Denmark Vesey and his fellow conspirators. This manuscript is not, however, the original record of the trials and does not appear to be any more complete than the Kennedy and Parker *Official Report* (*supra*, n. 2). The Archives Department manuscript was in fragile condition and was not available for detailed inspection by the author at the time of the completion of this work.

## Chapter 1

1. Smyth, *A Tour of the United States*, II, 81. Until its incorporation in 1783, the South Carolina city was called Charles Town. but throughout this work it will be referred to by its incorporated name of Charleston.

2. *South Carolina and American General Gazette* (Charleston), July 18, Aug. 20, 1770; Jan. 20, 1775. (Although the *South Carolina and American General Gazette* carried below its nameplate the dates for a full week—i.e., "July 18 to July 25, 1770,,—in the interest of simplicity, only the initial date will be cited in this work.) *South Carolina Gazette and Country Journal* (Charleston), July 31, 1770; May 7, 1771; Jan. 7, 1772; *South Carolina Gazette* (Charleston), March 22, 1773; Feb. 14, 1774; Miscellaneous Records, Book ZZ, p. 434, Office of Judge of Probate, Charleston.

3. *Register of Shipping*, Hamilton, Bermuda; Letter to author from Col. Henry Wilkinson, Bermuda historian, July 19, 1956.

4. *S. C. Gazette and Country Journal*, July 31, 1770; *S. C. and American General Gazette*, Aug. 20, 1770.

5. *Ibid.*

6. Donnan, "Slave Trade in South Carolina before the Revolution," *American Historical Review, XXXIII* (June, 1928), 823.

7. *S. C. and American General Gazette*, Jan. 20, Aug. 18, 1775.

8. Charleston newspaper files for the remainder of 1775 were examined.

9. *S. C. and American General Gazette*, Sept. 8, 15, 1775; Kennedy and Parker, Official Report, p. 42 n.

Great Britain during the Revolution forbade the Bermudians to trade with the North American mainland, which may have had something to do with Captain Vesey's absence from Charleston during the war. The islanders at this time, however, had little reason to be friendly with the mother country even though they remained in the empire. Bermuda, having no commodities to trade with Britain for foodstuffs, was at times reduced to dire straits and acquired necessary supplies only by surreptitious dealings with the rebelling Americans. Strode, *Story of Bermuda*, pp. 56-58. Thus Joseph Vesey had provocation for and examples in disloyalty growing out of the war.

10. Miscellaneous Records, Book ZZ, p. 434, Office of Judge of Probate, Charleston.

11. *Ship Register*, 1765 *et seq.*, South Carolina Archives Department, Columbia, S.C.

FOR OTHER AUTHORITIES USED, SEE:

On Bermuda—Kerr,*Bermuda*; Strode, *Story of Bermuda*.

On Charleston trade—Sellers, *Charleston Business*; Wallace, *South Carolina*.

## Chapter 2

1. A contemporaneous sketch of Denmark Vesey's life (presumably supplied by Captain Vesey) is available. This sketch, however, records no details about his birthplace or boyhood. See Hamilton, *Negro Plot*, pp. 17-18 n. and Kennedy and Parker, *Official Report*, p. 42 n. Though some accounts of Denmark Vesey's life have given Africa as his birthplace and others have given St. Thomas, there seems to be no document to firmly sustain either view. Aptheker in *American Negro Slave Revolts*, p. 268, says it was reported that Vesey was born in Africa. Aptheker mentions Hamilton, *Negro Plot*, and Kennedy and Parker, *Official Report*, as his sources; but these accounts do not give Africa as Vesey's birthplace. Among the writers who identify Africa as the place of birth are Victor, *History of American Conspiracies*, p. 375,, and Phillips, by implication, in *American Negro Slavery*, p. 477. Victor gives Higginson, "Denmark Vesey," *The Atlantic Monthly*, June, 1861, as his source, but Higginson's statement is not supported. Phillips, who states that Vesey was brought from Africa in his youth, cites no document to support his statement. Denmark is referred to as "a native of St. Thomas" by Wish, "American Slave Insurrections Before 1861," *Journal of Negro History*, XX11, 316. But Wish does not document his assertion.

2. Donnan, *Documents*, II, xvi.

3. Campbell, "St. Thomas Negroes," *Psychological Monographs*, LV, No. 5, pp. 4, 12. Captain Vesey gave 1767 as the year of Denmark's birth.

4. Another source indicates that 106 men and 285 women and children constituted the "free colored population of St. Thomas," in 1772. Pendleton, "The Danish West Indies," *Journal of Negro History*, II, 275.

5. Clarkson, *Impolicy of the American Slave Trade*, p. 146.

6. Hamilton, *History of Moravian Church*, pp. 53, 182, 268, 269, 328.

7. *Ibid.*, p. 268; Pendleton, "The Danish West Indies," *Journal of Negro History*, II, 275.

8. In 1781, the year of Captain Vesey's arrival at St. Thomas, the island's population was not appreciably greater than in 1775—judging by the figures for 1789, the next year of record.

9. Contemporary chroniclers said that Captain Vesey and his colleagues named their captive Telemaque, and explained that the name, through gradual corruption in Negro usage, later became Denmark, or sometimes Telmak. Kennedy and Parker, *Official Report*, p. 42 n. This may be correct. But it seems more logical to surmise that Denmark was the name originally used by his captors because of the young slave's connection with the Danish island of St. Thomas. Denmark seems rather strained as a corruption of Telemaque.

10. It was reported that Captain Vesey was forced to take Denmark back at the time of his next voyage to the Cape. Kennedy and Parker, *Offiicial Report*, p. 42 n. If the records of the captain's voyages from the West Indies to the Carolina coast are an indication of the time lapses between return calls at the same port, Vesey was probably back at Cape Francais in three months or less. Vesey's travel schedule suggests that the return voyage was surely not delayed for more than a year. *S. C. Gazette and Country Journal*, May 7, Sept. 3, Dec. 17, 1771; May 19, July 7, 1772; *S. C. Gazette* Nov. 26, 1772, March 22, 1773; Feb. 14, Sept. 12, 1774; *S. C. and American General Gazette*, Jan. 20, May 26, Aug. 18, 1775.

11. Hamilton, *Negro Plot*, pp. 17-18 n.; Kennedy and Parker, *Official Report*, p. 42 n.; Grimké, *Right on the Scaffold*, p. 5. No other reference to Denmark's reported affliction occurs in the contemporary accounts, and Grimké has suggested that the young slave may have pretended to have epilepsy in order to get back to the people who had treated him kindly. Furnas, in *Road to Harpers Ferry*, p. 419, n. 12, draws inferences about Vesey's eccentricity which seem to this author unjustified without knowing more about the degree of his affliction.

12. Verrill, *The Bermuda Islands*, pp. 560, 561, 563, 564.

FOR OTHER AUTHORITIES USED, SEE:

On St. Thomas—Campbell, "St. Thomas Negroes," *Psychological Monographs*, LV; Pendleton, "The Danish West Indies," *Journal of Negro History*, II, 275.

On the slave trade—Phillips, *American Negro Slavery*; Sellers, *Charleston Business*.

On St. Domingue—Blake, *Slavery and the Slave Trade*; Davis, *Black Democracy*; Phillips, *American Negro Slavery*; Vandercook, *Black Majesty*.

On Bermuda—Kerr, *Bermuda*.

On slavery in the West Indies—Blake, *Slavery and the Slave Trade*.

## Chapter 3

1. Although Captain Vesey's exact activities and whereabouts from 1781 to 1783 (Denmark's first years of service) are not known, it is known that he was a slave trader in the West Indies during the American Revolution and at Charleston in 1783. Therefore it is reasonable to assume that he followed the same occupation in the intervening years.

2. Kennedy and Parker, *Official Report*, p. 98; [Higginson], "Denmark Vesey," *Atlantic Monthly*, VII (June, 1861), 730 (Higginson is identified as the author in Brawley, *Social History of American Negro*, pp. 387, 406).

Many of the writers refer to the fact that Denmark learned several languages in his travels with the captain. It seems probable to this writer that he learned Danish while a resident of St. Thomas and English after becoming Vesey's slave. He no doubt picked up some French while living at St. Domingue, and he would certainly have encountered that language as well as Spanish in West Indian voyages. One of Denmark Vesey's associates said Vesey spoke French fluently. Kennedy and Parker, *Official Report*, p. 98.

3. Higginson, "Denmark Vesey," *Atlantic Monthly*, VII, 730.

4. *S. C. Gazette and Country Journal*, Dec. 18, 1770; Sept. 3, 1771: May 19, 1772; Dec. 8, 1772; Aug. 30, 1774; *S. C. Gazette*, March 22, 1773; *S. C. and American General Gazette*, April 15, 1774; Feb. 17, June 9, Aug. 18, 1775.

5. Donnan, *Documents*, II, p. xvii.

6. Spears, *Slave Trade*, pp. 69, 70.

7. This was the size of the *Penelope* of Liverpool, which had a capacity of 389 slaves. Vesey, however, might have had a smaller vessel and still carried as many as 390 slaves, since on the relatively short haul from St. Thomas to St. Domingue, it would not have been necessary to take on as much food and water as was needed for the passage from Africa. Donnan,

*Documents*, II, 646. See Kennedy and Parker, *Official Report*, p. 42 n., on Vesey's slave cargo.

8. Phillips, *American Negro Slavery*, pp. 33, 34-35; Blake, *Slavery and the Slave Trade*, p. 128.

9. Description of sloop *Adventure* which cleared Newport for Sierra Leone in 1773. Dow, *Slave Ships*, pp. 259, 260.

10. Canot, *Adventures of an African Slaver*, p. xi. Reference is to the 300-ton English ship, *Kitty's Amelia*, which put out from Liverpool in 1807.

11. Dow, *Slave Ships*, p. 260. Upon the Newport slaver's return, her master reckoned a net profit of 23 per cent.

12. [Johnston], *The Journal of an African Slaver*, pp. 3-5.

13. Kennedy and Parker, *Official Report*, p. 98.

14. Dow, *Slave Ships*, pp. xxii-xxv.

FOR OTHER AUTHORITIES USED, SEE:

On slavery in St. Domingue—Blake, *Slavery and the Slave Trade*.

On the slave trade in Africa—Davidson, *Lost Cities of Africa*.

On slave voyages—Blake, *Slavery and the Slave Trade*; Phillips, *American Negro Slavery*; Sypher, *Guinea's Captive Kings*.


## Chapter 4

1. La Rochefoucauld-Liancourt, *Travels*, II, 373-374.

2. Sellers, *Charleston Business*, p. 64. One ship, the *Maria Wilhelmina*, which appeared in April of 1775, was reported to be 800 tons burden and the largest ship ever to enter the harbor up to that time.

3. *South Carolina Gazette and General Advertiser*, July 19, 1783.

4. "Charleston, S.C., in 1774, as Described by an English Traveller," *The Historical Magazine, and Notes and Queries Concerning the Antiquities, History and Biography of America*, IX (1865), 341; Smyth, *Tour of the United States*, II, 81; De Brahm, "Hydrogeography of S.C.," *Documents*, p. 195.

5. The displacement of the *Dove* is actually given in the advertisement as "230 barrels Rice burthen." The tonnage was computed by using the formula of four barrels of rice to the ton. Sellers, *Charleston Business*, p. 63. Lease by Vesey recorded in Book H-5, p. 265, Register of Mesne Conveyance, Charleston.

6. It is possible that there was some error in the listing of names and that the *Dove* and the *Eagle* were the same ship, since David Miller is given as the master of each. Miller is listed as

master of the *Dove* in the *S. C. Gazette and General Advertiser*, Sept. 27, 1783; Miller is listed as master of the *Eagle* in Donnan, *Documents*, IV, 474.

7. This address would have been close to the spot which Charleston historian Samuel Gaillard Stoney orally identified for the writer as the location of sheds for the sale of slaves. The now vanished sheds, according to Mr. Stoney, stood on Vendu Range close to East Bay. The auction block was about opposite Prioleau Street on the north side of the Range, he said.

8. *S. C. Gazette and General Advertiser*, Sept. 23, 27, 1783; *Gazette of the State of South Carolina*, Sept. 24, 1783.

9. Donnan, *Documents*, IV, 474; *S. C. Gazette and General Advertiser*, Sept. 16, 1783; *Supplement to General Advertiser*, Sept. 20, 1783; *Gazette of S. C.*, Sept. 24, 1783.

10. La Rochefoucauld-Liancourt, *Travels*, II, 410.

11. *S. C. Gazette and General Advertiser*, Sept. 27, Oct. 7, 14, 1783.

12. Ralph Izard in 1785 had advocated a three-year ban on the importation of Negroes to help check the flow of capital from the state. Wolfe, *Jeffersonian Democracy*, p. 16. When the ban was later imposed, the reason given for it was the debt the planters had contracted. The legislature found it necessary to provide for payment by postponing installments and preventing the opening of a new source of debt before the old debt was discharged. La Rochefoucauld-Liancourt, *Travels*, II, 409. Travelers could take slaves and free Negroes within two years. McCord, *Statutes of S.C.*, VII, 447, 448.

13. Cooper and McCord, *Statutes of S. C.*, IV, 608; VII, 430, 431-448.

14. Schoepf, *Travels*, II, 221 n.

15. The Duke de la Rochefoucauld-Liancourt reported the price of the best Negro in 1796 as $300-$350, the common Negro as $200, and the common Negress as $100 to $150. La Rochefoucauld-Liancourt, *Travels*, II, 410.

16. *Ship Manifests, 1784*, pp. 97, 99, 101, 102, 115, 133, 141, 151, 154, 156. South Carolina Archives Department.

17. *S. C. Gazette and General Advertiser*, Nov. 11, 1783; *Supplement to General Advertiser*, Nov. 18, 1783; *The Courier*, Oct. 11, 1803.

18. *The Charleston Directory for 1790*, p. 39.

19. La Rochefoucauld-Liancourt, *Travels*, II, 381; Spears, *American Slave Trade*, pp. 160, 162. Most of the American slaves carried away by the English during the war were taken to Nova Scotia. Negroes from Nova Scotia were later (1787 and after) taken to Sierra Leone to be colonized. DuBois, *Suppression of the*

246                                    DENMARK VESEY'S REVOLT

*African Slave Trade*, p. 11, reports that South Carolina lost 25,000 Negroes from 1775 to 1783.

20. *South Carolina Weekly Gazette*, March 22, 1783.

21. Uhlendorf, *The Siege of Charleston*, pp. 199, 379.

22. Aptheker, *American Negro Slave Revolts*, p. 22. Southerners frequently exhibited a fear of slave unrest while male citizens were absent on military duty. *Ibid.*, pp. 23, 24, 91.

23. Up to this time it had been officially designated as Charles Town.

24. *Year Book - 1880, Charleston*, p. 257; *S. C. Weekly Gazette*, Sept. 13, Oct. 4, 1783.

25. Asbury, *Journal*, I, 184, 506; Phillips, *American Negro Slavery*, p. 134. Quincy quoted in Sellers, *Charleston Business*, p. 154.

26. [Washington], *Diaries of George Washington*, IV, 174.

27. Bernard, *Retrospections of America*, pp. 216-217.

28. *S. C. Weekly Gazette*, Dec. 19, 1783.

29. Ford, "Diary of Timothy Ford, 1785-1786," ed. by Joseph W. Barnwell, *South Carolina Historical and Genealogical Magazine*, XIII, 203-204.

FOR OTHER AUTHORITIES USED, SEE:

On Charleston shipping—Phillips, *American Negro Slavery*; Sellers, *Charleston Business*; Wallace, *South Carolina*.

On the South Carolina slave trade—Jervey, *Slave Trade*; Petty, *Population*; Phillips, *American Negro Slavery*; Sellers, *Charleston Business*; Wolfe, *Jeffersonian Democracy*.

Effect of war on S.C. economy—Wallace, *South Carolina*.

Charleston after the Revolution—Krout and Fox, *Completion of Independence*; Molloy, *Charleston*; Petty, *Population*; La Rochefoucauld-Liancourt, *Travels*, II; Schoepf, *Travels*, II.


## Chapter 5

1. St. Mery, *American Journey*, pp. 306-307; La Rochefoucauld-Liancourt, *Travels*, II, 408.

2. Moreau de St. Mery reported that each Negro cultivating rice brought in to his master $257 a year, while his cost to his master was only $13. St. Mery, *American Journey*, pp. 307-308. But a second French traveler about the same time gave a far more conservative estimate of the return a slave's labor produced for his owner. La Rochefoucauld-Liancourt noted that, in a plantation with seventy slaves, no more than forty worked—the rest being old, sick or children. He said a single black laborer produced on an average of seven barrels of rice a year. Valuing

a barrel at his figure of $19.28, and multiplying this by seven and then by forty, one gets $5,398.40 as the gross return from 40 slaves. From this deduct his amounts of $80 for the overseer's wages, $128 for the expense of attending the sick, $70 for the poll tax of one dollar each on seventy Negroes, $300 for the clothing for seventy Negroes—bringing the average maintenance cost to $8.25 per individual slave. The net return was thus $4,820.40. This would mean a net of $68.86 on each slave (though by the Frenchman's computation it was for some reason $58). La Rochefoucauld-Liancourt, *Travels*, II, 492. Various other visitors to South Carolina gave different reports of the slave's productive capacity. De Brahm, "Hydrogeography of S. C.," *Documents*, said the slave annually produced four acres of indigo or four acres of rice; J. F. D. Smyth put the figure at seventy-five bushels of rice; George Washington said it was five or six barrels of rice. Quoted in Ryan, "Travelers," master's thesis, U. of N. C., p. 137. In 1822 General Thomas Pinckney put the annual maintenance cost of a South Carolina slave at $35. This figure included food, clothing, taxes, overseer's wages, medicine, tools, etc. Aptheker, *American Negro Slave Revolts*, pp. 128-129.

3. By 1790 the requirement of licenses for hired slaves had been discontinued. Sellers, *Charleston Business*, p. 105. But badge and tax requirements were reimposed in 1800. Aptheker, *American Negro Slave Revolts*, p. 151, n. 8.

4. *Ibid.*, pp. 102-104.

5. Quoted in Sellers, *Charleston Business*, p. 81.

6. *City Gazette and Daily Advertiser*, Oct. 28, 1793.

7. *Ibid.*, Oct. 15, 1799.

8. Ryan, "Travelers," p. 138.

9. *City Gazette and Daily Advertiser*, Oct. 4, 1800.

10. Ford quoted in Sellers, *Charleston Business*, p. 27; La Rochefoucauld-Liancourt, *Travels*, II, 378-379.

11. La Rochefoucauld-Liancourt, *Travels*, II, 395, 397. Smith, *South Carolina as a Royal Province*, pp. 179-180, 181.

12. La Rochefoucauld-Liancourt, *Travels*, II, 391-392.

13. St. Mery, *American Journey*, p. 307; Jervey, *Hayne*, p. 31.

14. Higginson, *Travellers and Outlaws*, p. 279; *The Times*, Jan. 9, 1802; *City Gazette and Daily Advertiser*, Nov. 1, 1793; Link, *Democratic-Republican Societies*, p. 97.

15. La Rochefoucauld-Liancourt, *Travels*, II, 393, 394.

16. *City Gazette*, June 30, 1800.

17. Schoepf, *Travels*, II, 220-221. It has been estimated that 22 slave revolts occurred in South Carolina between 1526 and 1784. Aptheker, *Negro Slave Revolts in U. S.*, pp. 71-72.

18. La Rochefoucauld-Liancourt, *Travels*, II, 410.

19. St. Mery, *American Journey*, pp. 308-309.

20. La Rochefoucauld-Liancourt reported that Negroes were employed almost exclusively to put out fires in Charleston. They were aided by a few whites and worked with zeal and spirit, he said, but their effectiveness was limited by a lack of proper direction. *Travels*, II, 418.

21. McCrady, *St. Philip's Church*, p. 35.

22. Schoepf, *Travels*, II, 147, 156-157, 220; La Rochefoucald-Liancourt, *Travels*, II, 411, 431, 451; Lambert, *Travels*, II, 210-211.

23. Davis, *Travels*, pp. 73-74.

24. Higginson, *Travellers and Outlaws*, p. 273.

25. Phillips, *Life and Labor*, p. 164.

26. *Ibid.*, p. 198; Helper, *Impending Crisis*, p. 406; *City Gazette*, Sept. 5, 1822.

27. Jackson, "Religious Instruction," *Journal of Negro History*, XV, 74, 80.

28. *Ibid.*, 80, 81.

29. Asbury, *Journal*, II, 331.

30. *Ibid.*, II, 47, 73, 184, 289, 290.

31. *Ibid.*, II, 218, 256, 292, 331, 336.

32. *Ibid.*, II, 178, 330.

33. Jackson, "Religious Instruction," *Journal of Negro History*, XV, 73.

FOR OTHER AUTHORITIES USED, SEE:

On population—Petty, *Population*; Phillips, *American Negro Slavery* and "Slave Labor," *Political Science Quarterly*, XXII, 426; Sellers, *Charleston Business*.

On occupations of slaves—Schoepf, *Travels*, II; Sellers, *Charleston Business*.

On slave control laws—Henry, *Police Control*; Phillips, *American Negro Slavery*; Wallace, *South Carolina*.

On slave living conditions—Aptheker, *American Negro Slave Revolts*; Sellers, *Charleston Business*.

On the education of slaves—Henry, *Police Control*; Wallace, *South Carolina*.

On the religious instruction of slaves—Henry, *Police Control*; Phillips, *American Negro Slavery*; Wallace, *South Carolina*.

## Chapter 6

1. Spears, *Slave Trade*, p. 111; Scott, *Journal of the Constitutional Convention*, p. 418.

2. Lander, "The South Carolinians at the Philadelphia Convention, 1787," *South Carolina Historical Magazine* LVII, 148.

3. Schaper, "Sectionism and Representation," *American Historical Association Annual Report 1900*, I, 423.

4. Ralph Izard to Thomas Jefferson, quoted in *S. C. Historical and Genealogical Magazine*, II, 197.

5. Quoted in Wallace, *South Carolina*, p. 357.

6. Laurens quoted in Sellers, *Charleston Business*, p. 146; Philodemus quoted in Helper, *Impending Crisis*, p. 228. See also Cash, *Mind of the South*, p. 61; Eaton, *Freedom of Thought*, pp. 22-23.

7. Klingberg, *Negro in Colonial S. C.*, p. 136; Weeks, *Quakers and Slavery*, p. 227 n.

8. Bassett, *Slavery in N. C.*, pp. 63, 71. In 1800 the First Presbytery of South Carolina defeated a resolution looking toward the emancipation of slave children. Howe, *Presbyterian Church in S. C.*, I, 634, 638; II, 171-172.

9. Asbury, *Journal*, II, 28, 48.

10. *Ibid.*, p. 220.

11. *Ibid.*, pp. 253, 286-287.

12. Bassett, *Slavery in N. C.*, pp. 53-54; Coulter, *Brownlow— Fighting Parson*, p. 90.

13. Jackson, "Religious Instruction," *Journal of Negro History*, XV, 78.

14. *Gazette of S. C.*, April 22, 1784.

15. Quoted in *Baltimore Daily Repository*, Sept. 18, 1793; also "Correspondence of the Republican Society of Charleston," Item 11.

16. Criticism of Washington quoted from *City Gazette*, March 17, 1794. Washington comment quoted in Wolfe, *Jeffersonian Democracy*, p. 81.

17. Toasts quoted *ibid.*, p. 79.

18. *City Gazette and Daily Advertiser*, *Aug.* 13, 1793.

19. *Heads of Families*, p. 40; *The Charleston Directory of 1790*, p. 39. *City Gazette and Daily Advertiser*, August 1, 1793; [Charleston] *Columbian Herald*, Aug. 24, 27, 29, Sept. 3, 5, 7, 1793.

20. Book YY, p. 330, Office of Judge of Probate, Charleston; Books C-7, p. 398; Q-6, pp. 428, 429; O-6, pp. 482, 484, Register of Mesne Conveyance, Charleston.

21. *City Gazette and Daily Advertiser*, Sept. 27, 1793; *The Act of the General Assembly Incorporating the City*, p. 152. Vesey had been a commissioner of pilotage for Charleston as early as 1788. *North and South Carolina and Georgia Almanac, 1788*

[no page numbers]. *City Gazette and Daily Advertiser*, A.ug. 13, Nov. 1, 1793. Book U-6, p. 9, Register of Mesne Conveyance.

22. *City Gazette and Daily Advertiser*, Aug. 26, Sept. 11, 1800.

23. *Ibid.*, Sept. 6, Nov. 29, 1793.

24. *Ibid.*, Sept. 10, 11, Oct. 3, 1793.

25. *Ibid.*, Sept. 14, 30, Oct. 3, 10, 17; Nov. 1, 15; Dec. 7, 1793.

26. *Ibid.*, Sept. 5, Oct. 5, Nov. 20, 21, 23, 28, 1793.

27. Logan, *Diplomatic Relations*, p. 48; Thomas, *Reminiscences*, I, 31-32; La Rochefoucauld-Liancourt, *Travels*, II, 426.

28. *City Gazette and Daily Advertiser*, Sept. 17, Oct. 17, 1793.

29. The Papers of Thomas Jefferson, vol. 96, items 16402, 16403.

30. Davis, *Black Democracy*, p. 30. Genet himself, according to later disclosures, was in favor of allowing the St. Domingue revolution to run its course on the ground that the blacks were the only ones capable of saving the colony by defeating a conspiracy between the English and royalist French colonists. He saw pride of skin uniting the English and the white French settlers who were ready to rebel against French authority and the decree of the National Assembly granting civic equality to mulattoes. Minnigerode, *Jefferson*, pp. 297-298

31. Logan, *Diplomatic Relations*, pp. 50, 79; La Rochefoucauld-Liancourt, *Travels*, II, 379; Lambert, *Travels*, II, 164.

32. Kennedy and Parker, *Official Report*, pp. 21, 62, 64, 67, 68, 73, 86.

33. Channing, *Jeffersonian System*, pp. 100-101; Jameson, *American Revolution*, pp. 22-23.

34. Lofton, "Enslavement of the Southern Mind: 1775-1825," *Journal of Negro History*, XLIII, 132-139; Weeks, *Quakers and Slavery*, p. 244; Eaton, *Freedom of Thought*, p. 315.

FOR OTHER AUTHORITIES USED, SEE:

On South Carolina constitutional history—Wallace, *South Carolina*; Wolfe, *Jeffersonian Democracy*.

On liberterian sentiment—Krout and Fox, *Completion of Independence*; Wallace, *South Carolina*.

On churches and slavery—Phillips, *American Negro Slavery*; Wallace, *South Carolina*.

On democratic organizations—Link, *Democratic-Republican Societies* and "Democratic Societies," *N. C. Review*, XVIII, 259; Wallace, *South Carolina*.

On revolution in St. Domingue—Davis, *Black Democracy*; Vandercook, *Black Majesty*.

On repercussions in South Carolina—Krout and Fox, *Com-*

*pletion of Independence*; Link, *Democratic-Republican Societies*; Molloy, *Charleston*; Wolfe, *Jeffersonian Democracy*.

On the shift in opinion on slavery—Krout and Fox, *Completion of Independence*; Wallace, *South Carolina*.

## Chapter 7

1. Though the account of Denmark's life in the *Official Report*, p. 42 n., says his good fortune came in 1800, documents of the turn of the century suggest that it was actually in 1799. The newspapers of the period indicate that the East Bay Street "second lottery" was completed on December 9, 1799, and the third lottery was not advertised until 1802. Ticket number 1884, worth $1,500, was drawn on November 8, 1799, though the money may not have been paid until early 1800. *City Gazette and Daily Advertiser*, Oct. 1, Nov. 9, Dec. 9, 1799; *The Times*, Jan. 18, 1802.

2. Phillips, "Slave Labor," *Political Science*, XXII, 426; Fitchett, "Free Negro in Charleston," *Journal of Negro History*, XXV, 142; *City Gazette and Daily Advertiser*, Oct. 28, 1793; Sellers, *Charleston Business*, p. 103.

3. The captain's address, which was 20 Queen Street just after Denmark's manumission, became successively King Street Road (1802), 13 N. W. Middle (now Alexander) Street (1806), 41 Anson Street (1819), 82 Anson Street (1822). *Nelson's Charleston Directory, 1801*, p. 19; *Charleston Directory, 1802*, p. 80; *Negrin's Directory for 1806*, p. 81; *Directory for Charleston, 1819*, p. 93; *Charleston Directory, 1822*, p. 84.

4. Kennedy and Parker, *Official Report*, pp. 43, 85, 98, 145.

5. *Ibid.*, pp. 85, 92, 95, 96, 98, 144.

6. *Heads of Families*, p. 40; Books P-6, pp. 467-468; L-7, p. 208, Register of Mesne Conveyance, Charleston; Book RR (1797-1803), p. 360; Inventories Book D (1800-1810), p. 80; Guardianship Book B, p. 22, Office of Judge of Probate, Charleston; *Charleston Directory*, 1829, p. 83; Charleston Directory, 1831, p. 178; Woodson, *Free Negro Heads of Families*, p. 157.

7. *City Gazette*, May 1, 1800; Book P-9, p. 52, Register of Mesne Conveyance, Charleston; Will Books, 1826-1834, Book G, p. 320, Charleston Free Library.

8. *The Times*, Oct. 10, 1803; *The Courier*, Oct. 11, 1803; *Charleston Directory*, 1806, p. 123; *Charleston Directory*, 1809, p. 137.

9. McCrady, *St. Philip's Church*, p. 35.

10. Henry, *Police Control*, p. 193. Following is an example of a South Carolina deed of manumission, the kind which Captain Joseph Vesey presumably used in freeing his slave, Denmark:

[*name of emancipator*]
Emancipates ——————.

Know all men by these presents That I ——————
of —————— District now in my proper memory & senses
do of my own free will and desire emancipate and set free my
negro [man or woman] named —————— & I do by these
presents discharge & forever renounce any right title or claim by
the said Negro [man or woman] named —————— & I
—————————— do nominate and appoint —————— &
—————————— as guardians for the safe protection & carrying
into Execution this my free will & desire.

Given under my hand & seal this ——— day of ——— in
the year ———.

Signed seald & delivered in the presence of
[*name of witness*]
[*name of witness*]                    [*name of emancipator*]
The State of South Carolina
—————————— District

Before me —————— Justice Quorum for said District personally appeared [*witness*] & made oath that he saw
[*name of emancipator*] . . . [*sign*] the within instrument of writing
& deliver the same to the within named [*name of slave*] also
that he saw [*second witness*] subscribe his name as witness with
himself to the same.

Sworn to before me this ——— day of —————— ———
[*name of justice*]                        [*name of emancipator*]

11. *Ibid.*, p. 189.

12. Phillips, "Slave Labor," *Political Science*, XXII, 426.

13. [U.S. Census], *Return of Persons within the U.S.*, 1800, p.
2M; *Persons within the U.S., 1810*, p. 79; *Fourth Census*, 1820,
p. 26; *Fifth Census*, 1830, pp. 94-95.

14. *Charleston Courier*, Dec. 12, 1820

15. McCord, *Statutes of S.C.*, VII, 433.

16. *Ibid.*, pp. 436-437, 440.

17. Hurd, *Law of Freedom and Bondage*, II, 95-96.

18. McCord, *Statutes of S.C.*, VII, 459.

19. *City Gazette*, June 30, 1800.

20. *City Gazette*, August 24, 1822; Hamilton, *Negro Plot*, p.
16; Kennedy and Parker, *Official Report*, pp. 85, 177. Not until
later years was Vesey designated as a mulatto. See William Gil-
more Simms, *History of South Carolina* [cited by Victor, *History
of American Conspiracies*, p. 375]; Dumas Malone, *The Public
Life of Thomas Cooper, 1783-1839* (New Haven: Yale University Press, 1926), p. 285. Jervey, *Hayne*, p. 131.

21. La Rochefoucauld-Liancourt, *Travels*, II, 457; Phillips,
*American Negro Slavery*, pp. 433-434, 437. Phillips surmises that

La Rochefoucald-Liancourt may have been mistaken and that Pindaim was James Pendarvis as reported in the first census.

22. *City Gazette*, Aug. 21, 1822.

23. *Ibid.*

24. Aptheker, "Petition of S. C. Negroes," *Journal of Negro History*, XXXI, 98-99.

25. *City Gazette and Daily Advertiser*, Sept. 7, 1793.

26. Quoted in Henry, *Police Control*, pp. 181-182.

27. For support of this point, see Henry, *Police Control*, p. 7.

28. Will Books, 1793-1800, Book A. vol. 25, p. 208, Charleston Free Library.

29. Henry, *Police Control*, pp. 134-135. Carter G. Woodson (*Education*, p. 118) suggests that the law against teaching was ignored by some masters.

30. Benedict, *History of Baptist Denomination*, II, 145-146.

31. Quoted in Henry, *Police Control*, p. 141.

32. Harrison, *Gospel Among the Slaves*, p. 114.

33. Kennedy and Parker, *Official Report*, pp. 22, 76, 115.

34. *Ibid.*, p. 22.

35. *Ibid.*, p. 82.

36. *Ibid.*, p. 120.

37. *Ibid.*, pp. 87-88.

38. "Letters to American Colonization Society," *Journal of Negro History*, X, 157-161.

39. Wallace, *History of South Carolina*, II, 414-415.

40. Boucher, *Nullification*, p. 4 n.

FOR OTHER AUTHORITIES USED, SEE:

On emancipation and immigration of Negroes—Henry, *Police Control;* Phillips, *American Negro Slavery* and *Life and Labor*, Wallace, *South Carolina.*

On caste among free Negroes—Birnie, "Education of the Negro," *Journal of Negro History*, XII, 15; Fitchett, "Free Negro in Charleston," *Journal of Negro History*, XXV, 143; Henry, *Police Control*; Jervey, *Hayne*; Phillips, *American Negro Slavery.*

On occupations of free Negroes—Birnie, "Education of the Negro," *Journal of Negro History*, XII, 15; Fitchett, "Free Negro in Charleston," *Journal of Negro History*, XXV, 143; Henry, *Police Control;* Phillips, *American Negro Slavery.*

On law for free Negroes—Henry, *Police Control*; Jervey, *Hayne*; Phillips, *American Negro Slavery.*

On education for free Negroes—Birnie, "Education of the Negro," *Journal of Negro History*, XII, 15; Fitchett, "Free Negro in Charleston," *Journal of Negro History*, XXV, 143; Henry, *Police Control*; Phillips, *American Negro Slavery*; Woodson, *Education*.

On churches for Negroes—Henry, *Police Control*; Jervey, *Hayne*; Phillips, *American Negro Slavery*.

On the American Colonization Society—Jervey, *Hayne*; Ottley, *Black Odyssey*.

### Chapter 8

1. [U.S. Census], *Return of Persons within the U. S.*, 1800 p. 2M.

2. *Negrin's Directory*, 1807, pp. 78, 80.

3. Adams, *The United States in 1800*, p. 107.

4. Lambert, *Travels*, II, 167-168.

5. *Ibid.*, p. 163.

6. Quoted in Jervey, *Hayne*, p. 68.

7. Quoted in Wolfe, *Jeffersonian Democracy*, pp. 231-232.

8. Quoted in Jervey, *Hayne*, p. 29.

9. Petty, *Population*, p. 214.

10. Gray, *History of Agriculture*, II, 1031.

11. Quoted in Wolfe, *Jeffersonian Democracy*, p. 244.

12. Quoted *ibid.*, p. 255.

13. Quoted *ibid.*, pp. 233-234.

14. Quoted *ibid.*, p. 283.

15. Gray, *History of Agriculture*, II, 1031; Petty, *Population*, p. 215; *Year Book - 1880*, Charleston, p. 314.

16. S.C. Congressman McDuffie quoted in Turner, *New West*, p. 307.

17. Doar, *Rice and Rice Planting*, pp. 18-19.

18. Hurd, *Law of Freedom and Bondage*, II, 96.

19. *Year Book - 1880*, Charleston, p. 263.

20. Dow, *Slave Ships*, p. 270.

21. Lambert, *Travels*, II, 165.

22. Hurd, *Law of Freedom and Bondage*, II, 96.

23. Turner, *New West*, p. 73.

24. *Ibid.*, p. 49.

25. Quoted in Hofstadter, *American Political Tradition*, p. 79.

26. Smith, *Wealth of Nations*, I, 364; see also *ibid.*, II, 181.

27. Cited in Phillips, *American Negro Slavery*, p. 347.

28. Quoted *ibid.*, p. 348.

29. Hinton Rowan Helper used the same approach in trying to convince the South of the error of its point of view. But his work came late (1857).

30. Gray, *History of Agriculture*, II, 1031.

31. Krout and Fox, *Completion of Independence*, pp. 222, 419.

FOR OTHER AUTHORITIES USED, SEE:

On Charleston in 1800—Jervey, *Hayne*; Molloy, *Charleston*; Wallace, *South Carolina*.

On Charleston society—Molloy,*Charleston*; Wallace, *South Carolina*; Wolfe, *Jeffersonian Democracy*.

On South Carolina politics—Wallace, *South Carolina*; Wiltse, *Calhoun, Nationalist and Calhoun, Nullifier*; Wolfe, *Jeffersonian Democracy*.

On crop and export statistics—Petty, *Population*; Wallace, *South Carolina*; Wolfe, *Jeffersonian Democracy*.

On economic currents—Wallace, *South Carolina*.

On the slave trade—Henry, *Police Control*; Petty, *Population*; Phillips, *Life and Labor*; Smith, *Economic Readjustment*; Wallace, *South Carolina*; Wolfe, *Jeffersonian Democracy*.

On people, industry and agriculture—Morison and Commager, *American Republic*, 3d, ed., I; Petty, *Population*; Phillips, *American Negro Slavery* and *Life and Labor*; Smith, *Economic Readjustment*; Wallace, *South Carolina*; Wolfe, *Jeffersonian Democracy*.

On the decline of cotton—Phillips, *American Negro Slavery*; Smith, *Economic Readjustment*; Wallace, *South Carolina*.

### Chapter 9

1. Quoted in Helper, *Impending Crisis*, p. 196.

2. See Chapter 6, text and note 23.

3. Kennedy and Parker, *Official Report*, pp. 118, 125, 126, 148, 167.

4. *City Gazette*, Oct. 11, 1800.

5. Kennedy and Parker, *Official Report*, pp. 67, 82.

6. Quoted in Aptheker, *American Negro Slave Revolts*, p. 76.

7. *Ibid.*, p. 72.

8. Quoted *ibid.*, pp. 257-258.

9. Quoted *ibid.*, p. 23.

10. Aptheker, "Maroons," *Journal of Negro History*, XXIV, 167.

11. The number of runaways in South Carolina was reported exceedingly high in 1765. *Ibid.*, p. 169. Militia from South Carolina and Georgia joined in attacking a Negro settlement in

1786, and in 1787 Governor Thomas Pinckney, in his annual legislative message, referred to the depredations of a group of armed fugitive slaves. *Ibid.*, p. 170. The number of runaways increased as abolitionists began to entice slaves to flee through the underground railroad. Henry, *Police Control*, p. 123.

12. The Georgetown difficulty was mentioned in the N.Y. *Evening Post*, June 11, 1821.

13. Kennedy and Parker, *Official Report*, p. 113.

14. See advertisements in *Charleston Courier*, Sept. 22, 1821.

15. Gordon, "Struggle for Physical Freedom," *Journal of Negro History*, XIII, 24.

16. Irving, *Day on Cooper River*, pp. 72-73.

17. McCord, *Statutes of S. C.*, VII, 460-461.

18. Kelly and Harbison, *American Constitution*, pp. 359-360; Peters, *U.S. Statutes at Large*, I, 302.

19. *City Gazette*, Sept. 12 and Nov. 11, 1800

20. *Ibid.*, July 30, 1800.

21. *Ibid.*, June 30, 1800.

22. Lambert, *Travels*, II, 164.

23. Quoted in Aptheker, *American Negro Slave Revolts*, p. 44, n. 78.

24. Quoted in Logan, *Diplomatic Relations*, p. 79.

25. *Ibid.*, p. 266; Schaper, "Sectionalism," *Historical Association Annual Report*, I, 393. See also Ramsay, *History of South Carolina*, II, 38. John Woolman, the great Quaker anti-slavery advocate, did not visit South Carolina. See Whitney, *John Woolman*.

26. Quoted in *Liberty*, 1837, p. 99 [abolitionist publication in which no publisher or place of publication are given]. Henry Grimké, brother of Sarah and Angelina Grimké, took a Negro mistress who bore him children whom he tried to protect from the horrors of slavery. Two of his sons by his mistress were Archibald and Francis. Archibald went to Lincoln University in Pennsylvania and Harvard Law School, became vice president of the National Association for the Advancement of Colored People, U.S. consul to Haiti and wrote biographies of Garrison and Sumner, also a pamphlet on the Vesey insurrection entitled, "Right on the Scaffold." Francis went to Princeton and became a minister. Johnson, *Lunatic Fringe*, pp. 39-40, 53.

27. Montesquieu quoted in Wallace, *South Carolina*, II, 414-415.

28. Cash, *Mind of the South*, p. 61.

29. Krout and Fox, *Completion of Independence*, p. 421.

30. Kennedy and Parker, *Official Report*, p. 18, n.

31. *Ibid.*, p. 18.

32. *Ibid.*, pp. 98, 118.

33. Hurd, *Law of Freedom and Bondage*, II, 97.

34. Kennedy and Parker, *Official Report*, pp. 118, 125, 126, 148, 167.

35. Quoted in Blake, *Slavery and the Slave Trade*, p. 411.

36. Quoted in Phillips, *American Negro Slavery*, p. 139.

37. Quoted *ibid.*, p. 142.

38. Kennedy and Parker, *Official Report*, pp. 18-19.

39. *Ibid.*, pp. 19, 21, 62, 64, 86, 126, 167.

40. *Ibid.*, p. 118.

41. *Niles Weekly Register* (Dec. 4, 1819) XVII, 215; King, *Two Speeches, 1819*; King, *Life of Rufus King*, VI, 233; Kennedy, and Parker, *Official Report*, p. 118.

42. Quoted in Turner, *New West*, p. 161.

43. King, *Life of Rufus King*, VI, 700; *Niles Weekly Register* (Dec. 4, 1819) XVII, 219.

44. *Congressional Globe, Debates of Second Session of Thirtieth Congress, Appendix*, p. 66; Kennedy and Parker, *Official Report*, p. 118.

FOR OTHER AUTHORITIES USED, SEE:

On channels of subversion—Blake, *Slavery and the Slave Trade*; Butcher, *Negro in American Culture*; Helper, *Impending Crisis*.

On fear of uprisings—Aptheker, *American Negro Slave Revolts*; Phillips, *American Negro Slavery*.

On runaway slaves—Aptheker *American Negro Slave Revolts*; Buckmaster, *Let My People Go*; Gordon, "Struggle for Physical Freedom," *Journal of Negro History*, XIII, 24; Henry, *Police Control*; Preston, "Genesis of Underground Railroad," *Journal of Negro History*, XVII, 150.

On relations with Haiti—Aptheker, *American Negro Slave Revolts*; Channing, *Jeffersonian System*; DeConde, *Entangling Alliance*; DuBois, *Suppression of the Slave Trade*; Logan, *Diplomatic Relations*; Montague, *Haiti and the U. S.*; Morison and Commager, *American Republic*, 2d ed., I; Vandercook, *Black Majesty*.

On internal anti-slavery spokesmen—Aptheker, *American Negro Slave Revolts*; Blake, *Slavery and the Slave Trade*; Channing, *Jeffersonian System*; Wallace, *South Carolina*.

On anti-slavery "infection" from outside—Aptheker, *American Negro Slave Revolts*; Birnie, *Grimké Sisters*; Blake, *Slavery and the Slave Trade*; Buckmaster, *Let My People Go*; King, *Life of Rufus King*; Morgan, *Johnson*; Morison and Commager, *American Republic*, 2d ed., I; Phillips, *American Negro Slavery*; Turner, *New West*.

## Chapter 10

1. Fitchett, "Free Negro in Charleston," *Journal of Negro History*, XXV, 143.

2. *City Gazette*, Aug. 21, 1822.

3. *Charleston Directory*, 1822, p. 109

4. Kennedy and Parker, *Official Report*, p. 95. Children born of a slave mother were consigned to bondage even though their father was free.

5. Kennedy and Parker, *Official Report*, p. 85. The master of a slave wife could set the visitation days of her husband. Henry, *Police Control*, p. 29.

6. See text, Chapter 7 at n. 35.

7. *Ibid.*, pp. 22-23, 76, 92, 115; A South Carolinian, *Practical Considerations*, p. 36. The Rev. John B. Adger (in *My Life and Times*, pp. 53-55) later expressed doubt that the African Church was the seat of insurrectionary activity. But his argument was obviously influenced by a desire to defend religious instruction of Negroes. The evidence as to the convenience of church meetings and the temptation to use them for covert purposes is more convincing.

8. Kennedy and Parker, *Official Report*, pp. 67, 82. In the interest of clarity and chronological simplicity, certain events are presented in narrative form in this chapter even though the testimony on which the narrative is based is scattered through the pages of the *Official Report*. Though no liberties have been taken with the reported facts, the sequence of events could only be determined by synchronizing the testimony of several witnesses.

9. *Ibid.*, pp. 116, 142. See James, *Andrew Jackson*, p. 242.

10. Kennedy and Parker, *Official Report*, p. 42, n. No reported testimony from any witness made light of Vesey's abilities.

11. *Charleston Directory*, 1822, p. 25.

12. Kennedy and Parker, *Official Report*, p. 118. Based on alleged confession by Jack Purcel. Governor Bennett evidently believed it. See Bennett, *Message No. 2*, p. 10.

13. *Ibid.*, p. 10.

14. Kennedy and Parker, *Official Report*, p. 45. This favorable evaluation of Peter's character, like similar assessments of the other leaders, was the estimate of white authorities who observed him and not of his Negro friends. See also *ibid.*, pp. 24, 44.

15. Ferguson, *Day on Cooper River*, p. 135.

16. Kennedy and Parker, *Official Report*, pp. 74, 80, 88, 106, 121. Governor Bennett is not convincing when he says the

conspiracy evidently did not embrace the country outside of Charleston because he found the countryside tranquil. Bennett, *Message No. 2*, p. 11. The governor was hardly in a position to observe unrest.

17. *Charleston Directory*, 1822, pp. VI-VII.

18. Kennedy and Parker, *Official Report*, pp. 41, 68, 83, 121. While some contemporary observers doubted the breadth, practicality and purposefulness of the reported plans, none doubted that insurrectionary agitation was afoot. It is this writer's contention that it matters little what the plan's prospects for success were but that what is important is that the white community was deeply stirred by the affair and that this had significant consequences, as will be shown.

In narrating the preparations for insurrection in this chapter, the writer is aware that much of the evidence as to what happened is hearsay. Some of it may also have been prompted by a desire on the part of the witnesses to gain clemency or turn attention from themselves. For these reasons, the narration is not being offered as a precise presentation of events as they occurred. Yet the narration is based on the evidence as recorded by and believed by the court. And since today we have little means of independently judging its probative value, the court record is the best source we have. With these reservations in mind, the writer has in this chapter made extensive use of the *Official Report* in the interest of relating a coherent story and of showing what contemporary Charleston authorities believed to have happened.

## Chapter 11

1. *Charleston Directory*, 1829, pp. 6-7.

2. Fraser, *Reminiscences*, pp. 15-16.

3. *Census for 1820*, p. 26.

4. Phillips, "Slave Labor," *Political Science*, XXII, 436.

5. Kennedy and Parker, *Official Report*, pp. 49-50. The names of neither Peter nor his owner, Colonel Prioleau, are given in the *Official Report*. They were revealed by the legislature in an act rewarding Peter for his services. See text at note 103, Chapter 12. Thomas Wentworth Higginson, who did research at Charleston on the Vesey plot, for some reason gives the name of the informing slave as Devany (*Travellers and Outlaws*, p. 215).

Fitzsimmons Wharf was identified for the writer by Samuel G. Stoney, Charleston historian, as the place where Peter and William Paul met. The schooner *Sally* from Cap Haitien (*City Gazette*, May 23, 1822) was the only ship entering the harbor at this time with a cargo consigned to a merchant using this wharf: John Stoney and Blake and Robertson. Therefore the *Sally* seems to have been the vessel observed by Peter and William. The address of J. and D. Paul comes from the *Charleston Directory*, 1822, p. 68.

6. Kennedy and Parker, *Official Report*, pp. 50-51. Pencil is identified in an act of the legislature rewarding him for his services (see text at note 103, Chapter 12). Higginson (*Travellers and Outlaws*, p. 215) identifies him as Pinceel. Pencil's residence is designated in the *Charleston Directory*, 1822, p. 108, and John C. Prioleau's, *ibid.*, p. 70.

7. Hamilton, *Negro Plot*, pp. 5-7.

8. Kennedy and Parker, *Official Report*, p. 53. John Wilson is not named in the *Official Report* but is identified in a letter from W. Hasell Wilson of Philadelphia to the Rev. D. Wilson of Charleston. Though no date is given on the letter, it was evidently written in 1900, since an accompanying note by Robert Wilson says W. Hasell Wilson was then 89 and was born in 1811. The W. Hasell Wilson letter is No. 98 in the manuscript collection of the Charleston Library Society. George Wilson is identified as a class leader in the *Official Report*, p. 114.

9. Letter from W. Hasell Wilson to Rev. D. Wilson.

10. *Charleston Directory*, 1822, p. 46.

11. Hamilton, *Negro Plot*, pp. 8-10.

12. *Ibid.*, pp. 8-10.

13. Letter from W. Hasell Wilson to Rev. D. Wilson.

14. Kennedy and Parker, *Official Report*, p. 28, n. Frank is referred to as a servant of Mrs. Ferguson in *Official Report*, pp. 80, 86, 90. Ferguson address in Charleston is given in *Charleston Directory*, 1822, p. 40.

15. Irving, *Day on Cooper River*, pp. 35, 112.

16. Kennedy and Parker, *Official Report*, p. 81. Monday Gell testified (*Official Report*, pp. 95-96) that Frank Ferguson had recruited four plantations of Negroes as early as three months before June 16. But this testimony is questionable as concerns dates, since Frank was also reported to have arranged at the time to bring the plantation slaves down on June 16. Yet June 16 was not set as the date of the uprising until about June 9.

17. *Ibid.*, pp. 81, 82, 89. Governor Bennett later expressed doubt as to Jesse's ability to carry out his assignment (*Message No. 2*, p. 15). But he made no allowance for the facts that Jesse was only a messenger, that the role of leading the country slaves had been assigned to others and that they were to come into the city by stealth, not march in.

18. Kennedy and Parker, *Official Report*, pp. 35-36, 163. Governor Bennett—in his determined effort to downgrade the significance of the insurrection (at least in part because of what it would do to the reputation of the state; see his letter in the *National Intelligencer*, Aug. 24, 1822)—at one point (*Message No. 2*, p. 16) pictures Vesey on Sunday as "shivering with fear."

This is wholly inconsistent with other reports of Vesey's behavior and character.

19. *National Intelligencer*, Aug. 24, 1822.

20. Hamilton, *Negro Plot*, p. 10.

21. Letter from W. Hasell Wilson to Rev. D. Wilson.

22. Bennett, *Message No. 2*, p. 3. A contemporary observer wrote that about 2,500 troops were under arms on the fateful night. Wish, "Slave Insurrections Before 1861," *Journal of Negro History*, XX, 299.

23. *National Intelligencer*, Aug. 24, 1822.

24. Hamilton, *Negro Plot*, pp. 10-19; *National Intelligencer*, Aug. 24, 1822.

25. Kennedy and Parker, *Official Report*, pp. iv-v; Hamilton, *Negro Plot*, pp. 10-11.

26. Letter from John Potter, Charleston, to Langdon Cheves, Philadelphia, June 29, 1822, in Cheves Collection, South Carolina Historical Society, Charleston.

FOR OTHER AUTHORITIES USED, SEE:

On Charleston in the 1820's—Jervey, *Hayne*; Molloy, *Charleston*; Petty, *Population*.

On the discovery of the plan for an insurrection—Kennedy and Parker, *Official Report*.

On preparations for the defense of Charleston—Kennedy and Parker, *Official Report*; Bennett, *Message No. 2*.

On the arrests—Kennedy and Parker, *Official Report*; Hamilton, *Negro Plot*.

On the occupations of court members—*Charleston Directory*, 1822.

On the Charleston atmosphere at the time of the arrests—Higginson, *Travellers and Outlaws*.

## Chapter 12

1. *Charleston Directory*, 1829, p. 10.

2. Higginson, *Travellers and Outlaws*, p. 265.

3. Kennedy and Parker, *Official Report*, pp. vi-vii; Higginson, *Travellers and Outlaws*, p. 265. For testimony on a contemplated later uprising and rescue efforts, see Kennedy and Parker, *Official Report*, pp. viii, 55, 148, 150, 163, 164. Two brigades were reported later by a contemporary to have been under arms to suppress any insurrection that might take place. Higginson, *Travellers and Outlaws*, p. 266.

4. See text of Chapter 5 at note 11.

5. See text of Chapter 7 at note 24.

6. Kennedy and Parker, *Official Report*, p. ix.

7. *Ibid.*, p. vi. Note that it was not the defendant's nearest of kin whose presence was guaranteed but his master's.

8. *Ibid.*, pp. vii, 56, 61 n., 64 n., 69 ns., 71 n.; Bennett, *Message No. 2*, pp. 7-8.

9. Kennedy and Parker, *Official Report*, p. 173. See criticism of the trial in T. Hamilton, *The Late Contemplated Insurrection*, p. 6.

10. See *National Intelligencer*, Aug. 24, 1822.

11. Inferences as to George's identity may be drawn from testimony reported in Kennedy and Parker, *Official Report*, p. 65.

12. The record indicates (*Official Report*, p. 67) that five witnesses appeared in Rolla's behalf but fails to identify their testimony.

13. Governor Bennett's letter in the *National Intelligencer*, Aug. 24, 1822, places the beginning date of Vesey's trial as June 22. But since Vesey was not arrested until June 22 (*Official Report*, p. 42 n.), the date of the trial opening was probably June 23. Governor Bennett also notes that, although Vesey was unquestionably the chief of the plot, no positive proof of his guilt appeared until June 25. This was evidently the testimony of the anonymous witness who was a friend of George Wilson. See text infra, at note 15.

14. Kennedy and Parker, *Official Report*, p. 85. Cross' first and middle names are given in Jervey, *Hayne*, p. 132.

15. Kennedy and Parker, *Official Report*, p. 86. The words of the fable are given as reported in the record, but punctuation and correct spelling have been supplied for the sake of clarity.

16. *Ibid.*, pp. 88-89. The exact span of the Vesey trial in days and hours is not recorded. But Frank and Adam Ferguson were not arrested until June 27 (*Official Report*, pp. 185, 187). And Governor Bennett notes (*National Intelligencer*, Aug. 24, 1822) that their evidence was important.

17. The record of the testimony at no point shows where defense counsel were able to confound the prosecution's witnesses.

18. Quoted in Kennedy and Parker, *Official Report*, pp. 177-178.

19. *City Gazette and Commercial Daily Advertiser,* Charleston *Courier, Southern Patriot and Commercial Advertiser,* Charleston *Mercury and Morning Advertiser*, June 29, 1822.

20. Charleston *Courier*, June 21, 1822.
21. *Ibid.*

22. Letter from John Potter, Charleston, to Langdon Cheves, Philadelphia, June 29, 1822.

23. Letter from John Potter, Charleston, to Langdon Cheves Philadelphia, July 5, 1822.

24. Charleston *Courier*, June 29, 1822.

25. *Ibid.*

26. Johnson pamphlet quoted in Morgan, *Johnson*, pp. 132-133.

27. Letter from John Potter, Charleston, to Langdon Cheves, Philadelphia, June 29, 1822.

28. Letter signed "Many Citizens" in *Southern Patriot and Commercial Advertiser*, July 1, 1822, and unsigned "communication" in Charleston *Courier*, July 1, 1822.

29. *Ibid.*

30. Letter from John Potter, Charleston, to Langdon Cheves, Philadelphia, June 29, 1822.

31. Irving, *Day on Cooper River*, pp. 22, 23.

32. Hamilton communication referred to in letter from John Potter, Charleston, to Langdon Cheves, Philadelphia, June 29, 1822.

33. *Ibid.*

34. *City Gazette*, July 2, 1800.

35. Use of irons mentioned in Kennedy and Parker, *Official Report*, p. 57.

36. While the *Official Report* (p. 26) indicates that none of the leaders except Monday Gell betrayed his associates, a confession by Rolla is reported on pp. 66, 67. Jesse, not a leader, was also reported to have confessed. *Official Report*, pp. 80, 81.

37. *Southern Patriot*, July 2, 1822; Charleston *Courier*, Charleston *Mercury*, July 3, 1822.

38. Charleston *Courier*, June 29, 1822.

39. *Ibid.*, June 29, July 6, 1822.

40. *Ibid.*, July 6, 1822. A Charleston pamphlet of the period recognized the explosive potential of public orations on liberty and urged that Negroes be barred from Fourth of July affairs. Higginson, "Denmark Vesey," *Atlantic Monthly*, VII, 743.

41. Charleston *Courier*, July 10, 1822.

42. "The Lines" followed the one-time defense fortifications of the city, a course corresponding to Calhoun Street today.

43. Charleston *Courier*, July 10, 1822.

44. *Southern Patriot*, July 12, 1822; Charleston *Mercury*, Charleston *Courier*, July 13, 1822.

45. *Southern Patriot*, July 12, 1822.

46. Monday Gell was the only one of Vesey's principal lieu-

tenants to furnish substantial evidence against his associates. Kennedy and Parker, *Official Report*, p. 26. The *City Gazette* observed that it was through his testimony principally that "the whole plot was unfolded, and the conspirators brought to justice." *City Gazette*, Aug. 21, 1822. Whether anything other than the hope of reprieve prompted Monday to talk was not revealed. Governor Bennett later wrote that "no means which experience or integrity could devise were left unessayed, to eviscerate the plot." He added that some of the confessing prisoners were motivated by an expectation of pardon or a spirit of retaliation growing out of a suspicion that they were the victims of treachery. *National Intelligencer*, Aug. 24, 1822.

During the planning of the uprising participants had reportedly been told that anyone who betrayed his fellows would be killed. Kennedy and Parker, *Official Report*, pp. 26, 64, 75, 79, 82, 105, 120. Most of the leaders, however, never had the opportunity to make good this threat. And, if others in the uncertainty of their predicament, yielded to the urge to implicate suspected betrayers, they were manifesting a not uncommon human attribute. Some of the informers were the targets of insults from other Negroes, and these hecklers were in turn punished by the authorities. Bennett, *Message No. 2*, p. 6.

47. Kennedy and Parker, *Official Report*, pp. 58-59. A confession by Gell was heard by the court on July 13. He and Drayton and Haig had been granted a respite by the governor in order to give them a chance to talk.

48. *National Intelligencer*, Aug. 24, 1822. It was at this time that the court adopted certain criteria by which the degree of guilt of the accused was to be judged. All of those who had attended meetings or engaged in some other overt act for the furtherance of the insurrection were to be in Class 1 and were to be sentenced to death. All of those who merely consented to join were to be in Class 2 and were to be sentenced to banishment. Kennedy and Parker, *Official Report*, p. 8. See *infra*, n. 74.

49. Letter from Governor Thomas Bennett to Secretary of War John C. Calhoun, July 15, 1822.

50. Letter from Secretary of War John C. Calhoun to Colonel A. Eustis, officer in command at St. Augustine, July 22, 1822.

51. Letter from Secretary of War John C. Calhoun to Major James Bankhead, officer in command at Charleston, July 22, 1822.

52. *Southern Patriot*, July 30, 1822.

53. *Ibid.*, Aug. 15, 1822.

54. Letter from Governor Thomas Bennett to Secretary of War John C. Calhoun, July 30, 1822.

55. Later Governor Bennett sought to persuade the legislature that, in asking for troops, he had only been concerned with

executing the quarantine laws. Bennett, Preamble, *Message No. 2*.

56. *Southern Patriot*, July 18, 22, 1822; Charleston *Mercury*, July 19, 23, 1822; Charleston *Courier*, July 19, 1822.

57. *Southern Patriot*, July 26, 1822.

58. *City Gazette*, July 27, 1822.

59. Charleston *Courier*, Charleston *Mercury*, July 27, 1822.

60. *Southern Patriot*, July 27, 1822.

61. Kennedy and Parker, *Official Report*, pp. 172, 183-188. Of the 59 defendants who were found guilty of attempting to raise an insurrection, 46 were sentenced to death by the court. But the tribunal recommended that the sentences of nine of these be commuted by the governor on condition that they be banished from the United States. The governor eventually commuted the sentences of the nine, as well as of three others, to banishment. One convicted defendant a Negro named Prince Graham, was allowed to choose his place of overseas exile and chose Africa. Kennedy and Parker, *Official Report*, p. 163.

62. See Henry, *Police Control*, p. 55, on transportation as punishment.

63. *City Gazette*, July 27, 1822.

64. *Southern Patriot, City Gazette*, July 27, 1822; Charleston *Mercury*, July 29, 1822.

65. *City Gazette*, July 27, 1822.

66. The arrest of Perault Strohecker on July 10 led to information on William Garner. *National Intelligencer*, Aug. 24, 1822.

67. *Southern Patriot*, July 26, 29, 1822.

68. *Ibid.*, July 27, 1822.

69. *City Gazette*, July 27, 1822.

70. *Southern Patriot*, Aug. 2, 1822.

71. *Ibid.*,

72. *City Gazette*, Aug. 9, 1822.
73. Kennedy and Parker, *Official Report*, Appendix, pp. i-x. William Allen, about forty-five, a Scotsman by birth and a sailor, was found guilty by a jury and sentenced to be imprisoned for twelve months, to pay a fine of $1,000 and to give security for his good behavior for five years after his release. *Ibid.*, Appendix, pp. ii-v. John Igneshias, another seafaring man, a Spaniard of about forty-five was convicted and sentenced to three months imprisonment, to pay a fine of $100 and to give security for five years' good behavior. *Ibid.*, Appendix, pp. v-vi. A similar sentence was imposed on Jacob Danders, a German peddler of about forty-five or fifty who had been overheard telling several Negroes that certain of the executed insurgents were innocent

and had been murdered and that his listeners ought to rescue those still to be hanged. *Ibid.*, Appendix, pp. vi-vii. The last white defendant was Andrew S. Rhodes, a former shopkeeper of about fifty who had lived in the state for about thirty years. He was found guilty and sentenced to six months in prison, to pay a fine of $500 and to give security for five years' good behavior. *Ibid.*, Appendix, pp. vii-ix.

74. Governor Bennett observed that, once the existence of the plot and the places of rendezvous were established, "all that was deememed requisite for conviction was to prove an association with the ringleaders and an expression of their assent to the measure." On "such, generally," he added, "the sentence of death has been executed. Others, who without actually combining, were proved to have known of the conspiracy, and to have given their sanction by any act, have been sentenced to die, and their punishment commuted to banishment from the United States." *National Intelligencer*, Aug. 24, 1822.

75. See text, *supra*, at n. 61.

76. Compare law for whites in Kennedy and Parker, *Official Report*, Appendix pp. ix-x.

77. *Ibid.*, pp. 58-59. Respite extended to July 19. Charleston *Courier*, July 12, 1822 Respite extended to July 26. *Southern Patriot*, July 18 1822.

78. But the man whose public letter aroused the suspicion against the governor later apologized. *Southern Patriot*, July 29, 1822,

79. *City Gazette*, Sept. 20, 1822.

80. Bennett, *Message No. 2*, p. 9. The court itself, though it sentenced Peter to death, had recommended that the governor pardon him on condition that he be banished from the United States. Kennedy and Parker, *Official Report*, pp. 154-155.

81. *City Gazette, July* 27, 1822.

82. Governor Bennett's publication was in the form of a letter. Written on August 10, 1822, and published first as a circular, it was picked up by the *National Intelligencer* and published in its issue of August 24, 1822. This edition was used as a source in this work.

In addiltion to Governor Bennett, a number of citizens expressed apprehension as to the effect the insurrection would have in depressing the value of slaves. Letter from Henry W. DeSaussure to Joel R. Poinsett, July 8, 1822; letter from John Potter to Langdon Cheves, July 5, 1822.

83. *City Gazette*, Charleston *Mercury*, Aug. 21, 1822; Carolina *Gazette, Aug.* 24, 1822.

84. See Hamilton, *Negro Plot*.

85. *City Gazette*, Aug. 21, 1822.

86. Higginson, *Travellers and Outlaws*, p. 268.

87. *Southern Patriot*, Nov. 9, 1822.

88. *City Gazette*, July 27, 1822.

89. *Ibid.*, Aug. 21, 1822.

90. Letter from John Potter, Charleston, to Langdon Cheves, Philadelphia, June 29, 1822.

91. The New York *National Advocate* called the executions "a necessary punishment." Quoted in Charleston *Mercury*, July 18, 1822.

92. *Niles Weekly Register* (July 13, 1822) XX, 320.

93. Richmond comment on insurrection mentioned in *Southern Patriot*, Aug. 7, 1822; news item on insurrection in *Arkansas Gazette*, Sept. 3, 1822; *Franklin Gazette* (Philadelphia) item reported and replied to in *City Gazette*, Aug. 15, 1822; New York *National Advocate* item reported in Charleston *Mercury*, July 18, 1822; Hartford *Courant* quoted in Higginson, *Travellers and Outlaws*, p. 266; letter to Boston *Recorder* republished in Charleston *Courier*, Nov. 15, 1822; mention of publication of insurrection news in British papers made in Charleston *Mercury*, Oct. 7, 1822.

94. Quoted in *City Gazette*, Aug. 14, 1822.

95. Quoted *ibid.*, Aug. 15, 1822.

96. *Ibid.*, Aug. 14, 1822.

97. Charleston *Courier*, Aug. 24, 1822.

98. Furman, *Exposition of the Views of Baptists*, p. 3.

99. Charleston *Mercury*, Nov. 19, 1822.

100. McCord, *Statutes of S. C.*, VI, 187-188.

101. Charleston *Courier*, Dec. 25, 1822.

102 *Southern Patriot*, Dec. 6, 1822.

103. McCord, *Statutes of S. C.*, VI, 194-195. The reward bill was introduced by the Charleston delegation. Charleston *Mercury*, Dec. 11, 1822.

As late as 1861 Peter Prioleau was still living in Charleston as a free man, having been established in business as a drayman and being the only man of property in the state who was exempt from taxation. Higginson, "Denmark Vesey," *Atlantic Monthly*, VII, 744.

104. Quoted in Aptheker, *American Negro Slave Revolts*, p. 224.

FOR OTHER AUTHORITIES USED, SEE:

On the trial setting, on the law for insurgents, on Vesey before his judges, on the trials in general, on the executions, on the dispute over procedure, on white accomplices in insurrection—Kennedy and Parker, *Official Report*.

On the trial scene—Higginson, *Travellers and Outlaws*.

On Justice Johnson's protest and the reaction of court officials and their sympathizers—Morgan, *Johnson*; Jervey, *Hayne*.

On the second court—Adger, *My Life and Times*.

On Governor Bennett's disagreement with the law enforcement authorities—Bennett, *Message No. 2*.

On the freeing of Peter Prioleau and George Wilson—Jervey, *Hayne*.

## Chapter 13

1. Letter from W. Hasell Wilson, Philadelphia, to Rev. D. Wilson, Charleston, June, 1900.

2. Higginson, "Denmark Vesey," *Atlantic Monthly*, VII, 742.

3. Letter from George Logan to Caesar Rodney, Dec. 19, 1822.

4. Higginson, *Travellers and Outlays*, p. 246.

5. Letter from John Potter to Langdon Cheves, July 5, 1822.

6. *City Gazette*, Sept. 5, 1822.

7. Higginson, *Travellers and Outlaws*, p. 274.

8. Charleston *Courier*, July 17, 1822; Charleston *Mercury*, Aug. 13, 1822; *Southern Patriot*, Aug. 16, 1822; *Carolina Gazette*, Aug. 24, 1822.

9. *Niles Weekly Register*, (July 27, 1822) XX, 352.

10. See text, Chapter 9 at note 10. One of the convicted conspirators had been a runaway. Kennedy and Parker, *Official Report*, p. 113.

11. Aptheker, *American Negro Slave Revolts*, p. 277.

12. Porter, "Relations Between Negroes and Indians," *Journal of Negro History*, XVII, 335.

13. Charleston *Directory*, 1822, p. 102.

14. See Chapter 6, text at note 13.

15. *City Gazette*, Aug 10, 1822.

16. *Ibid.*, In later years there was a tendency among Carolinians to exonerate the African church, evidently because an incriminating view interfered with religious objectives. Adger, *My Life and Times*, pp. 53-55.

17. Hamilton, *Negro Plot*, p. 30.

18. Charleston *Mercury*, Sept. 24, 1822.

19. Charleston *Mercury*, Oct. 23, 1822. Some slaves were still in the Charleston workhouse in December, 1822, awaiting

arrangements for their banishment to be made. Charleston *Courier*, December 25, 1822.

20. Achates [Pinckney], *Reflections*, pp. 6-7.

21. *Ibid.*, p. 8.

22. The newspaper strategists of slave security ranged far and wide in their search for causes and cures. Readers were advised that the evil of the incipient rebellion could be traced to the hiring out of slaves for jobs where they were removed from the watchful eyes of their masters (letters in *Southern Patriot*, July 19, 1822, and the Charleston *Mercury*, Oct. 30, 1822), to the laxity of the patrols (letters in *Southern Patriot*, July 5, 1822, and Charleston *Courier*, July 10, 1822), to the pernicious influence of dram shops in many parts of the city (letters in *Southern Patriot*, July 5 and 19, 1822; Charleston *Courier*, July 17, 1822) where Sunday was profaned by the sale of liquor to Negroes and where fuel was supplied for the incubation of who knows what manner of diabolical schemes. A merchant came to the defense of the "honest" owners of dram shops in a letter to the *Southern Patriot*, July 20, 1822.

Among the remedies which the correspondents proposed were the extensive reorganization of the patrol system (Charleston *Courier*, July 10, 1822), the revision of the law on slaves working for wages (Charleston *Mercury*, Oct. 30, 1822), the exiling of free Negroes from the state (Charleston *Courier*, Nov. 13, 1822) and the raising of a standing army for the lowcountry (Charleston *Mercury*, Dec. 4, 1822).

23. Letter from John S. Cogdell, Charleston, to Langdon Cheves, Philadelphia, July 6, 1822. Cogdell position identified in Charleston *Courier*, Dec. 12, 1822.

24. The grand jury recommended that the legislature regulate the clothing worn by persons of color, since expensive dress tended to subvert the servile demeanor desirable in such persons; that it limit the number of slaves which any one owner might hire out; and that it direct its attention to the number of dram shops permitted in the city. Finally, the presentment emphasized as a growing evil the frequent introduction of slaves from other states. *City Gazette*, Oct. 15, 1822.

25. The Turnbull grand jury complained about the destructive effect of dram shops on the morals of Negroes, about the number of free Negroes living in Charleston and its environs and their unfortunate competition with the "poorer classes of white persons," and about the number of schools kept by persons of color within the city. Charleston *Courier*, Jan. 31, 1823.

26. Charleston *Mercury*, *Aug.* 19 and 20, 1822; *Southern Patriot*, Aug. 21, 1822.

27. Charleston *Mercury*, Nov. 30, 1822; *City Gazette,* Dec. 4, 1822.

28. The witnesses referred to were Bacchus Hammett, Smart Anderson and Pharo Thompson.

29. Charleston *Mercury*, Dec. 4, 1822.

30. *City Gazette*, Dec. 4, 1822.

31. Charleston *Mercury*, Dec. 5, 1822.

32. *Ibid.*, Dec. 11, 1822.

33. *Carolina Gazette*, Dec. 14, 1822.

34. *Ibid.*,

35. Quoted in Morgan, *Johnson*, p. 138.

36. Charleston *Mercury*, Dec. 7, 1822.

37. *Ibid.*, Dec. 11, 1822.

38. *Ibid.*,

39. McCord, *Statutes of S. C.*, VI, 177.

40. *Ibid.*, VII, 461-462.

41. Charleston *Mercury*, Dec. 7, 1822.

42. Jervey, *Hayne*, p. 134; Charleston *Courier*, Dec. 25, 1822.

43. *Niles' Register* (March 15, 1823) XXIV, 31-32.

44. Hamer, "Negro Seaman Acts," *Journal of Southern History*, I, 4. The text of Canning's note was printed in the *City Gazette*, Dec. 7, 1824.

45. Hamer, "Negro Seaman Acts," *Journal of Southern History*, I, 5, n. 10; Morgan, "Johnson on the Treaty-Making Power," *Geo. Wash. L. Rev.*, XXII, 5. Elkinson's status given in 8 Fed. Cas. 493.

46. Morgan, *Johnson*, p. 193. Commercial Convention of 1815 quoted in Morgan, "Johnson on the Treaty-Making Power," *Geo. Wash. L. Lev.*, XXII, 5, n. 10.

47. Morgan, *Johnson*, p. 194, n. 19. The jurisdiction of federal courts to issue the writ of habeas corpus on application of state prisoners was not authorized by statute until 1867. 108 *U. Pa. L. Rev.* 461, n. 1.

48. Morgan, *Johnson*, p. 195. The famous case of Gibbons v. Ogden, also bearing on the commerce clause, was not decided until seven months later. Morgan, "Johnson on the Treaty-Making Power," *Geo. Wash. L. Rev.*, XXII, 5, n. 9.

49. Quoted in Morgan, *Johnson*, p. 195.

50. *Caroliniensis*, p. 41.

51. *Ibid.*, pp. 37-38.

52. McCord, *Statutes of S. C.*, VII, 461; Hamer, "Negro Seamen Acts," *Journal of Southern History*, I, 9.

53. The Wirt opinion was printed in the *City Gazette*, Dec. 7, 1824.

54. Adams letter. *Ibid.*

55. Quoted in *City Gazette*, Dec. 7, 1824.

56. Hamer, "Negro Seamen Acts," *Journal of Southern History*, I, 12. In *Niles Weekly Register*, Dec. 18, 1824, the editor expressed the opinion that the issue of the Negro Seaman Act was potentially as dangerous as the Missouri question. Cited in Bedford, "Johnson and the Marshall Court," *S. C. Historical Magazine*, LXII, 170.

57. James, *Andrew Jackson*, p. 511.

58. Swisher, "Mr. Chief Justice Taney," *Mr. Justice*, pp. 210-211.

FOR OTHER AUTHORITIES USED, SEE:

On Charleston's reaction to insurrection—Kennedy and Parker, *Official Report*.

On suggested causes and cures—Kennedy and Parker, *Official Report*; Phillips, *Plantation and Frontier Documents*, II.

On Governor Bennett's observations to the legislature on insurrection—Bennett, *Message No. 2*.

On legislative reaction—Jervey *Hayne*; Morgan, *Johnson*; Morgan, "Johnson on the Treaty-Making Power," *Geo. Wash. L. Rev.*, XXII, 1-29.

On the Negro Seamen Act—Ames, *State Documents*; Hamer, "Negro Seamen Acts," *Journal of Southern History*, I, 3-28; Morgan, *Johnson*; Morgan, "Johnson on the Treaty-Making Power," *Geo. Wash. L. Rev.*, XXII, 1-29.

## Chapter 14

1. Bennett, *Message No. 2*, p. 23.

2. Turner, *New West*, *p.* 308; Franklin, *Slavery to Freedom*, p. 257; Morgan, *Johnson*, p. 126; Wiltse, *Calhoun, Nationalist*, p. 256.

3. Wallace, *South Carolina*, pp. 481-482.

4. Professor Basil L. Gildersleeve quoted in Wallace, *South Carolina*, p. 408.

5. Quoted in Jervey, *Hayne*, pp. 96-97.

6. Quoted in Wallace, *South Carolina*, p. 387.

7. Logan, *Diplomatic Relations*, p. 79. See Chapter 9, text at note 24.

8. See Chapter 9, text at note 19.

9. Kennedy and Parker, *Official Report*, pp. 62, 64, 67, 68, 73, 82, 83, 86, 93, 94, 96, 118, 120, 121, 125, 146, 153.

10. Quoted in Jervey, *Hayne*, p. 192.

11. Quoted in Wallace, *South Carolina*, p. 385.

12. Ames, *State Documents*, pp. 203-204.

13. *Ibid.*, pp. 207-208.

14. Turner, *New West*, p. 304; Eaton, *Freedom of Thought*, p. 90.

15. Dumond, *Antislavery*, p. 191.

16. Quoted in Aptheker, *Negro in Abolutionist Movement*, pp. 25-26.

17. Furnas, *Road to Harpers Ferry*, p. 419, n. 13.

18. Neilson, *Zamba*, pp. 236-237.

19. Hamilton, *Late Contemplated Insurrection*, p. 6.

20. Helper, *Impending Crisis*, p. 128.

21. *Ibid.*. pp. 225-226, 227.

22. One author, as early as 1830, felt that the tariff was being exaggerated as a cause of distress. Quoted in Smith, *Economic Readjustment*, p. 36; see also Wallace, *South Carolina*, p. 428.

23. House resolution quoted in Turner, *New West*, pp. 308-309.

24. McDuffie and House committee report quoted in Turner, *New West*, pp. 308-309; see also Wallace, *South Carolina*, p. 390.

25. Degler, "There Was Another South," *American Heritage*, XI, 53; Boucher, *Nullification*, p. 1.

26. *Ibid.*, p. 1. Boucher mistakenly, it seems to this author, says the 1825 anti-tariff resolutions marked the "beginning of the formidable anti-nationalist movement in the state."

27. Holland, *Refutation of Calumnies*.

28. Wiltse, *Calhoun, Nationalist*, p. 356; Wallace, *South Carolina*, p. 391; Hofstader, *Great Issues*, I, 275.

29. *Ibid.*, pp. 277-278.

30. *Ibid.*, pp. 278-281.

31. Wallace, *South Carolina*, p. 400. See Chapter 6.

32. Quoted *ibid*, p. 400; Wiltse, *Calhoun, Nullifier*, pp. 147, 148.

33. Hofstadter, *Great Issues*, I, 284, 288.

34. *Ibid.*, p. 289.

35. *Ibid.*, p. 290.

36. Quoted in Wallace, *South Carolina*, p. 511.

37. Quoted *ibid.*, p. 403.

38. Quoted *ibid.*, p. 396.

39. *Ibid.*, p. 408

40. Quoted *ibid.*, p. 507.

41. Quoted *ibid.*, pp. 500, 513, 514, 515.

42. Stampp, *Causes of Civil War*, pp. 125-126

43. Kirwan,*Confederacy*, p. 23.

44. Bennett, *Message No. 2*, p. 22.

45. Kirwan, *Confederacy*, p. 34; Stampp, *Causes of Civil War*, p. 37.

46. Kirwan, *Confederacy*, p. 51.

47. *Ibid.*, p. 25.

48. Wallace, *South Carolina*, p. 527; Stampp, *Causes of Civil War*, p. 108.

49. Quoted in Wallace, *South Carolina*, p. 529.

50. Kirwan, *Confederacy*, p. 30.

51. *Ibid.*, p. 30.

52. Hofstadter, *Great Issues*, I, 400.

53. Kirwan, *Confederacy*, p. 47.

54. Quoted *ibid.*, p. 50.

55. Stampp, *Causes of Civil War*, pp. 140-142.

56. Hughes and Maltzer, *Pictorial History of the Negro*, p. 172.

FOR OTHER AUTHORITIES USED, SEE:

On slavery as a way of life—Turner, *New West*; Wallace, *South Carolina*; Wiltse, *Calhoun, Nationalist.*

On relations with Haiti—Logan, *Diplomatic Relations*; Montague, *Haiti.*

On reaction to abolitionism—Jervey, *Hayne*; Wallace, *South Carolina*, Wiltse, *Calhoun, Nullifier.*

On the tariff controversy—Boucher, *Nullification;* Degler, "There Was Another South," *American Heritage*, XI (Aug. 1960); James, *Andrew Jackson;* Jervey, *Hayne;* Morgan, *Johnson;* Morison and Commager, *American Republic*, 2d ed., Smith, *Economic Readjustment;* Turner, *New West;* Wallace, *South Carolina;* Wiltse, *Calhoun, Nationalist* and *Calhoun, Nullifier.*

On the trend from nullification to insurrection—Angle, *Nation Divided*; Boucher, *Nullification*; Franklin, *Militant South*; James, *Andrew Jackson*; Jervey, *Hayne*; Smith, *Economic Readjustment*; Wallace, *South Carolina.*

# • BIBLIOGRAPHY

## Letters

Bennett, Gov. Thomas, to John C. Calhoun, Secretary of War, July 15, 1822. Register of Letters Received, File No. 30 B (16), War Records Branch, National Archives.

Bennett, Gov. Thomas, to John C. Calhoun, Secretary of War, July 30, 1822. Register of Letters Received, File 55 B (16), War Records Branch, National Archives.

Calhoun, Secretary of War John C., to Col. A. Eustis, officer commanding at St. Augustine, July 22, 1822. Item 324, Record Group 107, National Archives.

Calhoun, Secretary of War John C., to Major James Bankhead, officer commanding at Charleston, July 22, 1822. Item 446/408, Record Group 107, National Archives.

Calhoun, Secretary of War John C., to Gov. Thomas Bennett, July 22, 1822. Item 424/53, Record Group 107, National Archives.

Cogdell, John (Charleston) to Langdon Cheves (Philadelphia), July 6, 1822. Cheves Collection, South Carolina Historical Society, Charleston.

DeSaussure, Henry W., to Joel R. Poinsett, July 8, 1822. Poinsett Papers, vol. 2, p. 65, Historical Society of Pennsylvania, Philadelphia, Pa.

Jefferson, Thomas, Papers of, Vol. 96, items 16402 and 16403, Library of Congress.

Logan, George, to Caesar Rodney, Dec. 19, 1822. Simon Gratz Collection, Case 7, Box 31, Historical Society of Pennsylvania, Philadelphia, Pa.

Potter, John (Charleston) to Langdon Cheves (Philadelphia) June 29 and July 5, 1822. Cheves Collection, South Carolina Historical Society, Charleston, S. C.

Wilson, W. Hasell (Philadelphia) to Rev. D. Wilson (Charleston), June 1900. Mss. No. 98 in manuscript collection of Charleston Library Society, Charleston, S.C. [Though no date is given on letter, the one specified above is inferred from accompanying note by Robert Wilson saying letter writer was then 89 and was born in 1811.]

## Public Documents

*The Act of the General Assembly Incorporating the City, and the Subsequent Acts to Explain and Amend the Same.* Charleston: John MacIver, 1796.

Ames, Herman V., ed., *State Documents on Federal Relations: The States and the United States*, No. V, "Slavery and the Constitution," Philadelphia: History Department, University of Pennsylvania, 1904.

*The Congressional Globe: New Series containing Sketches of the Debates and Proceedings of the Second Session of the Thirtieth Congress*. Washington: Blair and Rives, 1849.

Cooper, Thomas and McCord, David J., eds., *Statutes at Large of South Carolina*. 10 vols. Columbia: 1836-1840.

Hurd, John Codman, ed., *The Law of Freedom and Bondage in the United States*. 2 vols. Boston: Little, Brown, 1862.

Peters, Richard, ed., *The Public Statutes at Large of the United States of America*. 8 vols.. Boston: Charles C. Little and James Brown, 1845.

Miscellaneous Records, Office of Judge of Probate, Charleston, S. C.

Miscellaneous Records, Office of Register of Mesne Conveyance, Charleston, S. C.

*Ship Manifests, 1784*. South Carolina Archives Department, Columbia, S.C.

*Ship Register, 1765 et seq*. South Carolina Archives Department, Columbia, S.C.

[U.S. Census], *Return of the Whole Number of Persons within the Several Districts of the United States According to "An act for the second Census or Enumeration of the Inhabitants of the United States*," 1800. [No place of publication given.]

*Aggregate amount of each description of Persons within the United States of America, and the Territories thereof, agreeably to actual enumeration made according to law, in the year 1810.*

*Fourth Census*, 1820. Washington: Gales and Seaton, 1821.

*Fifth Census; or Enumeration of the Inhabitants of the United States, 1830*. Washington: Duff Green, 1832.

*Heads of Families at the First Census of the United States Taken in the Year 1790, South Carolina*. Washington: Government Printing Office, 1908.

Will Books. Charleston Free Library, Charleston, S. C.

### Diaries, Memoirs, Autobiographies, Reminiscences

Adger, John B., D.D., *My Life and Times, 1810-1899*. Richmond: The Presbyterian Committee of Publication, 1899.

Asbury, Francis, *The Journal of the Rev. Francis Asbury*. 3 vols. New York: Easton and Maine, 1821.

Bernard, John, *Retrospections of America, 1797-1811*. Edited by Mrs. Bayle Bernard. New York: 1887.

Ford, Timothy, "Diary of Timothy Ford, 1785-1786," *South Carolina Historical and Genealogical Magazine*. Edited by Joseph W. Barnwell. Vol. XIII, 203.

Fraser, Charles, *Reminiscences of Charleston*. Charleston: 1854.

Thomas, E. S. *Reminiscences of the Last Sixty-Five Years, Commencing with the Battle of Lexington. also, Sketches of His Own Life and Times*. Hartford: Case, Tiffany and Burnham, 1840.

Uhlendorf, Bernard A., ed. and trans., *The Siege of Charleston—With an Account of the Province of South Carolina: Diaries and Letters of Hessian Officers from the von Jungkenn Papers in the William L. Clements Library*. Ann Arbor: University of Michigan Press: 1936.

[Washington, George], *The Diaries of George Washington, 1748-1799*. Edited by John C. Fitzpatrick. Boston: Houghton Mifflin Company, 1925. Vol. IV.

*Wilson, William Hasell, Reminiscences of*. Elizabeth B. Pharo, ed. Philadelphia: Patterson and White Co., 1937.

### Contemporary Accounts

[Canot, Theodore], *Adventures of an African Slaver—Being a True Account of the Life of Captain Theodore Canot, Trader in Gold, Ivory, & Slaves on the Coast of Guinea; His Own Story as told in the Year 1854 to Brantz Mayer*. Malcolm Cowley, ed. New York: Albert & Charles Boni, 1928.

*The Charleston Directory for 1790*. [In Charleston Library Society collection; no publisher or place of publication given.]

*Nelson's Charleston Directory, and Stranger's Guids. for the Year of Our Lord, 1801 Being the Twenty-Fifth Year of the Independence of the United States of America, Until July Fourth*. Charleston: John Dixon Nelson, 1801.

*New Charleston Directory, and Stranger's Guide, for the Year 1802. Being the Twenty-Sixth and Twenty-Seventh Years of the Independence of the United States of America*. J. J. Negrin, ed. Charleston: John A. Dacqueny, 1802.

*Negrin's Directory and Almanac for the Year 1806: Containing Every Article of General Utility*. Charleston: J. J. Negrin, 1806.

Hrabowski, Richard (compiler), *Directory for the District of Charleston, Comprising the Places of Residence and Occupation of the White Inhabitants of the Following Parishes, to wit—St. Michael, St. Philip, St. Philip on the Neck, St. John (Colleton), Christ Church, St. James (Santee), St Thomas and St. Dennis, St. Andrew, St. John (Berkley), St. Stephen, and St. James (Goose Creek)*. Charleston: John Hoff, 1809.

*The Directory and Stranger's Guide, for the City of Charleston; also a Directory for Charleston Neck, Between Boundary-Street and the Lines, For the Year 1819. To which is added An Almanac; The Tariff of Duties on all Goods Imported into the United States; Rates of Wharfage, Weighing, Storage, Cartage and Drayage, &c. &c.* Charleston: Schenck & Turner, 1819.

*The Directory and Stranger's Guide for the City of Charleston, also a Directory for Charleston Neck, Between Boundary-Street and the Lines; Likewise for the Coloured Persons Within the City, and another for Coloured Persons Residing on the Neck, for the Year 1822, To which is added, An Almanac; the Tariff of Duties on all Goods Imported into the United States; and the Rates of Wharfage, Weighing, Storage, Dockage and Drayage, &c.* Charleston: James R. Schenck, 1822.

Cromwell, O. (compiler), *Directory, or Guide to the Residences and Places of Business of the Inhabitants of the City of Charleston and its Environs: Prefaced with a Description of Our Various Public Buildings, and other Local Information. Taken Down for the Year of Our Lord 1829.* Charleston: James S. Burges, 1828.

Goldsmith, Morris (compiler), *Directory and Strangers' Guide for the City of Charleston and its Vicinity.* Charleston: 1831.

"Charleston, S.C., in 1774, as Described by an English Traveller," *The Historical Magazine, and Notes and Queries concerning the Antiquities, History and Biography of America,* IX (1865), 341.

Davis, John, *Travels of Four Years and a Half in the United States of America during 1798, 1799, 1800, 1801 and 1802.* New York: Henry Holt and Company, 1909.

De Brahm, William Gerard, "Philosophic-Hydrogeography of South Carolina, Georgia and East Florida," *Documents Connected with the History of South Carolina.* Edited by Plowden C. J. Weston. London: 1856.

Donnan, Elizabeth, *Documents Illustrative of the History of the Slave Trade to America.* Washington: Carnegie Institution of Washington, 1931. Vol. II.

Furman, Rev. Richard, *Exposition of the Views of Baptists Relative to the Colored Population of the United States in a Communication to the Governor of South Carolina.* Charleston: A. E. Miller, 1823.

Hamilton, James Jr., *Negro Plot, An Account of the Late Intended Insurrection Among a Portion of the Blacks of the City of Charleston, South Carolina.* Boston: Joseph W. Ingraham, 1822.

[Johnston, John], *The Journal of an African Slaver, 1789-1792*. Worcester, Mass.: American Antiquarian Society, 1930.

Kennedy, Lionel H. and Parker, Thomas, *An Official Report of the Trials of Sundry Negroes, Charged with an Attempt to Raise an Insurrection in the State of South Carolina*. Charleston: James R. Schenck, 1822.

Lambert, John, *Travels Through Canada and the United States of North America in the Years 1806, 1807 & 1808*. London: C. Cradock and W. Joy, 1814. Vol. II.

La Rouchefoucault-Liancourt, Francois, Alexander du Frederic, Duke de. *Travels Through the United States of America*. London, 1799. Vol. II. [As indicated here, the author's name is spelled "La Rochefoucault-Liancourt" on the title page of this edition of his work. But elsewhere in the present work the usual spelling of this well-known family name (with a "d") is used.]

St. Mery, Moreau de, *American Journey*. Translated and edited by Kenneth and Anna M. Roberts. New York: Doubleday and Company, Inc., 1947.

Schoepf, Johann David, *Travels in the Confederation*. edited by Alfred J. Morrison. Philadelphia: William J. Campbell, 1911. Vol. II.

Scott, E. H. (ed.), *Journal of the Constitutional Convention Kept by James Madison*. Chicago: Scott Foresman Company 1893.

Smyth, J. F. D., *A Tour of the United States of America*. London: G. Robinson, 1784. Vol. II.

*The Southern States Ephemeris: or the North and South Carolina and Georgia Almanac, For the Year of Our Lord, 1788*. Charleston: Brown, Vandle and Andrews. (In College of Charleston Library).

## Newspapers

*Arkansas Gazette* (Little Rock), 1822.

*Carolina Gazette* (Charleston), 1822.

Charleston *Courier*, 1820. 1822, 1823.

Charleston *Mercury and Morning Advertiser*, 1822.

Charleston *Mercury*, 1822.

*City Gazette* (Charleston), 1794, 1800, 1822, 1824.

*City Gazette and Commercial Daily Advertiser*, 1822.

*City Gazette and Daily Advertiser* (Charleston), 1793, 1799, 1800.

*Columbian Herald* (Charleston), 1793.

*The Courier* (Charleston), 1803.

*Gazette of the State of South Carolina* (Charleston), 1783.

*National Intelligencer* (Washington), 1822.

*Niles Weekly Register* (Baltimore), 1819, 1822, 1823, 1824.

*South Carolina and American General Gazette* (Charleston), 1770, 1774, 1775.

*South Carolina Gazette* (Charleston), 1772, 1773, 1774.

*South Carolina Gazette and Country Journal* (Charleston), 1770, 1771, 1772, 1774.

*South Carolina Gazette and General Advertiser* (Charleston), 1783.

*South Carolina Weekly Gazette* (Charleston), 1783.

*Southern Patriot* (Charleston), 1822.

*Southern Patriot and Commercial Advertiser* (Charleston), 1822.

*The Times* (Charleston), 1802, 1803.

## Monographs and Special Accounts

Aptheker, Herbert, *The Negro in the Abolitionist Movement*. New York: International Publishers, 1941.

Aphetker, Herbert, *Negro Slave Revolts in the U. S.—1526-1860*. New York: International Publishers, 1939.

*Caroliniensis*. Charleston: A. E. Miller, n. d. [Robert J. Turnbull and Isaac E. Holmes identified as authors in pencil notation on pamphlet. No place of publication given, but Miller was a Charleston printer. Original series of Caroliniensis letters appeared in Charleston newspapers in 1823].

Clarkson, T., *An Essay on the Impolicy of the African Slave Trade. To which is added, An Oration Upon the Necessity of Establishing at Paris, a Society to Promote the Abolition of the Trade and Slavery of Negroes* [by J. P. Brissot de Warville]. Philadelphia: Francis Bailey, 1788.

Doar, David, *Rice and Rice Planting in the South Carolina Low Country*. No. VIII, *Contributions from the Charleston Museum*. ed. E. Milby Burton. Charleston: The Charleston Museum, 1936.

Grimké, Archibald H., *Right on the Scaffold, or the Martyrs of 1822*. Washington: American Negro Academy, 1901.

[Hamilton, T.] A Colored American (of Philadelphia), *The Late Contemplated Insurrection in Charleston, S. C. . . .* New York 1850. ["Supposed author" identified in pencil notation on pamphlet.] Schomburg Collection, New York Public Library.

[Holland, E. C.], A South Carolinian, *A Refutation of the Calumnies Circulated Against the Southern and Western States*

*Respecting the Institution and Existence of Slavery Among Them.* Charleston: A. E. Miller, 1822.

King, Rufus, *Substance of Two Speeches, Delivered in the Senate of the United States on the Subject of the Missouri Bill.* New York: Kirk and Mercein, 1819.

Lesesne, Thomas P., *History of Charleston County, South Carolina.* Charleston: 1931.

*Liberty*, 1837. [No publisher or place of publication given.]

McCrady, Edward, *A Sketch of St. Philip's Church, Charleston, S. C.* Charleston: 1901.

Neilson, Peter, *The Life and Adventures of Zamba, An African Negro King, And His Experience of Slavery in South Carolina. Written by Himself.* London: Smith, Elder and Co., 1847. Schomburg Collection, New York Public Library.

[Pinckney, Thomas] Achates, *Reflections Occasioned by the Late Disturbances in Charleston.* Charleston: A. E. Miller, 1822. New York Public Library.

Ryan, Frank, "Travellers in South Carolina in the Eighteenth Century," Unpublished master's thesis, University of North Carolina, 1949.

A South Carolinian, *Practical Considerations Founded on the Scriptures, Relative to the Slave Population of South Carolina.* Charleston: A. E. Miller, 1823. New York Public Library.

Woodson, Carter G., *Free Negro Families in the United States in 1830.* New York: Association for the Study of Negro Life and History, 1925.

### Articles and Essays in Periodicals, Annuals and Publications of Learned Societies

Aptheker, Herbert, "Eighteenth Century Petition of South Carolina Negroes," *Journal of Negro History*, XXXI, 98 (January, 1946).

Bedford, Henry F., "William Johnson and the Marshall Court," *South Carolina Historical Magazine*, LXII, 165 (July, 1961.)

Birnie, C. W., "Education of the Negro in Charleston, S. C., Prior to the Civil War," *Journal of Negro History*, XII, 17 (January, 1927).

Campbell, Albert A., "St. Thomas Negroes—A Study of Personality and Culture," *Psychological Monographs*. Edited by John F. Dashiell. Vol. LV, Number 5. Evanston, Ill.: American Psychological Association, Inc., 1943.

Degler, Carl N., "There Was Another South," *American Heritage*, XI, no. 5, 52 (August, 1960).

"Documents—Letters to the American Colonization Society," *Journal of Negro History*, X, 157 (April, 1925).

Donnan, Elizabeth, "Slave Trade in South Carolina Before the Revolution," *American Historical Review*, XXXIII, 823 (June, 1928).

Fitchett, E. Horace, "The Traditions of the Free Negro in Charleston, S. C.," *Journal of Negro History*, XXV, 142 (April, 1940).

Gordon, A. H., "The Struggle of the Negro Slaves for Physical Freedom," *Journal of Negro History*, XIII, 24 (January, 1928).

Hamer, Philip May, "Great Britain, the United States and the Negro Seamen Acts, 1822-1848," *Journal of Southern History*, I, 3-28 (February, 1935).

[Higginson, Thomas Wentworth], "Denmark Vesey," *Atlantic Monthly*, VII, 730 (June, 1861).

"Izard, Ralph to Thomas Jefferson," *South Carolina Historical and Genealogical Magazine*, II, 197.

Jackson, Luther P., "Religious Instruction of Negroes, 1830-1860, with Special Reference to South Carolina," *Journal of Negro History*, XV, 74 (January, 1930).

Lander, Ernest M. Jr., "The South Carolinians at the Philadelphia Convention, 1787," *South Carolina Historical Magazine*, LVII, 316 (July, 1956).

Link, Eugene Perry, "The Democratic Societies of the Carolinas," *The North Carolina Historical Review*, XVIII, 259-277 (July, 1941).

Morgan, Donald G., "Justice William Johnson on the Treaty-Making Power," *George Washington Law Review*, XXII, 1-29, (December, 1953).

Pendleton, Leila Amos, "Our New Possessions—The Danish West Indes," *Journal of Negro History*, II, 275 (July, 1917).

Phillips, Ulrich B., "Slave Labor in the Charleston District," *Political Science Quarterly*, XXII, 426 (September, 1907).

Porter, Kenneth W., "Relations Between Negroes and Indians Within the Present Limits of the U.S., *Journal of Negro History*, XVII, 335 (July, 1932).

Preston, E. Delorus Jr., "Genesis of the Underground Railroad," *Journal of Negro History*, XVIII, 150 (April, 1933).

Schaper, William A., "Sectionalism and Representation in South Carolina," *American Historical Association Annual Report 1900*, I ,423.

Wish, Harvey, "American Slave Insurrections Before 1861," *Journal of Negro History*, XXII, 316 (July, 1937).

*Year Book—1880, City of Charleston, So. Ca.* Charleston: The News and Courier Book Presses.

## General Accounts

Adams, Henry, *The United States in 1800.* Ithaca, N.Y.,: Great Seal Books, A Division of Cornell University Press, 1955.

Angle, Paul M., ed., *The Nation Divided—Selected from the American Reader.* Greenwich, Conn.: Fawcett Publications, Inc., 1960. Vol. III.

Aptheker, Herbert, *American Negro Slave Revolts.* New York: Columbia University Press, 1943.

Bassett, John Spencer, *Slavery in the State of North Carolina,* Johns Hopkins University Studies in Historical and Political Science, Nos. 7-8 of Series XVII. Edited by Herbert B. Adams. Baltimore: Johns Hopkins University Press, 1899.

Benedict, David, *A General History of the Baptist Denomination in America and Other Parts of the World.* 2 vols. Boston: Manning and Loring, 1813. Vol. II.

Birney, Catherine H., *The Grimké Sisters—Sarah and Angelina Grimké.* Boston: Lee and Shepard, 1885.

Blake, W. O., *The History of Slavery and the Slave Trade, Ancient and Modern.* Columbus, Ohio: H. Miller, 1860.

Boucher, Chauncey Samuel, *The Nullification Controversy in South Carolina.* Chicago: University of Chicago Press, 1916.

Brawley, Benjamin, *A Social History of the American Negro.* New York: Macmillan, 1921.

Butcher, Margaret Just, *The Negro in American Culture—*Based on materials left by Alain Locke. New York: Mentor Book, New American Library, 1956.

Cash, W. J., *The Mind of the South.* New York: Alfred A. Knopf, 1941.

Channing, Edward, *The Jeffersonian System, 1801-1811.* Vol. XII of *The American Nation: A History.* Edited by A. B. Hart. 28 vols. New York: Harper & Bros., 1904-1918.

Coulter, E. Merton, *William G. Brownlow—Fighting Parson of the Southern Highlands.* Chapel Hill: University of North Carolina Press, 1937.

Davis, H. P., *Black Democracy, the Story of Haiti.* New York: Dodge Publishing Company, 1928.

DeConde, Alexander, *Entangling Alliance—Politics and Diplomacy under George Washington.* Durham, N.C.: Duke University Press, 1958.

Dow, George Francis, *Slave Ships and Slaving*. Salem, Mass.: Marine Research Society, 1927.

Du Bois, W. E. Burghadt, *The Suppression of the African Slave Trade to the United States of America—1638-1870*. New York: Longman's Green & Co., 1896.

Dummond, Dwight Lowell, *Antislavery—The Crusade for Freedom in America*. Ann Arbor: University of Michigan Press, 1961.

Eaton, Clement, *Freedom of Thought in the Old South*. Durham, N.C.: Duke University Press, 1940.

Elkins, Stanley M., *Slavery—A Problem in American Institutional and Intellectual Life*. Chicago: University of Chicago Press, 1959.

Franklin, John Hope, *The Militant South: 1800-1861*. Cambridge: The Belknap Press of the Harvard University Press, 1956.

Furnas, J. C., *The Road to Harpers Ferry*. New York: William Sloane Associates, 1959.

Gray, L. C., *History of Agriculture in the Southern United States to 1860*. 2 vols. Washington: Carnegie Institution, 1933. Vol. II.

Hamilton, J. Taylor, *A History of the Church Known as the Moravian, or the Unitas Fratrum, or the Unity of the Brethren, During the Eighteenth and Nineteenth Centuries*. Bethlehem, Pa.: Times Publishing Company, 1900.

Helper, Hinton Rowan, *The Impending Crisis of the South: How to Meet It*. New York: Burdick Brothers, 1857.

Henry, H. M., *The Police Control of the Slave in South Carolina*. Emory, Va., 1914.

Higginson, Thomas Wentworth, *Travellers and Outlaws, Episodes in American History*. Boston: Lee and Shepard, 1889.

Hofstadter, Richard, ed., *Great Issues in American History —A Documentary Record, 1765-1865*. New York: Vintage Books, 1958. Vol. I.

Hofstadter, Richard, *The American Political Tradition and the Men Who Made It*. New York: Vintage Books, 1954.

Howe, George, *History of the Presbyterian Church in South Carolina*. Columbia: Duffie and Chapman, 1870.

Irving, John B., M. D., *A Day on Cooper River*. 2d ed. edited and enlarged by Louisa C. Stoney. Columbia: R. L. Bryan Co., 1932.

James, Marquis, *The Life of Andrew Jackson*. Indianapolis: Bobbs-Merrill Co., 1938.

Jameson, J. Franklin, *The American Revolution Considered as a Social Movement*. Boston: Beacon Press, 1956.

Jervey, Theodore D., *Robert Y. Hayne and His Times*. New York: The Macmillan Company, 1909.

Jervey, Theodore D., *The Slave Trade, Slavery and Color*. Columbia: The State Company, 1925.

Johnson, Gerald W., *The Lunatic Fringe*. New York: Lippincott, 1957.

Kelly, Alfred H. and Harbison, Winfred A., *The American Constitution—Its Origins and Development*. Revised ed. New York: Norton, 1955.

Kerr, Wilfred B., *Bermuda and the American Revolution: 1760-1783*. Princeton: Princeton University Press, 1936.

King, Charles R., ed., *The Life and Correspondence of Rufus King—Comprising His Letters, Private and Official, His Public Documents and His Speeches*. 6 vols. New York: G. P. Putnam's Sons, 1900. Vol. VI (1816-1827).

Kirwan, Albert D., ed., *The Confederacy*, Vol. I of *Meridian Documents of American History*, edited by George F. Scheer. New York: Meridian Books, Inc., 1959.

Klingberg, Frank J., *An Appraisal of the Negro in Colonial South Carolina*. Washington: Associated Publishers, 1941.

Krout, John Allen and Fox, Dixon Ryan, *The Completion of Independence, 1790-1830*. Vol. V of *A History of American Life*. Edited by Arthur M. Schlesinger and Dixon Ryan Fox. 12 vols. New York: The Macmillan Company, 1944.

Link, Eugene Perry, *Democratic-Republican Societies, 1790-1800*. New York: Columbia University Press, 1942.

Logan, Rayford W., *The Diplomatic Relations of the United States with Haiti—1776-1891*. Chapel Hill: University of North Carolina Press, 1941.

Malone, Dumas, *The Public Life of Thomas Cooper, 1783-1839*. New Haven: Yale University Press, 1926.

Minnigerode, Meade, *Jefferson, Friend of France, 1793, the Career of Edmund Charles Genet, Minister Plenipotentiary from the French Republic to the United States, as Revealed by His Private Papers, 1763-1834*. New York: G. P. Putnam's Sons, 1928.

Malloy, Robert, *Charleston—A Gracious Heritage*. New York: D. Appleton Century, Inc. 1947.

Montague, Ludwell Lee, *Haiti and the United States, 1714-1938*. Durham: Duke University Press, 1940.

Morgan, Donald G., *Justice William Johnson, the First Dissenter*. Columbia: University of South Carolina Press, 1954.

Morison, Samuel Eliot and Commanger, Henry Steele, *The Growth of the American Republic*. 2 vols. (2d ed., 1937; 3rd ed., 1942) New York: Oxford University Press.

Ottley, Roi, *Black Odyssey—The Story of the Negro in America*. New York: Charles Scribner's Sons, 1948.

Petty, Julian J., *The Growth and Distribution of Population in South Carolina*. Columbia: State Council for Industrial Development Committee, 1943.

Phillips, Ulrich Bonnell, *American Negro Slavery*. New York: Peter Smith, 1952.

Phillips, Ulrich Bonnell, *Life and Labor in the Old South*. Boston: Little, Brown, and Company, 1939.

Phillips, Ulrich B., ed., *Plantation and Frontier Documents: 1649-1863—Illustrative of Industrial History in the Colonial & Ante-Bellum South*. Vols. I and II of 10 vol. Documentary History of American Industrial Society. Cleveland: Arthur H. Clark Co., 1909. Vol. II.

Ramsey, David, *The History of South Carolina from Its First Settlement in 1670, to the Year 1808*. Charleston: David Longworth, 1809. Vol. II.

Sellers, Leila, *Charleston Business on the Eve of the American Revolution*. Chapel Hill: The University of North Carolina Press, 1934.

Smith, Adam, *An Inquiry Into the Nature and Causes of the Wealth of Nations*. 2 vols. edited by Edwin Cannan. New York: G. P. Putnam's Sons, 1904.

Smith, Alfred Glaze Jr., *Economic Readjustment of an Old Cotton State, 1820-1860*. Columbia: University of South Carolina Press, 1958.

Smith, W. Roy, *South Carolina as a Royal Province*. New York: Macmillan, 1903.

Spears, John R., *The American Slave Trade—An Account of Its Origin, Growth and Suppression*. New York: Charles Scribner's, 1900.

Stampp, Kenneth M., ed., *The Causes of the Civil War*. Englewood Cliffs, N.J.: Prentice-Hall, Inc., 1959.

Swisher, Carl Brent, "Mr. Chief Justice Taney," *Mr. Justice*, edited by Allison Dunham and Philip B. Kurland. Chicago: University of Chicago Press, 1956.

Sypher, Wylie, *Guinea's Captive Kings: British Antislavery Literature of the XVIII Century*. Chapel Hill: University of North Carolina Press, 1942.

Turner, Frederick Jackson, *Rise of the New West—1819-1829*. Vol. XIV of *The American Nation: A History*, edited by A. B. Hart. 28 vols. New York: Harper and Brothers, 1904-1918. (1906).

Vandercook, John W., *Black Majesty*. New York: The Literary Guild of America, 1928.

Verrill, Addison E., *The Bermuda Islands, An Account of Their Scenery, Climate, Physiography, Natural History and Geology, With Sketches of Their Discovery and Early History, and the Changes in Their Flora and Fauna due to Man*. New Haven, Conn. Published by the Author, 1902.

Victor, Orville J., *History of American Conspiracies: A Record of Treason, Insurrection, Rebellion, Etc. in the United States of America From 1760 to 1860*. New York: James D. Torrey, Publisher, 1863.

Wallace, David Duncan, *History of South Carolina*. 4 vols. New York: American Historical Co., 1934. Vol. II.

Wallace, David Duncan, *South Carolina—A Short History, 1520-1948*. Chapel Hill: The University of North Carolina Press, 1951.

Weeks, Stephen B., *Southern Quakers and Slavery*. Baltimore: The Johns Hopkins Press, 1896.

Whitney, Janet, *John Woolman, American Quaker*. Boston: Little, Brown, and Company, 1942.

Wiltse, Charles M., *John C. Calhoun, Nationalist, 1782-1828*. Indianapolis: Bobbs-Merrill Company, Inc., 1944.

Wiltse, Charles M., *John C. Calhoun, Nullifier, 1829-1839*. Indianapolis: Bobbs-Merrill Company, Inc., 1949.

Wolfe, John Harold, *Jefferson Democracy in South Carolina*. Chapel Hill: The University of North Carolina Press, 1940.

Woodson, Carter G., *The Education of the Negro Prior to 1861*. 2d ed. Washington: Associated Publishers, Inc., 1919